Praise for *Learning GitHub Copilot*

Learning GitHub Copilot is practical, thoughtful, and grounded in how developers work on code every day.

—*Andrew Stellman, developer, team lead, instructor, and author*

Every programmer should understand AI-assisted programming. And GitHub Copilot is the clear leader. Brent's book is the ultimate guide to mastering this powerful tool.

—*Tom Taulli, author of* AI-Assisted Programming

This book is the missing link between using Copilot and truly mastering its potential. It's an invaluable resource for developers who want to elevate their workflow.

—*Balaji Dhamodharan, data science leader*

This book will help to unlock the future of coding. It's a guide to the tool that simplifies the entire coding process, code explainability, and optimization by offering clear lessons and examples on Github Copilot. Whether you're new to coding or a seasoned coder, this book will help you increase your productivity.

—*Aditya Goel, GenAI consultant and assistant vice president at a global bank*

Learning GitHub Copilot is a comprehensive description of Github Copilot's features along with usage examples. I found it very informative.

—*Chhaya Methani, Microsoft*

This book expertly balances foundational knowledge with practical applications, making it a must read for anyone eager to explore AI-enhanced software development.

—*Sundeep Goud Katta, lead software engineer*

Learning GitHub Copilot
Multiplying Your Coding Productivity Using AI

Brent Laster
Foreword by Andrew Stellman

Learning GitHub Copilot

by Brent Laster

Copyright © 2025 Tech Skills Transformation, LLC. All rights reserved.

Printed in the United States of America.

Published by O'Reilly Media, Inc., 1005 Gravenstein Highway North, Sebastopol, CA 95472.

O'Reilly books may be purchased for educational, business, or sales promotional use. Online editions are also available for most titles (*http://oreilly.com*). For more information, contact our corporate/institutional sales department: 800-998-9938 or *corporate@oreilly.com*.

Acquisitions Editor: John Devins, Louise Corrigan
Development Editor: Michele Cronin
Production Editor: Jonathon Owen
Copyeditor: Sharon Wilkey
Proofreader: Heather Walley

Indexer: Potomac Indexing, LLC
Cover Designer: Susan Thompson
Cover Illustrator: Monica Kamsvaag
Interior Designer: David Futato
Interior Illustrator: Kate Dullea

July 2025: First Edition

Revision History for the First Edition
2025-07-09: First Release

See *http://oreilly.com/catalog/errata.csp?isbn=9781098164652* for release details.

The O'Reilly logo is a registered trademark of O'Reilly Media, Inc. *Learning GitHub Copilot*, the cover image, and related trade dress are trademarks of O'Reilly Media, Inc.

The views expressed in this work are those of the author and do not represent the publisher's views. While the publisher and the author have used good faith efforts to ensure that the information and instructions contained in this work are accurate, the publisher and the author disclaim all responsibility for errors or omissions, including without limitation responsibility for damages resulting from the use of or reliance on this work. Use of the information and instructions contained in this work is at your own risk. If any code samples or other technology this work contains or describes is subject to open source licenses or the intellectual property rights of others, it is your responsibility to ensure that your use thereof complies with such licenses and/or rights.

978-1-098-16465-2

[LSI]

To Anne-Marie, coauthor of the amazing book that is our life together.

To Ace,

Thanks for your interest in the book! Hope it's useful!

Brent

Table of Contents

Foreword... xi

Preface.. xiii

1. **Foundations**.. 1
   What Is GitHub Copilot?   2
   How Does Copilot Work?   3
      Large Language Models   4
      Code and Generative AI   5
      High-Level Flow   7
   Usage Considerations   11
      Timeliness   12
      Relevance   13
      Completeness   13
      Accuracy   14
      Privacy   14
      Security   16
   Copilot Versus ChatGPT   17
   Copilot Plans   18
   Conclusion   22

2. **Coding with Copilot**.. 23
   Inline Suggestions   24
   Getting Additional Suggestions   28
   Leveraging Comments   30
      Directive Comments   31
      Questions via Comments   34
   Copilot and the Context Menu   35

Using Copilot to Review Your Code	39
Using Copilot's Default Review Options	39
Creating Custom Review Instructions	42
Configuring Copilot in the IDE	44
Conclusion	49

3. Chatting with Copilot in the IDE... 51

Accessing Chat's Main Interface	52
Understanding Chat Output	55
Managing Chat Sessions	59
Prompt Engineering for Copilot	62
Making Effective Use of the Prompt Dialog	63
Adding Context Elements	64
Adding Participants	66
Understanding Options for Submitting Your Prompt	67
Using the Editor Inline Chat Interface	69
Using the Quick Chat Interface	73
Chat Shortcuts	74
Chat Participants	77
@workspace	78
@vscode	80
@terminal	81
Chat Variables	83
Chat in the Terminal	86
Creating Custom Code-Generation Instructions	87
Dealing with Hallucinations and Bad Answers	90
Conclusion	91

4. Advanced Editing and Autonomous Workflows in the IDE......................... 93

Predictive Edits with Next Edit Suggestions	93
Copilot Edits	97
Agent Mode	104
Copilot Vision	111
Debugging with Copilot	119
Conclusion	123

5. Testing with Copilot... 125

How Do I Test?	126
Creating Unit Tests	132
Using the /tests Command	133
Creating Tests from Explicit Prompts	136
Creating Tests from Comments	137

	Validating Inputs	139
	Creating Integration Tests	141
	Defining Custom Testing Instructions	144
	Testing Before the Coding and Leveraging Frameworks	145
	Leveraging Agent Mode for Testing Workflows	151
	Conclusion	154

6. Using Copilot to Document and Explain Code.................................. 155

Documenting Content	156
Generating Documentation Inline	156
Generating Documentation Through Chat	159
Generating Framework-Compatible Documentation	162
Generating Documentation for APIs	164
Creating Functional Documentation	165
Extracting Summary Documentation from the Code	167
Explaining Content	169
Understanding Code in a Language New to You	169
Understanding Generated Code and Conventions	170
Explaining the Logic Used in a Section of Code	172
Explaining What Might Go Wrong with a Set of Code	173
Explaining Items from the Terminal	174
Explaining How to Do Something in the Terminal	177
Conclusion	178

7. Keeping Copilot Timely and Relevant.. 181

Where Context Originates	182
How Timeliness and Relevancy May Be Affected	183
Training Cutoffs	183
Hallucinations	186
Lack of Real-Time Validation	187
Misplaced Context	188
Missing Context	189
User-Based Coping Strategies	191
Telling Copilot What to Use for Context	191
Changing the Model	194
Querying the Model to Determine Which Version Is Current	195
Guiding Copilot by Example	198
Adding Context to Make Code More Relevant	199
Conclusion	202

8. Other Ways to Leverage Copilot.. 203

Using Copilot with SQL	204

	Queries	204
	Stored Procedures	207
	Optimizations	209
	Working with YAML and Kubernetes	210
	Generating Regular Expressions	215
	Automatic Data Generation	216
	GitHub CLI and Copilot	218
	Conclusion	220

9. Using Copilot in GitHub. 223
    Using Chat with GitHub Repositories   224
    Using Copilot for Change Workflows   231
    Using Copilot with Pull Requests   237
        Having Copilot Review Pull Requests   238
        Leveraging Copilot to Simplify Initiating Pull Requests   241
    Exploring Code Changes with Copilot   245
    Using Copilot with GitHub Issues   249
    Conclusion   251

10. Extending Copilot's Functionality. 253
    Copilot Extensions Versus VS Code Extensions for Copilot   253
    What Are Copilot Extensions?   254
    Getting Copilot Extensions from the Marketplace   255
    Understanding Copilot Extension Implementation Types   263
    Assembling Building Blocks for Extensions   264
        GitHub Apps   264
        Endpoint Server   266
    Implementing an Extension as an Agent   266
        Performing a Basic Implementation   267
        Configuring a GitHub App for a Copilot Agent Extension   272
    Implementing an Extension via Skillsets   280
        Performing a Basic Implementation   281
        Configuring a GitHub App for a Copilot Extension Using Skillsets   285
    Creating VS Code Extensions for Copilot   289
    Conclusion   296

Index. 297

Foreword

I've spent a lot of time helping developers learn how to use AI tools as part of their daily work—by mentoring people, running training sessions, and writing about them in books—and I've relied on those same tools myself while building real software. One really stands out to me: GitHub Copilot.

It's a game-changer. I use it all the time.

I've been coding for decades, and like every developer, sometimes I get stuck. Maybe it's when I'm using a new technology or API, and I'm dreading going through poorly written documentation. Maybe it's when I'm refactoring a particularly nasty bit of code that everyone on my team has been avoiding. Or maybe I just don't feel like writing dull boilerplate code that has to get written but is going to cost me a half hour of my life that I'll never get back.

That's where Copilot can really make a difference. It might give me all the code I need, complete and working. Or it might give me just a starting point—something we'll iterate on together. Either way, it's valuable to me, and it almost always gives me enough to get things moving again.

But working with Copilot isn't a one-way street—it comes with responsibility. Copilot can write code that compiles, runs, even passes tests. But if you don't understand what it gave you, or why it works—or, most importantly, how you got it to produce that result—you're not really in control of what's going into your codebase. This book puts you in control.

Good developers need to do more than just learn Copilot's features. We need to learn an effective way to work with AI, one that supports us in what we already do: write code, make decisions, and solve problems alongside other people.

That learning starts with understanding that Copilot isn't perfect—and it isn't trying to be perfect. It's trying to help you move forward by offering suggestions based on the patterns and context in your code. And a lot of the time, it gets satisfyingly close.

But like any tool, it works best when you know how to guide it—and when to slow down and double-check what it gave you.

And that's why this book matters. *Learning GitHub Copilot* is practical, thoughtful, and grounded in how developers work on code every day. Brent Laster has done a masterful job because he doesn't just list off Copilot's features; he shows you how to use them when you're doing real work—when things are messy, nonlinear, and often under a deadline.

He starts with Copilot's built-in strengths, like explaining code and writing tests, and then moves into showing you how it helps with things that trip people up—SQL queries, regular expressions, YAML files, and all the other small (and sometimes not so small!) tasks that eat up time. I appreciate all the examples throughout the book because they reflect the kinds of problems developers face in real life. I think you'll appreciate them too.

Copilot works as an important everyday development tool—not because it promises magic, but because it respects how developers think. This book does the same thing. It assumes you're thoughtful, capable, and still learning, and it gives you space to make good decisions with the tool instead of just following along.

In my own teaching and writing, I've seen how quickly developers improve when they get clear, honest guidance—especially when it helps them make better decisions when they're doing real work. That's exactly what this book provides. It's not hype. It's not oversimplified. It's a practical guide to a powerful tool, written for developers who want to stay in control of their code.

If you're new to Copilot, this book is a great place to start. If you've been using it for a while, you'll pick up techniques that make it more effective and easier to trust. And if you've been skeptical, that's healthy. This book meets you where you are, and it'll show you how to get the most out of the tool without giving up what makes you a good developer.

— Andrew Stellman
Developer, team lead, instructor,
and author of Learning Agile, Head First C#,
and many other O'Reilly books
Brooklyn, New York, April 2025

Preface

The winds and the waves are always on the side of the ablest navigators.
    —Edward Gibbon

I've been writing code for a very long time now—longer than I care to admit—and I've seen the winds and waves of change that have swept across the software development industry multiple times (and written about or trained on many of them). From the internet to CI/CD to containers to cloud, the paradigm shifts have upended the old ways of doing things, and spawned innovation, incredible tools, and turnarounds in our approaches to creating software. And, broadly, those shifts have also generated uncertainty and confusion as individuals tried to understand them and figure out how to adapt and apply their skills..

Now we have generative AI, arguably the biggest wave of change we have encountered in tech, especially for those developing software. Just like the others, it is inspiring massive innovation and driving massive changes. But in some respects, it resembles more of a tsunami where new tools, new models, and new capabilities exhibit tremendous power, all while coders are being swept along and trying to keep our collective heads above water.

This book is my attempt to help you surf the wave—at least as far as using the AI powerhouse that is GitHub Copilot. I won't claim it will answer all your questions, but hopefully it will help you get to a very good comfort level with the tool, let you understand its capabilities (from basic to advanced topics), and inspire you to make your coding tasks simpler and easier than they've ever been before.

I've been using Copilot in multiple ways for several years: in personal projects, as a former DevOps director piloting it in a corporate R&D organization, as a trainer on Copilot for multiple vendors, as a skeptic, and as an enthusiast. Regarding those last two roles, I wasn't as impressed with Copilot in its early days as I was with other tools. But over the course of writing this book, developing courses on it, and watching it evolve, it's become one of the primary tools I use on a regular basis when working in my integrated development environment (IDE) or in GitHub. Copilot has come a long way, even in the last few months. There's been some impressive progress with features and functionality. I've tried to capture as many of those as I could in the book.

One of my goals in writing these chapters is to share the benefits and the challenges of using Copilot, and try to help you avoid surprises. So, before you jump in, here's a few things to be aware of:

- For the last year or so, GitHub Copilot has changed the appearance and location of at least one dialog or control with nearly every release. I've done my best to update screenshots and descriptions as they are at the time of writing. But it's certain that some will have been moved, changed in appearance, etc. by the time you are reading this.

- Copilot is now releasing new features on a fairly regular basis. So, over time there will be new features that are not represented in the book. Likewise, some functionality in Copilot is noted as being in *preview* or *experimental* as of the time of writing. Those may have been moved to production by the time you read this or may have been removed if they didn't make the cut.

- Copilot runs in many different environments, including multiple IDEs. In each IDE, there can be (and are) differences in integration, appearance, and even functionality. GitHub has historically prioritized Visual Studio Code and the environments that use the same interface (like GitHub Codespaces) to roll out new features and to contain the superset of functionality. For that reason, all screenshots and examples in the book are done with either VS Code or in a Codespace.

- For those of you using non-VS Code IDEs, some features or functions may have not been implemented by GitHub in that environment. Please consult the Copilot and/or IDE documentation (*https://docs.github.com/en/copilot*) for the latest information.

- Similarly, IDEs that integrate with Copilot can usually be run on multiple platforms including Windows, Mac, and Linux. Since it's not practical to cover all the variations in the book, the examples were done on a Mac. So the windows and controls shown may reflect the Mac style. Also keyboard shortcuts will differ among the platforms. To avoid having to list all keyboard shortcuts each time we reference them, we've adopted *Meta* as a notation that means to insert the appropriate shortcut for your platform.

All of these things apply across the entire structure of the book, which was written to take you from the *What is it* basics to the advanced *Here's how you go beyond the core functionality*. Most of the chapters can be read standalone, and you should feel free to skip between chapters as your needs and comfort level dictate.

The Structure of This Book

Since you're reading this book, I imagine you're interested in GitHub Copilot as a potential AI coding assistant or at least looking to learn more about how it and similar coding assistants can be used to help you work more quickly and efficiently.

To help with that, an outline of the book's structure follows.

Chapters 1, 2, and 3 guide you through the foundations you need to understand what Copilot is and how to interact with it in its two main modes—code completion and the chat (conversational) interface.

Chapter 4 explores advanced ways of interacting with Copilot to do more autonomous editing as well as using Agent mode to drive changes from prompt to finish automatically. This chapter also explores the unique interface of Copilot Vision as well as debugging with Copilot.

Chapters 5 and 6 show you how you can leverage Copilot to create rich sets of tests and multiple kinds of documentation to simplify those tasks and give you more time to focus on other coding tasks.

Chapter 7 focuses on how you can improve the timeliness and relevance of results from Copilot.

Chapter 8 explores how you can use Copilot to handle a number of less common but useful tasks.

Chapter 9 explores Copilot's chat interface in GitHub and how Copilot can help you understand more about your projects and simplify working with GitHub Issues and pull requests.

Finally, Chapter 10 provides information on enhancing Copilot's functionality through the integration of GitHub Extensions and shows how to build your own.

As you start reading, you don't have to know anything about Copilot to use this book. But I do assume you're familiar with basic coding skills and have a basic working knowledge of Git and GitHub. The next section explains a bit more about the types of readers who may benefit from the book.

Intended Audience

This book is for anyone who is trying to learn more about using AI assistants for developing software. Yes, it's specifically about GitHub Copilot, but many of the examples and flows have parallels in other AI coding tools and environments. To get the most out of this book, you should already have experience coding in an IDE and have a basic knowledge of GitHub. To be clear, this book is not going to teach you how to code, how to use an IDE, or how to use GitHub. But it will help you multiply your productivity in all of those areas through using Copilot. Whether you are a software developer, quality engineer, SRE, or someone who is just looking to understand how an AI assistant like Copilot can benefit them, I believe you'll find meaningful information and insights.

Here are some audiences that I had in mind while writing the book and that I think can benefit from it:

- Those who are new (or newish) to AI coding assistants and looking to understand what they are all about and how to best make use of them
- Those who already understand the concepts and flow of using AI coding assistants and want to understand what GitHub Copilot has to offer
- Those who want to understand and evaluate GitHub Copilot as a possible tool to use on a wider scale in their organization or business
- Those who already have some experience with GitHub Copilot and want to take full advantage of its features and functionality
- Those who are looking to understand how to compensate for some of GitHub Copilot's shortcomings
- Those who want to understand the new features of Copilot, such as Agent mode
- Those who want to create their own GitHub Copilot extensions
- Those who work with GitHub and want to take advantage of the Copilot integration there

If one of these fits your use case, I hope the book will provide you with the value you're looking for. If you read it and have the opportunity, feedback is always welcome through reviews or interactions at future conferences or training venues. Info about how to ride the wave of Generative AI in coding begins in Chapter 1. Happy surfing!

Conventions Used in This Book

The following typographical conventions are used in this book:

Italic
  Indicates new terms, URLs, email addresses, filenames, and file extensions.

`Constant width`
  Used for program listings, as well as within paragraphs to refer to program elements such as variable or function names, databases, data types, environment variables, statements, and keywords.

`Constant width bold`
: Shows commands or other text that should be typed literally by the user.

Constant width italic
: Shows text that should be replaced with user-supplied values or by values determined by context.

This element signifies a tip or suggestion.

This element signifies a general note.

This element indicates a warning or caution.

Using Code Examples

Supplemental material (code examples, exercises, etc.) is available for download at *https://github.com/techupskills/learning-github-copilot*.

If you have a technical question or a problem using the code examples, please send an email to *support@oreilly.com*.

This book is here to help you get your job done. In general, if example code is offered with this book, you may use it in your programs and documentation. You do not need to contact us for permission unless you're reproducing a significant portion of the code. For example, writing a program that uses several chunks of code from this book does not require permission. Selling or distributing examples from O'Reilly books does require permission. Answering a question by citing this book and quoting example code does not require permission. Incorporating a significant amount of example code from this book into your product's documentation does require permission.

We appreciate, but generally do not require, attribution. An attribution usually includes the title, author, publisher, and ISBN. For example: "*Learning GitHub Copilot* by Brent Laster (O'Reilly). Copyright 2025 Tech Skills Transformation, LLC, 978-1-098-16465-2."

If you feel your use of code examples falls outside fair use or the permission given above, feel free to contact us at *permissions@oreilly.com*.

O'Reilly Online Learning

For more than 40 years, *O'Reilly Media* has provided technology and business training, knowledge, and insight to help companies succeed.

Our unique network of experts and innovators share their knowledge and expertise through books, articles, and our online learning platform. O'Reilly's online learning platform gives you on-demand access to live training courses, in-depth learning paths, interactive coding environments, and a vast collection of text and video from O'Reilly and 200+ other publishers. For more information, visit *https://oreilly.com*.

How to Contact Us

Please address comments and questions concerning this book to the publisher:

> O'Reilly Media, Inc.
> 1005 Gravenstein Highway North
> Sebastopol, CA 95472
> 800-889-8969 (in the United States or Canada)
> 707-827-7019 (international or local)
> 707-829-0104 (fax)
> *support@oreilly.com*
> *https://oreilly.com/about/contact.html*

We have a web page for this book, where we list errata, examples, and any additional information. You can access this page at *https://oreil.ly/learning-github-copilot*.

For news and information about our books and courses, visit *https://oreilly.com*.

Find us on LinkedIn: *https://linkedin.com/company/oreilly-media*.

Watch us on YouTube: *https://youtube.com/oreillymedia*.

Acknowledgments

Learning GitHub Copilot marks my fourth published book, alongside many technical guides, reports, articles, and other documents I've written over the years. Getting from a proposal to a finished product is an incredible investment of time and energy not only from the author, but from a team of people to bring things to production. I am incredibly grateful to the following group of people who contributed their time and energy to bring this project to the point where you can read it and hopefully get value from it.

First, many thanks to John Devins, my acquisitions editor at O'Reilly who believed in, and advocated for, this book—as he did on my behalf for so many other projects. John, I hope you're enjoying a well-deserved retirement! And thanks to Louise Corrigan for picking up from John to continue the effort. Over my time working with O'Reilly, I have truly come to respect and appreciate the role of acquisition editors to support meaningful projects and to provide quality training opportunities and find new ways to bridge learning gaps. Their roles are most often behind the scenes, but their efforts are core to much of the learning that I and other content creators get to bring to the attendees of O'Reilly Learning.

When I first started writing this book, I specifically asked to work again with Michele Cronin as the development editor for the project. Michele was also the development editor on *Learning GitHub Actions*, so I knew she was the right person to make this project complete, polished, and successful. Behind the scenes, Michele has put in many hours keeping the project (and me) on track, helping resolve any potential roadblocks, lining up reviewers and consolidating feedback, and always being available for any questions. As well, she has provided sage advice on how to navigate any and all challenges that have come up along the way. She has been an optimistic and supportive guide throughout the process, and I am very much appreciative of all that she has done and the experience and guidance she provided that made this book possible.

There are numerous other people at O'Reilly that have had a hand in the process that I want to also call out. Sharon Wilkey and Jonathon Owen have been exceptional in proofreading and clarifying the content to make it clear and readable. Kate Dullea has helped keep me straight on the images and make sure they are usable and legible. And thanks to Susan Thompson for the cool cover picture and David Futato for the interior design.

Many noted experts from GitHub and other areas contributed their time and resources as reviewers for some or all of the book content. Without a doubt, the book is much better for their efforts. Many thanks to Andrew Stellman, Steffen Bjerkenås, Chhaya Methani, Balaji Dhamodharan, Aditya Goel, Sundeep Katta, Jess Males, and Tom Taulli for providing their feedback, impressions, and suggestions. I feel very fortunate and appreciative that these individuals were willing to take time from their busy schedules and provide their feedback, suggestions, and thoughts to make things better for the readers. The book benefitted greatly from their collective technical backgrounds and collective eye for detail. Additional thanks to Andrew Stellman for writing the foreword for the book, which I hope you can find a few minutes to read.

I would be remiss not to give a shout-out here to Jay Zimmerman, director of the No Fluff Just Stuff (NFJS) conferences, and Todd Lewis, chairman of the All Things Open (ATO) organization, for providing me with opportunities to speak and present at their respective conferences over the years. The material in this book is better because of the multiple presentations I've done on related topics in virtual workshops and conferences for NFJS and ATO. If you ever have a chance to attend one of these conferences or a meetup or virtual event sponsored by these organizations, I encourage you to do so.

Thanks also to my colleague and friend, Bob Pacheco, for regularly engaging in technical and non-technical discussions that helped to provoke perspective and lighten the mood when needed.

Most importantly, I want to thank my wife, Anne-Marie, for being my supportive soulmate, forever friend, and partner in life. Through her and our kids, Walker, Chase, Tanner, and Katie, I am constantly reminded that those closest to us and that share our daily world are what make each day worth living and each meaningful task worth doing, despite whatever else is going on.

Finally, thanks to you, the reader, for getting this book and reading it. I sincerely hope that you will find it useful and something that helps you achieve the goals that you're looking for as you start or continue your journey with GitHub Copilot. Feel free to reach out on social media or catch me at a conference or event sometime to discuss AI, Copilot, or just chat.

CHAPTER 1
Foundations

Welcome to *Learning GitHub Copilot*! I'm excited you're reading this book and hope you find it useful. AI tools like ChatGPT and AI agents have changed, and will continue to change, how we interact with software applications. GitHub Copilot and similar tools have changed, and will continue to change, how programmers create software applications. Through its ability to take context from existing code or natural language prompts, GitHub Copilot provides a richer and more powerful code-generation capability than any we've seen before.

In this book, I'll help you understand how to use GitHub Copilot's capabilities—from performing code generation and completion, forming tests, and translating and explaining code, to working with repositories, pull requests, and issues directly in GitHub. You'll see examples of using Copilot across multiple domains and programming languages. You'll learn to leverage it to your advantage and craft prompts to get the best results. You'll even learn how to add your own custom functionality to it. And you'll understand how it does what it does, including why it sometimes doesn't provide the results you expect—and how to mitigate those situations.

Some foundational knowledge is required to begin with, though. That's the purpose of this chapter. I'll start by explaining GitHub Copilot at a high level. We'll then explore the key underlying technology, its overall flow, some usage considerations, how it differs from tools like ChatGPT, and what you need to know about getting and installing it. So, let's get started.

Copilot Catchall

As we begin this discussion, be aware that *copilot* is a popular term for AI applications that collect information, formulate prompts, and return answers and suggestions. For example, Microsoft has an Office 365 Copilot (*https://oreil.ly/DaSLT*) that does this for Microsoft Office applications. It analyzes context from Word, Teams, Outlook, etc., and provides summarizations, suggested responses, and other valuable interactions.

In this book, I use *Copilot* to mean *GitHub Copilot*. The only exceptions will occur when I am referring to another system that uses the same word. In those cases, I'll explicitly identify them with their formal names, such as *Office 365 Copilot*.

What Is GitHub Copilot?

GitHub Copilot is a cloud-based, generative artificial intelligence (AI) tool. Let's break down these buzzwords. We can generically define AI as *computers doing tasks that previously only humans were thought to be able to accomplish because of required reasoning and skills*. More recently, this has also taken on the aspect of interacting with humans in a natural and human-like way through natural language processing (NLP), chat interfaces, and automated processing and decision making with AI agents.

AI Concerns

When we talk about AI, popular culture would have us think of machines becoming conscious, sentient, and taking over the world. While many of us in the technical professions understand that that is not realistic, programmers using tools like GitHub Copilot may think of AI (in the coding domain) as potentially taking over their jobs.

Some job displacement has undoubtedly taken place due to the use of AI. But this is not the intended purpose of Copilot. For all the seeming intelligence that Copilot may display in some use cases, it is still subject to creating incorrect or unusable code. And it still needs human oversight and review. The hope is that the information in this book will help make this particular AI tool a valuable tool in your toolbox to assist you in your project and in your role.

Cloud-based refers to the pathway through which Copilot returns suggestions and generates answers. It refers to a cloud environment managed by GitHub that facilitates interaction with the AI models. *Generative* expresses the AI's ability to *generate* new results from the context it takes in. Copilot can offer responses and suggestions for software development based on the context and prompts from the user's environment. How well it does this depends on several factors that we'll talk about in the next section. But, as a quick example, Figure 1-1 shows using Copilot to suggest optimizations based on a project in Visual Studio (VS) Code.

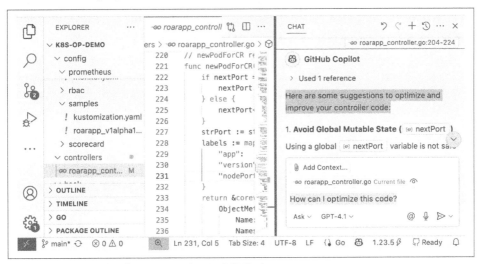

Figure 1-1. Using Copilot on a project in VS Code

Default IDE

Because it's not possible to represent all integrated development environments (IDEs) in this book, we'll be using VS Code or GitHub Codespace in our examples where an IDE is involved. If you use a different IDE, please consult the Copilot documentation for any differences in use, controls, etc.

How Does Copilot Work?

To understand how Copilot works, we need to understand some of the pieces that underpin its functionality and that of similar AI tools. These details include where it gets information to base responses on and its overall flow.

Copilot and most AI applications get their data from large language models (LLMs) trained on extensive data collections. If you're unfamiliar with term LLM, the following section provides a brief explanation.

Large Language Models

It's challenging to discuss AI tooling today without mentioning LLMs. LLMs are AI models trained on vast amounts of existing data to predict the next words or other types of content (e.g., *tokens*) that *fit* given some input (a *prompt*).

LLMs differ from traditional computer models that can process formatted data or respond to a math problem because LLMs are taught to understand context, syntax, and structure. This is done by algorithms that consider vast numbers of parameters to figure out what words or tokens make the most sense to come next. In this way, the models statistically craft responses based on how the input is presented, not just the input itself.

The model's prediction capabilities are learned and tuned from extensive collections of existing content. In this training process, the models map how the various pieces of information relate in any given domain. Technically, given a sequence of tokens as a query, LLMs can assess the input's syntax and structure, infer context based on the model's training data, and predict the sequence of tokens that would likely come next. Simply put, LLMs can figure out what would sound right based on all the data they've digested and continue the conversation.

> ### Not Just LLMs
> There are more variants of AI models than just *traditional* LLMs, such as small language models and reasoning models. Copilot continues to be updated to use various models with different capabilities and training, but we're using the LLM terminology to keep explanations simple.

To appreciate the difference from traditional processing, think of learning a language and then conversing with someone who speaks it as a first language. You can learn the vocabulary and individual words and phrases. But in a conversation with someone who speaks this language well, you also need to gather and understand the context of what the other person is saying. This is so you can choose the right words or phrases to respond with. You also need to be able to frame your response in a context that will make sense to the other person. Language has syntax and structure, but the context of a conversation is how we ensure that syntax and structure make sense and convey meaning. LLMs can assess context from the inputs and supply relevant context in their outputs.

Turning back to Copilot, it uses, by default, LLMs developed and managed by OpenAI (*https://openai.com*), the same company behind ChatGPT (*https://chat.openai.com*). In conjunction with OpenAI, GitHub developed Copilot over several years. Recently, they have added options to use several other families of models, including ones from Claude by Anthropic and Google Gemini. Across models, the common characteristic of Copilot is the focus on creating software, and its conversational language is code.

Code and Generative AI

Programming languages, by definition, have specific, required syntax and semantics that differ for each language. When coding in Python versus Go, you use different tokens and structures to create the program. However, the tokens and structure you use have rules. They are well-defined and form a closed set. Copilot's abilities are targeted to provide coding suggestions and related information that match syntax and structure. But the real value-add is providing responses that are relevant to what the coder is creating or prompting about. The context that gets fed into Copilot can come from several sources, including these:

- A set of code being written in an editor in a development environment
- Interactions with the model via direct natural language prompts or queries, aka *chat models*
- Typical development activities in GitHub itself, such as pull requests

I'll discuss these interactions more throughout the book. But regardless of the interface, the context (code, directives/input, or GitHub elements you work with) gets turned into a *prompt*—your side of the conversation that you expect the AI to respond to. Processing those and deciding on a response based on context and the model's training and capabilities is the *generative* part of Copilot's *generative AI* functionality. The response can be suggested code, an answer to a question, or step-by-step directions. It is what the AI thinks completes the code, satisfies the prompt, or answers the query.

> ### Chat Models
> Most of the time, we think of programming as sitting in front of a terminal and typing code into an IDE. However, a programmer often needs to answer some questions or gain some understanding before entering the code. For example, if learning a new language, they may need to understand how to implement a data structure or control flow. Or they may need to know how to open files or read and write to a database. Going further, they might want to understand the differences in versions of a third-party platform or whether a certain functionality is deprecated. These are the kinds of details you might ask a colleague about or search for on Stack Overflow. If you're

> using AI instead, you need to be able to communicate questions or directives to the AI (have the ability to *chat* with it).
>
> Typical *social* implementations of generative AI (like ChatGPT) have gained broad appeal because they can converse and respond in a human-friendly way. Copilot adds this ability through *Copilot Chat*. Using this chat interface, it's simple to prompt Copilot for tasks like "generate unit tests for the code" as well as ask it questions like "What is the current version of Kubernetes?" and even "What does this code do?" Generating answers based on directives or questions in the chat interface is another example of the *generative* part of *generative AI*.

You can think of this process like describing a set of symptoms to a doctor over a Zoom call so they can try to reach a diagnosis based on their years of training. Or describing to the car mechanic over the phone an issue that you are seeing with your vehicle so that they can suggest a fix. In these cases, the communication and context you provide, with the professional's training, make all the difference. The interaction can result in suggestions to address the issue (some of which may not apply) or indicate that the professional didn't have enough context or understanding to help. Generative AI behaves the same way.

When Copilot offers suggestions as you're coding, items in your coding environment provide the context to create a prompt for the AI model. Copilot can produce suggestions that follow the coding style used in the files that are part of the project you're working on. This can be both good and bad.

It can be good that Copilot's suggestions are often similar to the users' existing coding styles if those coding styles reflect best practices. It can be bad if Copilot sometimes skews too much towards bad practices in existing code. The latter situation can lead to reinforcing limited and inefficient coding practices—or you may have to wade through a more extensive set of suggestions to find the one that fits. The quality and quantity of the examples that Copilot has to draw on from your environment, and its own training, can affect its responses.

Ultimately, the generative AI employed with Copilot can be very useful. Still, be aware that the coding suggestions will be biased by the context and training Copilot has to work with. You can use this to your advantage to provide Copilot with more examples of the style of suggestions it should return. However, this bias can also be a disadvantage if the context that Copilot has to work with is limited. We'll discuss how to help Copilot return the best results throughout the book.

Let's briefly look at Copilot's high-level flow to understand more about how it interacts with context to respond to you.

High-Level Flow

To understand how Copilot works at a high level, we can trace the basic workflow from the perspective of working in one of the supported IDEs. Currently, the supported IDEs for Copilot include Visual Studio, VS Code, NeoVim, any of the JetBrains family of IDEs, and others. Copilot also works in selected other environments, such as GitHub Codespaces (*https://oreil.ly/QyEks*).

GitHub has also released the Copilot Language Server SDK (*https://oreil.ly/6rDHq*), which can be used to integrate GitHub Copilot into any editor or IDE. So, expect to see more applications integrated with Copilot in the future.

About Codespaces

GitHub Codespaces utilize virtual machines (VMs) running in the cloud that provide a full-featured and customizable development environment for GitHub users. Their interface is similar to that of VS Code; they can be tailored with the same extensions used in VS Code in a browser or connected to several IDEs. GitHub provides them as an optional service.

When writing code in an editor and using Copilot to suggest coding completions, several pieces of information are automatically scanned to gather context about what you're working on:

Current file
　The current file that a user is editing is one key source of context for Copilot.

Name of the currently active file
　When named descriptively, this can provide Copilot with clues about what the code is intended to do, such as *TestConfig.go*.

Content before and after the current cursor position
　Copilot can draw context from the code and comments immediately before and after the cursor position in the file. This can help it decide what to fill in and/or understand gaps in the code.

Comments
　Like human pair programmers or reviewers, Copilot can use comments to understand what code is doing and the intent of code that has yet to be written. This is one of the primary ways to provide context for Copilot—the more precise and detailed the comments, the more likely the code that Copilot suggests will be relevant.

Other open files in the editor
> Copilot uses the code being developed in any open files as context. This is key to gathering information about the current task and augmenting information in the model. For example, one strategy for dealing with deprecated features stored in the LLM is to open a file in the editor with the replacement approach for the deprecated feature. From this example, Copilot can interpret preferred alternatives for coding instead of relying on the deprecated approach used to train the LLM.

Local index
> Copilot automatically parses most files in a project opened in IDEs like VS Code and builds an advanced local *index* for the project. (See the following sidebar for more info.)

Indexing

In the context of Copilot, *indexing* refers to a process of scanning and organizing the codebase to create a structure that can be searched quickly and accurately. This enables Copilot to provide more accurate and context-aware coding suggestions and responses than it could without the index.

A *local index* is created and updated automatically as changes are made and stored on the user's machine. When used in GitHub (Chapter 9), Copilot creates a *remote index* paired to the repository there.

If you are using the chat interface, it will usually be pre-populated with a file, selection, or terminal command as context, depending on what you were most recently working on. However, you can explicitly change that before submitting your prompt. (More on this in Chapter 3.)

So, when you're using one of the interfaces with Copilot installed and activated, Copilot gathers context from these sources as you enter code (Figure 1-2).

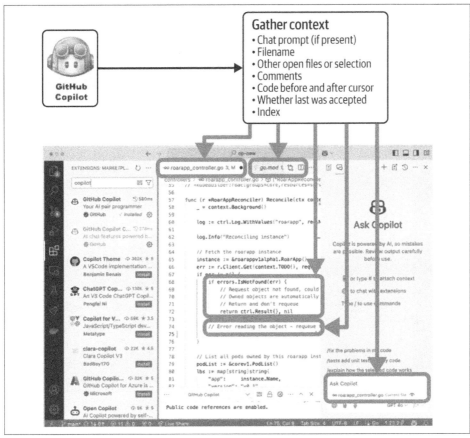

Figure 1-2. Gathering context from the IDE environment

That context is processed and ultimately sent to GitHub, synthesized into a prompt (Figure 1-3).

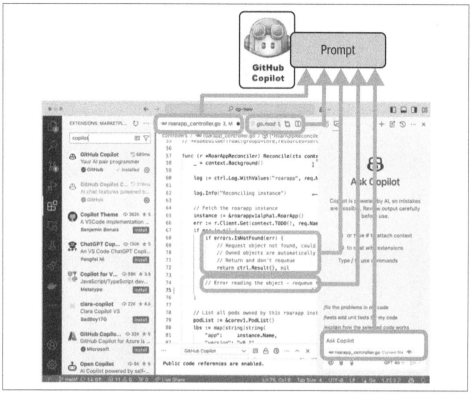

Figure 1-3. Synthesizing the prompt

The prompt is then passed through GitHub to the LLM, and possible completions or answers are returned. Once results are generated from the prompt to the LLM, GitHub's Copilot systems perform additional processing on the result (more on that later). After that, the response is returned to the IDE, where you can evaluate it and choose how to proceed. See Figure 1-4 for the flow for code completion.

This process continues and repeats with the user/Copilot interactions. In this way, Copilot acts as an assistant to help you with whatever use case you are working on, whether crafting boilerplate code, searching for a sophisticated algorithm, generating data or queries, writing unit tests, or learning a new programming language.

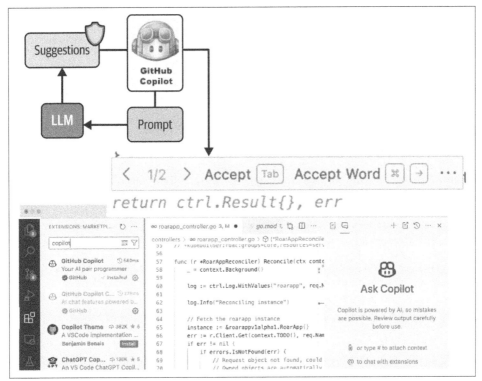

Figure 1-4. Flow from the prompt to suggestions

You'll see more of how the flow happens as we discuss how to use Copilot throughout the remaining chapters. But at this point, it's worth understanding some of the usage considerations when using Copilot to help you produce software.

Usage Considerations

Now that you know what Copilot is and how it works, here's a key point to understand: Copilot, like any AI, can give incorrect or incomplete answers. It can be wrong, or it can give you unexpected results. This is not common, but you should keep some important things in mind when using it so you can be aware. In this section, we'll look at the following considerations:

- Timeliness
- Relevance
- Completeness
- Accuracy
- Privacy
- Security

And by the way, these aren't unique to Copilot. They can apply to any current AI tool assisting you with a task.

Timeliness

Timeliness here refers to the currency of Copilot's suggestions. This may seem like an odd choice to start with, but it can intersect with all of the others.

Copilot relies on models trained initially at a point in time, so its data is based on what was current in the training data at that point. For example, if the model Copilot uses was trained two years ago, it does not necessarily know about changes since then.

Your everyday use of Copilot can produce outdated suggestions and answers. Results could contain deprecated code that no longer works with your compiler or interpreter. You could get a suggestion that references a version of a dependency with a known vulnerability or a response that might include an outdated approach.

You might ask the chat interface in Copilot, "Is X deprecated?" and get an answer that X is *not* deprecated when, in fact, it is. Copilot is answering as of the point in time when the model it is using was trained. Or you might ask, "What is the current version of X?" and get a result from two years ago. I'm sure you can see how this could cause issues. Results can also vary significantly depending on the model you've chosen (from the ones that Copilot supports) for the current interaction.

> ### Getting Current Version Info
>
> Say you ask Copilot through the chat interface, "What is the current version of X?" In most cases, the response will vary depending on the model being used. In some cases, the response will include "as of the date of training" or something similar. In other cases, Copilot will recommend that you consult the documentation for the latest information.
>
> You can't expect a model to know what the latest version is, so asking it isn't usually useful. The question can *sometimes* be useful, to give you an idea of which version was current when the model was trained, but the correctness and detail of that response will vary by model.

Chapter 7 discusses techniques for providing Copilot with more up-to-date context for deprecated items within your environment, increasing the likelihood of returning more up-to-date responses.

Relevance

Copilot's suggestions and chat responses are based on LLMs trained on large sets of code. If you're using the default OpenAI models, that codebase is the public code hosted on GitHub. GitHub arguably has the most comprehensive collection of repositories for open source software. This includes code written in today's most popular programming languages, such as Python, Go, and JavaScript.

Given the training, it stands to reason that Copilot will be most effective when you're working in one of the more common programming languages or frameworks represented in the codebase used for training. The more a language or framework is represented in that collection (GitHub repositories for the OpenAI models), the more references Copilot can learn from. Think of it like the subjects you spent more time studying in school—those are the ones you know the most about.

If you're working in a less represented language or framework, the suggestions may not be as useful. That doesn't imply you can't get relevant suggestions and answers, but you may find them less helpful in answering your exact query.

A key factor beyond Copilot's control is the amount of context it has to work with. For example, if your code consists of a function named `ParseData` or you supply a generic or ambiguous prompt, such as "Create a function to parse data," without additional context, the results returned from Copilot are likely to also be generic.

Completeness

Generative AI can sometimes return incomplete or unusable suggestions. This rarely happens in the chat interface, but it's not uncommon for Copilot's code completion to return a set of suggestions that are only partial solutions.

The same caveat discussed at the end of the previous section on relevancy applies here. If your code or query is generic or ambiguous, Copilot may not have enough context to draw on to return a complete result.

In other instances, you might provide specific context to Copilot, but it suggests only a comment or the first line of a function. This is generally seen when working through the suggestion process in the IDE rather than in the chat interface. You may need to provide additional prompting or supply more context for Copilot. Sometimes you can *nudge* Copilot by giving it a hint (typing a keyword, for example), and that will be enough to make it return a more complete suggestion. At other times, Copilot may simply respond with a blank line, and accepting that response may cause it to continue generating code.

Copilot does offer options to get more suggestions if the immediate one isn't a good fit, but those can be of limited utility. I'll delve into details on those approaches in Chapter 2.

Accuracy

Except in the simplest of cases, you cannot assume that any response from Copilot is entirely correct or the best answer. You should always carefully review Copilot responses. It's not hard to find stories of AI results in other domains that made their way into official records with references that don't exist. For example, there have been reports of court briefs that were filed referencing previous cases that didn't happen. I know of people who have tried to use AI to plan vacation itineraries and received a promising agenda—only with hotels that didn't exist.

Likewise, Copilot may return a response that is valid syntax but references constructs or variables that do not exist in the code. This is a coding form of AI *hallucination*: the AI presents information that is incorrect, made up, or otherwise not grounded in reality as a valid solution or suggestion. This is rare but can still occur. Sometimes this can be because Copilot needs to create suggestions around elements that don't exist yet. For example, if you ask Copilot how to open and write to a file without specifying the name, it may use a filename that has no meaning in your code within its example.

Regardless of the circumstances, the user is always responsible for reviewing Copilot's responses for accuracy. This should be no different from reviewing a human's contributions to your code; you want to ensure they are correct and do no harm.

Prompts and Accuracy

The results from Copilot can often be improved by developing a better prompt for the AI. We'll cover more about prompting throughout the book.

Privacy

Another aspect of working with Copilot is data privacy. As previously noted, several information sources (including open files and current files) are read, and information is collected and transferred through Copilot to factor into the prompt for the LLM. That means some data is going across the web and being processed outside your control. This may seem like a potential security risk. However, Copilot includes options when signing up to specify whether or not you want to allow GitHub to include your context information as part of its data to help Copilot get better. (See the bottom part of Figure 1-5.) If you do not, while the information will be gathered, it will not be retained. It will be collected to construct the prompt and then discarded.

Copilot Trust Center

GitHub has a Trust Center (*https://oreil.ly/0GM3-*) to help with any privacy-related content issues or concerns.

Figure 1-5. Options at sign-up for data privacy

Copilot intersects with user data in three areas: user engagement, prompts, and suggestions. Here's a summary:

User engagement
 This is usage data about how you interact with Copilot (telemetry). It can include whether you accept or dismiss suggestions from Copilot, how you interact with the chat UI, and metrics such as latency and error messages.

Prompts
 As previously discussed, the context information taken from your environment, or a chat query passed back to GitHub.

Suggestions
 The suggested code completions returned by Copilot and/or the responses to chat queries.

User engagement data is tracked by default and could include anonymized data, although there are nuances depending on the particular Copilot plan you're using. (See the Trust Center (*https://oreil.ly/rC8Rm*) documentation for more information.) Mechanisms exist to encrypt data in transit and at rest. GitHub has controls to strictly limit who can access data on their side.

GitHub Repositories and Legal Concerns

The legality of using the *public* repositories on GitHub to train some LLMs has been questioned in public opinion and in courts. We will leave those considerations for others to sort out, and we won't focus on, or comment on, those aspects of the initial training process in this book.

One other concern is often raised about Copilot when using a model trained on licensed repositories: Copilot could generate suggestions that closely match content from that codebase. The implication is that users could end up unwittingly violating licensing terms and intellectual property rights by having the duplicated code included in their work. Copilot includes an option for individuals and administrators to block public code matches if those are generated as part of the AI's process. (See the top part of Figure 1-5.) If that option is selected, Copilot will alert you to the situation and filter out matches from the public code base.

Why Allow Matching Content?

Matching content refers to exact or near-exact matches between code in GitHub repositories and code suggested by Copilot. You may wonder what value there would be in having an option to allow matching content. In actuality, there may not be much. However, if you were generally researching how to do something and either did not intend to use it if there was a match, or use it under the terms of the license if it represented the best approach, that might be an acceptable use case.

Security

Last but certainly not least is the area of security in the results that Copilot returns. Security is an ever-present concern in any product or application used today. Addressing that concern starts with secure coding practices.

I stated earlier that once Copilot receives potential results from the LLM, GitHub performs some additional processing on them. This processing includes running algorithms to quickly look for possible vulnerabilities. GitHub does not run a security scanning application against the result, which would take too long. Instead, it quickly scans for patterns indicating vulnerabilities and/or insecure coding practices. If those are identified, the proposed suggestion is flagged.

Even with these measures, there is no guarantee that something hasn't slipped through. Since the processing isn't the same as running full scans with an application focused on finding vulnerabilities, the results from Copilot should still be subject to whatever other security checks you would use for any code.

The clear and ever-present requirement when using generative AI is that you must always review and assess any suggestions it returns. You should not assume that it completely and correctly interpreted the context. And, in all but the simplest of cases, you cannot assume that the result is perfect.

To state this another way, while Copilot is often referred to as an *AI pair programmer*, it does not have the same understanding and level of familiarity with your code as an actual human pair programmer would. Instead, it is best to think of Copilot as a skilled programmer new to the project. A programmer in that position can create useful code based on what they can observe and what has been shared with them, but they can't possess all of the larger context, project history, or backstory. As a result, you must be diligent in ensuring that the code they produce is accurate, secure, and suitable to merge. Copilot's answers and suggestions should be treated the same way.

And, as when working with a new programmer on the team, the more details you provide (whether code to use as context or specific directions), the better the result will usually be. Giving Copilot more coding examples to draw on and more specifics in your prompt in the chat can go a long way towards getting a better result from the AI.

Another consideration may come up as you start to work with or consider using an assistant like Copilot: why not just use ChatGPT or a similar chatbot to produce code? The answer is that you certainly can. However, the two approaches and interfaces have key differences. The following section provides a quick comparison, using ChatGPT to represent other generalized AI applications that can create code.

Copilot Versus ChatGPT

You might wonder how Copilot or similar coding assistants differ from ChatGPT or similar chatbots, given both may use the same underlying models to produce responses. The general distinction is that Copilot is focused only on the coding domain and provides functionality to specifically help with that. ChatGPT, on the other hand, is targeted more broadly across any domain and doesn't provide the same level of integration. Table 1-1 highlights differences in several more specific categories.

Table 1-1. Comparison of Copilot to ChatGPT

Category	GitHub Copilot	ChatGPT
Primary function	Understanding and generating code or code-related prompts	Understanding and generating any natural language
Primary user interface	Code editors, chat	Chat
Developer	GitHub with OpenAI	OpenAI
Primary use cases	Writing and augmenting code and code documentation	Conversational responses with text generation

Category	GitHub Copilot	ChatGPT
Pricing model	Subscription based with usage tracking for premium models	Usage based and subscription based
Training data	Code repos, documentation	Diverse, broad text content
Public APIs	Limited to telemetry, monitoring, and license management	Broad API surface for interaction

In general, you can think of Copilot as a very domain-specific implementation of generative AI. This is as opposed to the broader (domain-less) implementation and function of ChatGPT and other general chat tools. ChatGPT can certainly be used for generating code, but it lacks the integration with development environments, coding focus, and GitHub support and features that Copilot has.

Although we've been discussing Copilot as a single application, it actually has five configurations. Let's finish up this introductory chapter by helping explain the plans available for you to choose from.

Copilot Plans

Copilot comes in five plans at the time of this writing: *Free*, *Pro*, *Pro+*, *Business*, and *Enterprise*. To understand the differences between them, you need to understand some common terms:

Code completions
   AI-suggested code for completing code being worked on in your IDE.

Chat request
   A prompt, which can be a direction or a question, that you pass to Copilot through a chat interface.

Agent mode
   An option in Copilot to have it act on a prompt by independently planning, executing, and iterating across files to suggest changes needed to accomplish a task.

Agent mode request
   A request made to Copilot to accomplish a task while it is in Agent mode.

Model access
   The LLMs that Copilot is allowed to access from the set of all LLMs it works with; a list of models currently available is included in the Copilot documentation.

Premium requests
   Interactions that use advanced AI models with operations such as Copilot Chat, Agent mode, code review, or extensions. These consume more compute resources and are counted separately from standard code completions.

> ## Understanding Premium Requests
>
> If you're using an advanced model, some Copilot features require more processing power. Those are considered *premium requests*. Essentially any type of model interaction can be a premium request, depending on the plan and model.
>
> If you're on the free plan, each of your requests counts as a premium. If you are on a paid plan, requests using the default base model (GPT-4o as of this writing) do not count as premium. Requests using any of the other models do.
>
> It is important to note that there is not always a one-to-one request-to-premium-request ratio. A single request made to some models can count as less than one premium request or more than one premium request, depending on the model. The current model multipliers can be found in the Copilot documentation.
>
> As an example, if you are on the Pro plan (at the time of this writing) and you do 20 chat interactions with the o1 model selected, you will have used 200 (20 × 10) of your 300 allocated premium requests for the month. (The number of premium requests per plan is shown in Table 1-2.)
>
> If you run out of premium requests and want more on a paid plan, you can purchase additional ones for $.04/premium request.

With those terms in mind, Table 1-2 explains the available plans and the key differences between them.

Table 1-2. Comparison of GitHub Copilot plans

	Free	Pro	Pro+	Business	Enterprise
Target users	Individual developers looking to explore Copilot	Individual developers who want unlimited access to Copilot but don't need to use all models	Individual developers who want maximum flexibility and access to all models	Organizations or enterprises that need unlimited access to core Copilot functionality and business management features but not all models	Organizations or enterprises that need unlimited access to core Copilot functionality and business management features with maximum flexibility and access to all models

	Free	Pro	Pro+	Business	Enterprise
Coding completions, chat requests, and Agent mode requests	50 chat requests or Agent mode requests/month (counted as premium) 2,000 code completion requests/month	Unlimited	Unlimited	Unlimited	Unlimited
Model access	Access to a small subset of models	Access to more models	Access to all models	Access to more models	Access to all models
Premium requests	50 premium requests/month	300 premium requests/month	1,500 premium requests/month	300 premium requests/month	1,000 premium requests/month
Additional features	Limited code review for selections in VS Code	• Code review • Pull request summaries	• Code review • Pull request summaries	• Code review • Pull request summaries • User management and metrics • Data privacy • IP indemnity	• Code review • Pull request summaries • User management and metrics • Data privacy • IP indemnity
Administration	Individual	Individual	Individual	Enterprise	Enterprise
Cost	Free	$10/month or $100/year (free trial available for 30 days)	$39/month or $390/year	$19/month/user	$39/month/user

Latest Info

The information in Table 1-2 is accurate as of the time of this writing. Consult the Copilot features page (*https://oreil.ly/ptoVy*) for the latest information.

Of course, cost is a significant factor. If you are an individual user who only uses Copilot on a limited basis in your IDE and doesn't need the extra features, the Free plan may make sense. If you're an individual user who wants to use Copilot on a regular basis and can benefit from the additional features, the Pro or Pro+ plans can provide a good match.

At a corporate or community level, if you need or want the extra ability to easily assign and manage licenses across multiple users, as well as additional administrative oversight, the Business subscription can provide that. And if, as a business or community, you you want to take full advantage of advanced features and have maximum access to models, then the Enterprise plan is your best option.

Mixing Plans

It is possible to mix plan types within an enterprise at the organization level. See the documentation (*https://oreil.ly/BZ1p6*).

Regardless of the plan you choose, the steps are similar:

- Sign up and register for license(s).
- Establish a payment process.
- Install Copilot via an extension or whatever process you use to add functionality in your IDE.

At an organization level, once the plan is set up, organization admins can add users and manage licenses as shown in Figure 1-6.

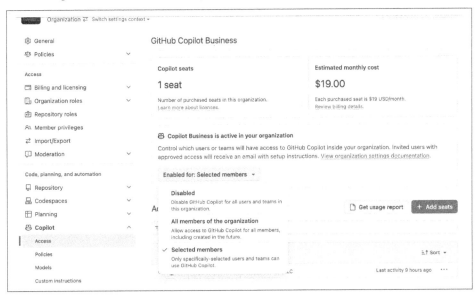

Figure 1-6. Managing a Copilot Business plan

Once you gain access to a Copilot subscription, you can install it into whichever IDE you use. The GitHub Copilot documentation (*https://oreil.ly/kF4rn*) provides links for installing the GitHub Copilot extension in your chosen IDE. As of this writing, the currently supported IDEs include the following:

- Azure Data Studio (*https://oreil.ly/uUNGn*)
- Eclipse (*https://oreil.ly/Mqdq2*)
- JetBrains IDEs (*https://oreil.ly/dlYdh*)
- Vim/Neovim (*https://oreil.ly/rA6oI*)
- Visual Studio (*https://oreil.ly/qYbh_*)
- Visual Studio Code (*https://oreil.ly/GYc9X*)
- Xcode (*https://oreil.ly/MGeCb*)

GitHub Copilot Language Server

GitHub also provides the Copilot Language Server SDK (*https://oreil.ly/008MF*). This SDK allows integrating Copilot with any editor or IDE that can use the Language Server Protocol (LSP) standard. So expect to see more integrations being developed.

Conclusion

I hope you're starting to have a better sense of what GitHub Copilot is all about and how it potentially can be used. I also hope you're finding yourself intrigued to learn and understand more about it.

In this chapter, I've provided an overview of what Copilot is, how it works, some key considerations to keep in mind when using it, and how to understand the plans it provides. This paints a picture of how Copilot fits in with the current use and potential of AI to help you in a given domain. In this case, that domain is creating software, and more generally, coding.

There are a few key points to take away from this text. One is that AI can greatly simplify and support your efforts as a coder. A second is that context is king when it comes to helping Copilot provide you with the best results. And a third, and arguably the most important one, is that you still have the ultimate responsibility to review and assess any suggestions and answers from the AI. Copilot is great at what it does, but it is only as good as the context we give it and the capabilities and training data of the model it is using. And as with human coders, those variables factor in to how complete, relevant, and accurate (or not) any result is.

There are a number of standard ways of leveraging Copilot to complete code. In the next chapter, you'll look at how to use and work with Copilot code completions in the IDE interfaces where you are coding. Understanding those will help get you to the next level of using the tool, completing the foundation you need for the rest of the book, and getting the most out of Copilot.

CHAPTER 2
Coding with Copilot

Now that you have the basic foundations of what Copilot is and how it works, we can move on to the key aspect of how to use it. Since Copilot is intended to function like an AI assistant, you need to understand how to work and communicate with your assistant. The mechanics of this boil down to learning to work with the integrations in the IDE. Learning those mechanics in this chapter and the next will set you up for success with the rest of the book. And they will also answer these questions:

- How do you query the assistant and provide directions for what you need?
- How do you follow up on responses or choose from multiple suggestions?
- Which ways are best to communicate with it for quick suggestions or longer explanations when needed?
- How can you best leverage the AI to help with coding tasks?

IDE = VS Code

GitHub Copilot can be installed and used with multiple IDEs, including VS Code, JetBrains IDEs, Eclipse, and NeoVim. Since we can't cover all of these in this book, we are using VS Code and GitHub Codespaces as our IDE examples throughout. Please consult your IDE's documentation for any differences in how to work with Copilot if needed.

Within the IDE, Copilot provides two primary modes of interaction. The first mode is integration within your editor and through the context menus and related controls. For simplicity, I refer to this as *inline* mode since it is most commonly used directly from the editor or related menus. This is the mode covered in this chapter.

The second interaction mode is through the separate *chat* interface bundled with Copilot. This approach offers expanded options for interaction and feedback. It also acts as a gateway to some of Copilot's more advanced functionality, including Copilot's *Agent* mode and an *advanced editing* mode. After we discuss the core inline use cases in this chapter, we'll cover chat ones in Chapters 3 and 4.

Most users will likely first engage with Copilot by working in an editor in their IDE. As you're coding, the installed Copilot extension gathers context and integrates with the remote components to provide you with suggestions. We discussed at a high level how that works in Chapter 1. Now, let's take a closer look at that flow.

Copilot uses different key combinations as shortcuts to invoke various functions. These key combinations are usually formed with a meta-key (Command, Ctrl, or Option key) plus a letter, number, or symbol. The meta-key will vary depending on which operating system you are using and possibly your keyboard. Instead of trying to list out each combination every time, I refer to these shortcuts by using the notation Meta-<character>, as in Meta-I instead of Option-I. You can find the list of keyboard shortcuts for your platform in the Copilot documentation (*https://oreil.ly/aAZ8S*).

Inline Suggestions

Suppose you are going to create a Python file to work with prime numbers. You might start by creating a file named *prime.py*. Visually, the first evidence of Copilot you will probably notice is an inline option to interact with *Copilot Chat* through the *Meta*-I keypress combination. This reminder will appear anytime you edit a file if Copilot is active and chat is enabled. See Figure 2-1.

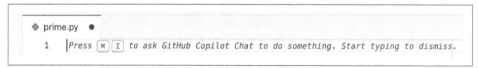

Figure 2-1. An option to invoke Copilot Chat inline

We'll defer discussing this interface until Chapter 3, after more basic interactions have been covered, since it will make more sense then. While this option is present by default, you can ignore it in the editor and start typing to proceed.

To provide an example to work with, let's create a relevant function in *prime.py* to check if a number is prime or not. You start typing:

```
def is_prime
```

At this point, Copilot will start suggesting possible completions. It might provide an option like Figure 2-2. The proposed text from Copilot is shown as *ghost text*. This means that until it is accepted, the suggested text will be displayed in an italicized lighter font rather than the regular dark font.

```
prime.py 1 ●      < 1/2 >  Accept [Tab]  Accept Word [⌘] [→] ...
1    def is_prime(n):
         if n < 2:
             return False
         for i in range(2, int(n ** 0.5) + 1):
             if n % i == 0:
                 return False
         return True
```

Figure 2-2. First suggestion

Your Suggestions May Be Different

While reading through this chapter and any places in the book showing suggestions or output from Copilot, remember that since this is generative AI, suggestions you get back with the same context may be very different.

Copilot's suggestion is one possible option for building out your function. In Figure 2-2, there's a gray bar above and to the right of the suggested text. This bar pops up when Copilot suggests text inline. The bar has controls to accept all or part of the suggestion. Other controls allow you to cycle through multiple suggestions if Copilot generates multiple choices.

Your IDE May Be Different

Throughout the book, we are using IDEs in the style of VS Code. If you are using a different IDE (such as one from JetBrains), your interfaces and controls may differ though similar functionality should be available.

The text in the bar also is a reminder of corresponding keyboard shortcuts and options. The ones available include accepting an entire suggestion (via the Tab key), accepting a word at a time (via the key combination shown in the bar and in the doc), and additional options that can be accessed via the More Actions menu, which is depicted as three dots (more about those later).

In the leftmost part of that bar is < 1/2 >. This text indicates that Copilot has generated two possible suggestions, and you are currently looking at option 1. To see the other options and rotate through the potential choices, click the > and < symbols in the bar or use the corresponding keys on your keyboard. For example, if you want to look at option 2, you can click the > symbol (see Figure 2-3).

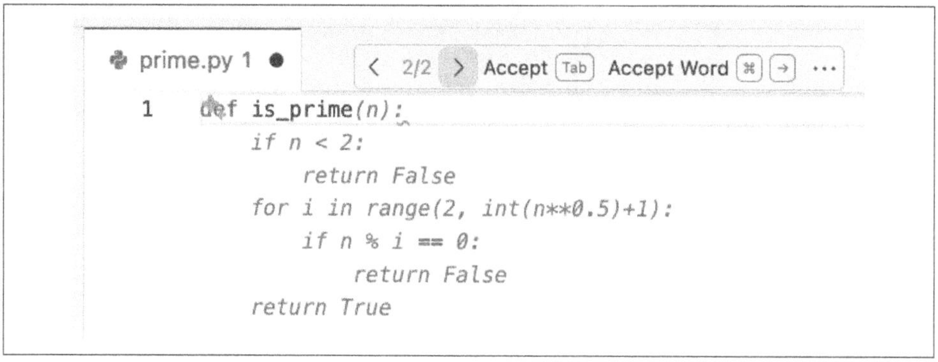

```
prime.py 1 ●        < 2/2 >  Accept [Tab]  Accept Word [⌘] [→]  ...
1   def is_prime(n):
        if n < 2:
            return False
        for i in range(2, int(n**0.5)+1):
            if n % i == 0:
                return False
        return True
```

Figure 2-3. Second suggestion

To accept either of Copilot's suggestions, you can rotate through the options and then hit the Tab key to select the one you want. If you don't like either suggestion, you can just continue typing.

The differences between option 1 and option 2 are subtle—just some whitespace. But Copilot still presents these as two separate options. Regardless of which option you choose, you have what looks like a viable function body that was automatically generated.

If you choose the first option, the full suggested text is inserted into your file after hitting Tab. This text no longer appears ghosted. It appears the same as any text you manually typed (Figure 2-4).

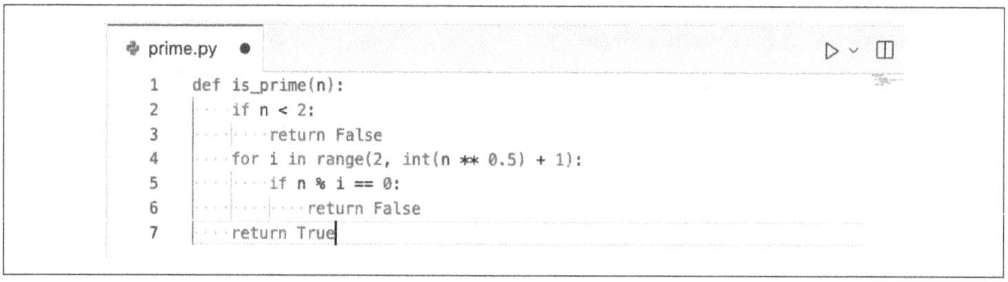

```
prime.py ●
1   def is_prime(n):
2       if n < 2:
3           return False
4       for i in range(2, int(n ** 0.5) + 1):
5           if n % i == 0:
6               return False
7       return True
```

Figure 2-4. Option 1 accepted

Once you've used it a few times, the interface starts to feel more predictable and helpful. From this point, the typical workflow as you are typing code becomes as follows:

1. Accept or discard a suggestion from Copilot.

2. Type additional code manually if needed/desired.

3. Pause slightly, if needed, to give time for Copilot to generate options.
4. Copilot offers suggestions.
5. Repeat steps 1–4 until you're done.

The *completeness* and *fit* of Copilot's suggestions can vary significantly. Depending on the context available to it, it may offer completion suggestions ranging from a comment, to a single line, to multiple lines that form a complete solution. As you are typing, you may get a full function definition suggested; at other times, you may only get a line or two. The flow in the preceding numbered steps is the same, whether the first suggestion is a complete option or you must work through multiple rounds of line-by-line suggestions.

Pausing for Suggestions

You may have wondered about step 3 in the previous list, which notes pausing (if needed) to give Copilot time to generate options. In between displaying suggestions, a lot of processing and communication takes place. As discussed in Chapter 1, Copilot does a lot in the background to generate coding suggestions. It gathers context, synthesizes it, ships it across the net, prompts the LLM, checks for any patterns that might indicate vulnerabilities, optionally checks against public code matches, and then makes the options available online.

This happens remarkably quickly. But occasionally, Copilot may take a moment to return the result after you hit Enter. For this reason, if you are in a mode of hitting Return and expecting to hit Tab right away to accept the next suggestions, you might get ahead of Copilot at times. If that happens, you may need to pause for a moment before trying to accept the next line. Note that sometimes Copilot may also generate a blank line as part of the output.

A couple of details about what's occurred so far with this simple interaction with Copilot are worth calling out:

- Copilot was able to suggest context-appropriate function definitions.
- The options only varied slightly in a *not technically significant* way but were still presented differently.
- How did Copilot get the specific context for the suggestions? It used the name of the file and the name we typed in for the function.
- If you were to repeat this same exercise, there is no guarantee that you would get the same suggestions or even more than one. Generative AI will not always return the same results, even given the same exact context again.

To that last point, while the inline suggestions presented by Copilot may often be good enough for what you need, sometimes you may want additional options. To help with that, Copilot includes a built-in mechanism to ask for additional *alternative suggestions*. We'll cover that next.

Getting Additional Suggestions

If Copilot's initial suggestions don't seem to be enough, you can ask it to generate others. To make Copilot generate a more extensive list of alternative completions, use the Ctrl-Enter key combination.

Trade-Offs of Using the Alternative Suggestions Functionality

While asking Copilot for additional suggestions can generate more completion options, it does so with the trade-off of taking longer to create and present them than the immediate inline options. Also, the alternative code may consist of partial implementations or sets of comments, making it less useful.

The best time to use this functionality is before accepting one of the inline suggestions. Let's return to where we were typing the function name but have not yet accepted a suggestion. At this point, you can hit Ctrl-Enter, and Copilot will generate a separate panel with alternative completions, as shown in Figure 2-5.

Copilot has suggested six alternatives, all likely plausible completions, with some implementations only slightly different.

The GitHub Copilot Suggestions tab is read-only. You can scroll through the set to see the alternative completions. If you find one you like, you can insert it into your file by clicking the "Accept suggestion #" button underneath it (where # represents the suggestion's number).

If you want to use the alternative suggestions functionality on code you've already completed, your results can vary even more. In this case, it's essential to make sure you highlight the code you want Copilot to target for the suggestions. Otherwise, you may not get any results.

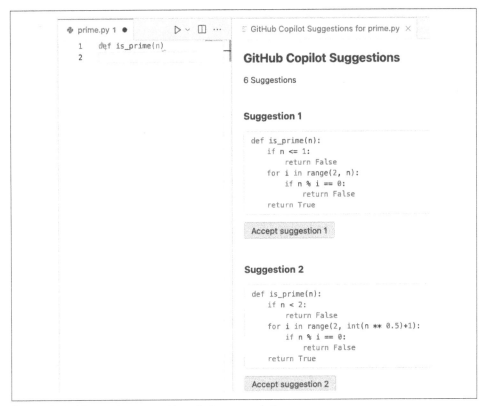

Figure 2-5. Alternative suggestions before completion

When asking Copilot for alternative suggestions on existing code, we can see the differences in quality and usability of the suggestions. Figure 2-6 shows a set of alternatives generated by starting with existing code.

Notice that in the suggestions tab that there are only three alternatives. None are complete implementations. So, if you have minimal context, your best bet is to ask for alternative suggestions before adding the code.

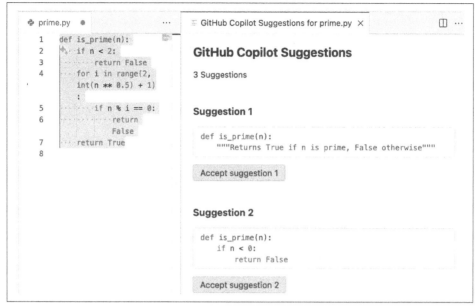

Figure 2-6. Request for alternative suggestions on existing code

As outlined in Chapter 1, Copilot bases suggestions not only on your actual code but also on related elements like comments. While we generally think of adding comments just to explain code, we can also leverage comments to drive Copilot's behavior in other ways.

Leveraging Comments

Comments can play a significant role in the context for Copilot. Say you enter the following single comment as the only line in a new file:

```
# a function to determine if a number is prime or not
```

Copilot may respond with a completion suggestion like that in Figure 2-7.

```
prime.py
1  # a function to determine if a number is prime or not
2  def is_prime(n):
3
```

Figure 2-7. A suggestion generated from a comment

If you accept that, code for the rest of the function body is suggested (see Figure 2-8).

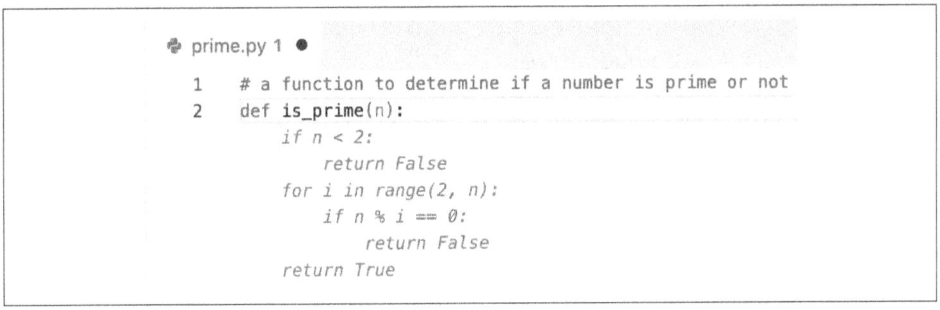

```
🐍 prime.py 1 ●
1    # a function to determine if a number is prime or not
2    def is_prime(n):
         if n < 2:
             return False
         for i in range(2, n):
             if n % i == 0:
                 return False
         return True
```

Figure 2-8. Completion generated from a comment

Beyond the passive context that Copilot can gather from standard comments, you can also use comments actively to tell Copilot what you want it to do. The difference is instead of writing comments as context, you are issuing instructions to Copilot. This involves phrasing the comment more as a directive.

Directive Comments

You can tell Copilot via comments what you'd like it to do. Suppose that in place of typing the function header as in the last section,

```
def is_prime
```

you instead enter a comment describing what you want to have happen. An example in our prime number-checking function might be this:

```
# create a function to determine if a number is prime
```

Depending on available context, Copilot might suggest a relevant completion of your comment, as shown in Figure 2-9. The suggested completion may or may not be what we intended.

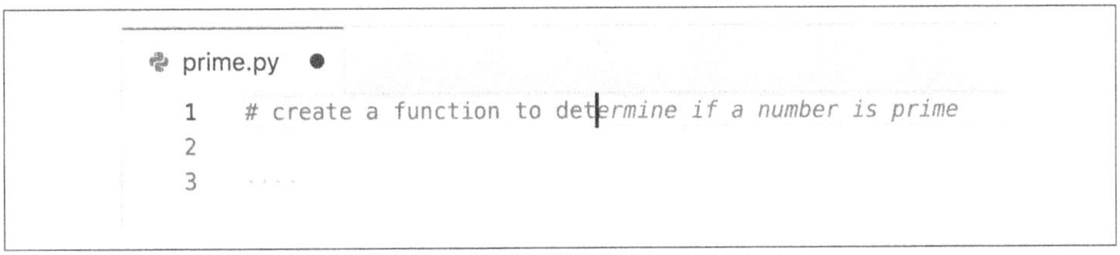

```
🐍 prime.py ●
1    # create a function to determine if a number is prime
2
3    ....
```

Figure 2-9. Auto-completion of a comment

This single line is enough to begin generating suggested code for the function. See the example in Figure 2-10.

Leveraging Comments | 31

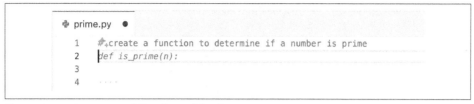

Figure 2-10. A generated first line of the function

The proposed name of the function is what you had before, but there is a difference in the options that Copilot provides. Instead of suggesting just one line, Copilot suggests multiple possible completions. One is a function header. The second option is a continuation of the comment. These options can be reviewed via the pop-up bar or keyboard shortcuts. See Figure 2-11.

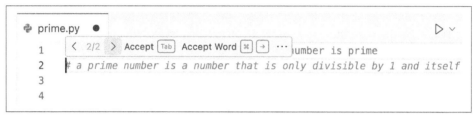

Figure 2-11. The second option—continuation of a comment

Options May Be Different

As a reminder, since you're working with generative AI, the suggestions you get when using Copilot in practice may be different from those in the book, even if using the same example code.

For this case, Copilot does not have enough context to know if you want to generate an extended comment or start creating the function code. So it gives you both options. After you accept the first option, Copilot has enough context and supplies a proposed function definition (Figure 2-12).

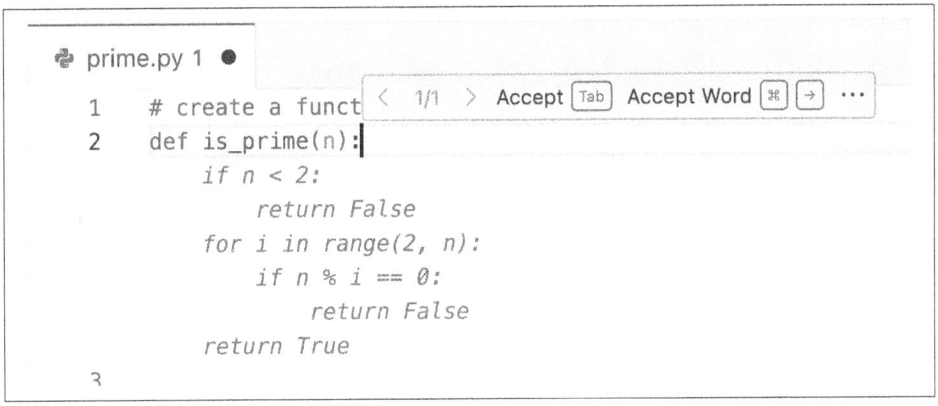

```
 prime.py 1 ●
1    # create a funct  < 1/1 >  Accept [Tab]  Accept Word [⌘] [→]  ...
2    def is_prime(n):
         if n < 2:
             return False
         for i in range(2, n):
             if n % i == 0:
                 return False
         return True
3
```

Figure 2-12. A full function suggestion

As another example, you can tell Copilot inline to explain existing code through a comment:

```
# explain the code above
```

Applied to the example you've been working with, Copilot responds with brief, commented output lines explaining how the code works. Figure 2-13 shows the generated comments. Copilot generated each of the three comment lines (11–13) after the `explain` directive.

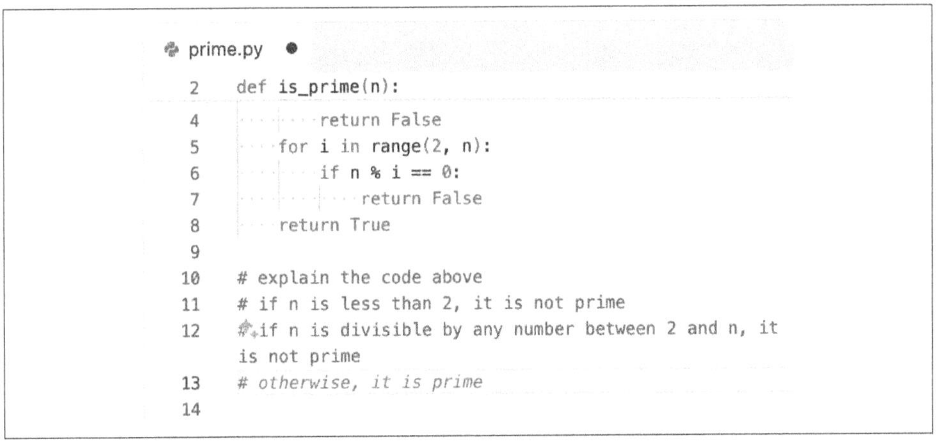

```
 prime.py  ●
2    def is_prime(n):
4            return False
5        for i in range(2, n):
6            if n % i == 0:
7                return False
8        return True
9
10   # explain the code above
11   # if n is less than 2, it is not prime
12   # if n is divisible by any number between 2 and n, it
     is not prime
13   # otherwise, it is prime
14
```

Figure 2-13. Output of telling Copilot to explain code via comments

You can also write a comment to get a more detailed response:

```
# explain the code above line-by-line
```

The results of using that comment are shown in Figure 2-14.

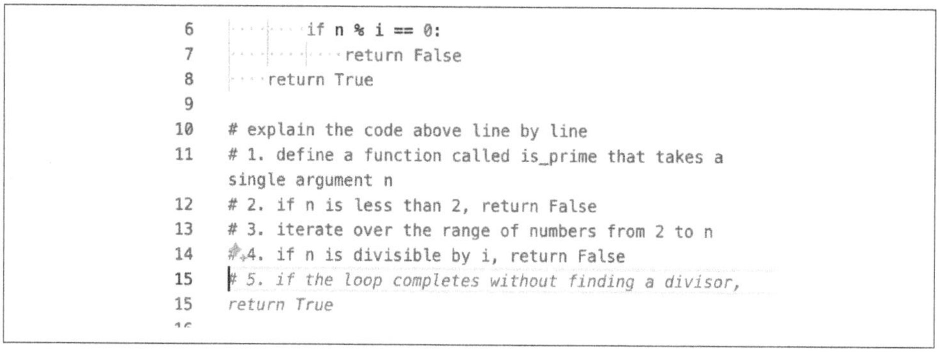

```
 6              if n % i == 0:
 7                  return False
 8          return True
 9
10      # explain the code above line by line
11      # 1. define a function called is_prime that takes a
        single argument n
12      # 2. if n is less than 2, return False
13      # 3. iterate over the range of numbers from 2 to n
14      # 4. if n is divisible by i, return False
15      # 5. if the loop completes without finding a divisor,
15      return True
```

Figure 2-14. Results of a more detailed `explain` directive in a comment

A helpful point to understand is that if you are using comments *to prompt Copilot to generate code*, Copilot should produce code based on the comment. For any other non-coding directive (such as `explain`), the results will be provided back as *additional comments*.

One other use case for comments is to ask Copilot direct questions.

Questions via Comments

Similar to giving Copilot directions through comments, you can also ask it questions. For example, instead of telling Copilot to explain the code, you can ask it a question like this:

```
# What does the code above do?
```

Figure 2-15 shows the result.

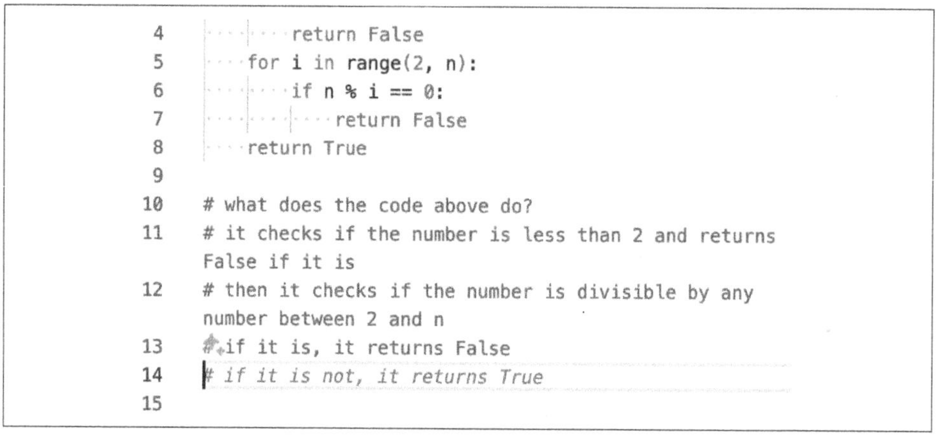

```
 4              return False
 5          for i in range(2, n):
 6              if n % i == 0:
 7                  return False
 8          return True
 9
10      # what does the code above do?
11      # it checks if the number is less than 2 and returns
        False if it is
12      # then it checks if the number is divisible by any
        number between 2 and n
13      # if it is, it returns False
14      # if it is not, it returns True
15
```

Figure 2-15. Using a comment to ask Copilot a question

You can also mark your comments as questions more formally by adding a `q:` after the comment character, but this is not required. If you do this, Copilot provides an answer back starting with an `a:`.

Q&A Context

Asking Copilot questions via comments historically provided a way to get chat-like answers before Copilot Chat was included with Copilot plans. Although this approach is typically less useful today than using the inline chat interface or the main chat window, it can still provide some value if you want brief answers included in the code.

Having completed our discussion of how we can interact with Copilot inline in the editor, let's look at how to use Copilot from the IDE menus.

Copilot and the Context Menu

Certain Copilot functions are available through your IDE's context menus. This integration provides a way to quickly run some advanced features without giving directions in chat. (The chat interfaces are discussed in Chapter 3.)

Contexts Meaning #2

When used with discussions about the menus in this section, *context* does not refer to the information that Copilot gathers to offer completion suggestions. Instead, the term refers to Copilot options available in the *context menus* of your IDE.

For example, you may have noticed some of the previous figures in this chapter show two small *four-point star* symbols at the start of the lines. These two stars form what is sometimes called the *sparkle* icon, which is a general symbol (beyond Copilot) for AI. In the IDE, the presence of the symbol usually indicates a link that you can click to interact with Copilot. That click, in turn, will open a menu with several advanced options.

In the cases we're discussing, the icon appears when the function definition is incomplete. However, the system can't distinguish between a function that is still being written and one that is broken. So, Copilot will suggest a completion and offer to *fix* it. Clicking the sparkle icon opens a pop-up menu, as shown in Figure 2-16. (Note that this may not show up in other IDEs.)

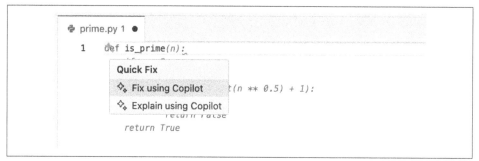

Figure 2-16. The Quick Fix option using Copilot

Leveraging Fix for Completion

The "Fix using Copilot" option can sometimes be an alternative to getting suggested completions. Selecting it may cause Copilot to generate partial code to get the system to a working state. However, you can't count on this functionality providing a full completion.

When you have more data for Copilot to work with (such as a completed function implementation), you can see additional options in the menu. (See Figure 2-17.)

Figure 2-17. Expanded context menu options

The options available in the menu (and what they refer to) also vary depending on what part of the IDE you're working with. For example, if you are working in the terminal, the Explain menu option refers to content in the terminal, not the editor. And, as shown in Figure 2-18, there are different options referring only to the terminal. (Since these are chat options, I'll explain them in the next chapter.)

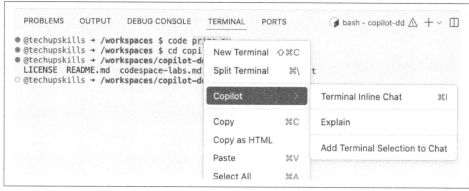

Figure 2-18. Copilot options in the terminal

So, context menus provide a subset of Copilot functionality that makes sense depending on your task. In VS Code and similar IDEs, you can also invoke Copilot-related commands through an interface called the *Command Palette*, as discussed in the following sidebar.

> ## Accessing Copilot Through the Command Palette
>
> VS Code–style IDEs have an interface for quick access to commands that are related to installed extensions. The interface, called the *Command Palette*, is accessed using *Meta*-P or F1. This brings up a dialog where you can scroll or type the name of the related extension, command, symbol, or file. For example, when you have the Copilot extension installed, you can get to commands related to it through the Command Palette by typing **Copilot** as shown in Figure 2-19.
>
>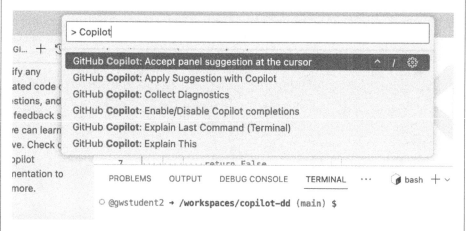
>
> *Figure 2-19. Accessing Copilot functionality from the Command Palette*

Entries in this list can be executed as commands. Figure 2-20 shows executing Copilot's Explain function from the list. This list is also helpful in showing all Copilot-related commands available to you.

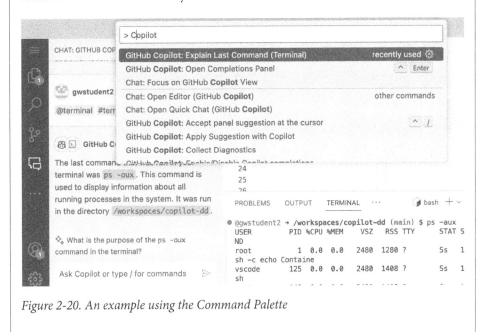

Figure 2-20. An example using the Command Palette

In addition to *standard* functions that we have discussed such as explaining code and fixing code, you can also use the context menu to have Copilot perform a useful and important task: reviewing your code and providing feedback on it. We'll discuss the mechanics of that next.

Using Copilot to Review Your Code

Copilot can act as a reviewer of your code. In GitHub, you can add Copilot as a reviewer on pull requests (see Chapter 9). In the IDE, you can have Copilot review your local code and provide feedback inline. This can be especially useful to catch problems before code is pushed. When doing reviews, you can use the default behavior of Copilot or customize the way it does the review.

Using Copilot's Default Review Options

Suppose we have the following code block that is intended to implement a simple class for a point:

```
class Point:
    def __init__(self, x, y, z=0): self.x = x; self.y = y
```

```
        def distance(self, other): return (self.x - other.x)**2 + \
        (self.y - other.y)**2 + (self.z - other.z)**2**0.5
p1 = Point(1, 2); p2 = Point(4, 6, 0)
print(p1.distance(p2))
```

If you are a Python programmer, you may be able to spot some of the issues with the code. Let's ask Copilot to review it. We do this by highlighting the code in the editor, then right-clicking and selecting Copilot > Review and Comment (see Figure 2-21).

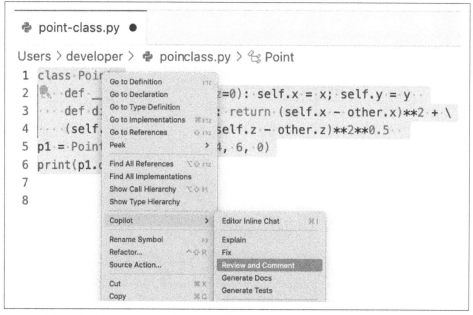

Figure 2-21. Selecting a code review from the menu

After Copilot processes the request, if it has any feedback about problems or recommended updates (including things as simple as adding documentation), it will provide the comments and suggested changes inline with the code. Figure 2-22 shows an example of a review item from Copilot.

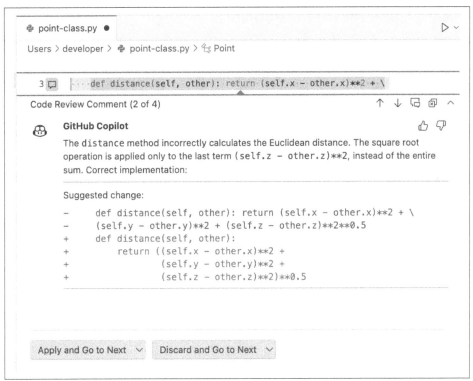

Figure 2-22. Feedback from Copilot's review

The review feedback dialog has arrow controls you can use to navigate to other review comments, as well as controls to see the feedback in chat, close the dialog and collapse it. Any suggested changes are shown as the current code in red (with the minus sign) and the suggested code in green (with the plus sign). Buttons at the bottom of the dialog make it simple to apply or discard the change and then advance to the next set of feedback.

In addition to the default review behavior, you can also customize what Copilot looks for during a review.

Creating Custom Review Instructions

By default, Copilot only reports issues that seem significant to it. So it's not uncommon for it to report that it has no feedback on your code when it includes elements that other reviewers might flag, such as those not conforming to best practices or style guidelines. Figure 2-23 shows an example of the message you see if Copilot doesn't find any issues.

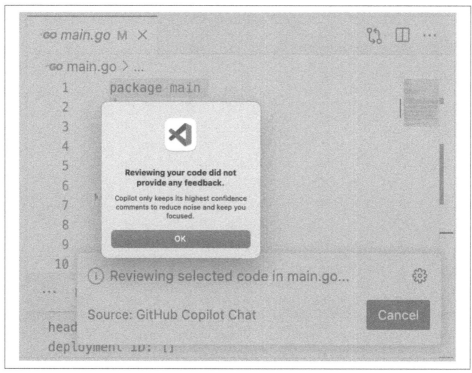

Figure 2-23. No feedback from Copilot's code review

If you want more detailed feedback, you can provide a set of custom review instructions for Copilot to use. There are two ways to do this.

First, you can edit the *settings.json* file and add custom instructions under `github.copilot.chat.codeReview.instructions`. Here's an example of a rule you can add:

```
"github.copilot.chat.reviewSelection.instructions": [
    {
        "text": "Ensure all functions have proper docstrings"
    }
]
```

After adding the rule in the user settings file, you can tell Copilot to review the same code again. This time, it flags the condition you specified in the settings file, as shown in Figure 2-24.

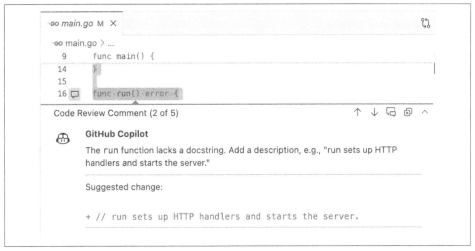

Figure 2-24. Flagged issue from the settings file

Optionally, you can also add your rule (and up to five more) as Markdown in a local file, save it with the specific path *.github/copilot-review-guidelines.md*, and Copilot will find and use it automatically.

If you prefer to have the instructions stored in a different file, you can create that file and then point to the local file in the *settings.json* file by using the `file:` key. Here's an example of what that might look like in the settings:

```
"github.copilot.chat.reviewSelection.instructions": [
    {
        "file": "./docs/review-guide.md"
    }
]
```

This assumes you have a local file in your codebase named *review-guide.md*, saved under the *docs* directory and with the contents shown here:

```
- Ensure all functions have proper docstrings.
```

Having Copilot Generate Automatic Commit Messages

After doing your code reviews, when you're ready to commit your changes, Copilot can assist there as well. As shown in Figure 2-25, when you are using the source control panel, instead of typing in your own commit message, you can have Copilot suggest one based on the changes. To do this, you click the sparkle icon at the end of the commit message field.

Figure 2-25. Having Copilot suggest commit messages

You can even set up custom instructions for commit message generation. Consult the VS Code documentation for more details on how to do that.

To conclude our discussion on coding with Copilot in the IDE, let's briefly examine a couple of additional controls and configuration settings to help you navigate and fine-tune your Copilot experience to what you want it to be.

Configuring Copilot in the IDE

In VS Code, after the Copilot extension is installed (and after you have authenticated, if needed), you can access Copilot functions through several controls. One control is located in the status bar at the bottom of the IDE. Clicking this gives you a quick way to turn off code completion suggestions for all files or only for the type of file you're currently working with. Figure 2-26 shows an example of the selected control providing an option to turn off code completion suggestions for Python files since that's the type that's currently active.

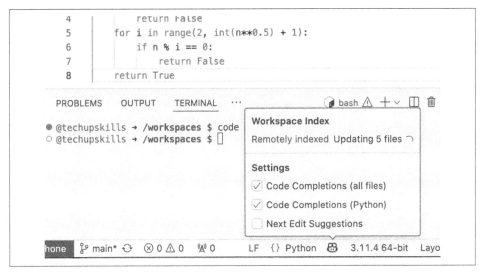

Figure 2-26. Bottom Copilot control

Why Turn Off Completions

You might wonder why there's an option to turn off code completions, given that that's one of Copilot's fundamental jobs. The answer is that sometimes the suggestions may become annoying or get in the way. For example, if you're trying to enter a lot of code in a hurry, or focus on creating code you already know how to do, you may not want the additional distraction of the Copilot suggestions popping up.

The Next Edit Suggestions option in the dialog refers to a type of automated *batch editing* functionality that is discussed in Chapter 4.

At the top of the IDE is another Copilot icon. This one allows you to open various chat interfaces, configure code completions, and manage your Copilot settings in GitHub. See Figure 2-27.

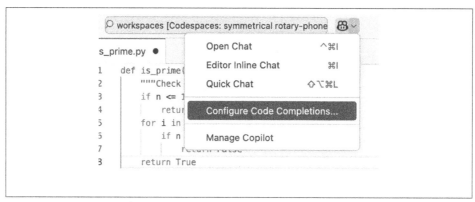

Figure 2-27. Top control options

We'll discuss the chat options in Chapter 3. The Manage Copilot selection will take you to the settings page (*https://oreil.ly/OlrYN*) for your Copilot account in GitHub (if you're logged in). And Configure Code Completions brings up a set of options (Figure 2-28) to customize code completions.

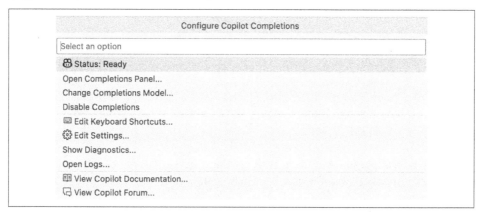

Figure 2-28. Configuring Copilot Completions

Some of these options are obvious, but a few are not. Here's a quick rundown of three of them:

Open Completions Panel
   Opens up a list of alternative completions for the currently active code. This is the same functionality we discussed earlier, invoking with Ctrl-Enter.

Change Completions Model
   Allows you to select a different AI model (other than the default) if another one is available. Note that this only affects the model used for code completions, not the model used for chats.

Disable Completions
> Similar to the earlier option from the other Copilot control, this lets you toggle completion suggestions on or off.

The Edit Settings option is a gateway to further customization and configuration for Copilot. Clicking it brings up the settings in the IDE with a search string of "GitHub Copilot". You could do the same thing by clicking the gear icon for Settings in the main IDE interface and then typing in "GitHub Copilot" to search for the related settings.

Figure 2-29 shows the Settings screen for items matching "GitHub Copilot". Notice the subcategories on the left for the editor, features, and a broader extensions group. Within the extensions group are settings for any extension related to GitHub Copilot.

Figure 2-29. GitHub Copilot settings in the IDE

In the settings, you can configure options at the *user level* (independent of workspace) and settings for the *workspace environment*. Tabs in the upper left allow you to switch between these categories.

When you drill in to some settings areas, you'll find ones marked Experimental or Preview. Both of these indicate an option or feature that is not in production yet. *Preview features* are closer to being officially released and are targeted for public testing and feedback if users opt in to using them. *Experimental features* are early concepts that you can use at your own risk. They may or may not move forward and may also be significantly changed before production.

Editing Files via the Settings

If you find a configuration option that can be persisted in a file (like *settings.json*), there will usually be a link to modify the file. As an example, if you want to add custom review rules (covered previously in this chapter), and you search for the option, you'll see a link to directly edit the *settings.json* file at the bottom (Figure 2-30).

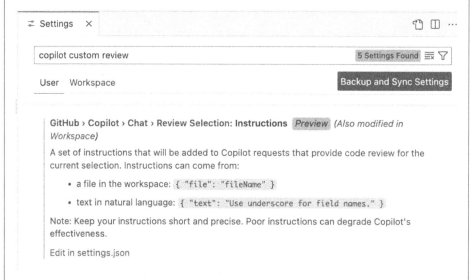

Figure 2-30. Accessing a file from the settings

Clicking that link opens the indicated file so you can edit it directly with some initial suggestions for content (Figure 2-31).

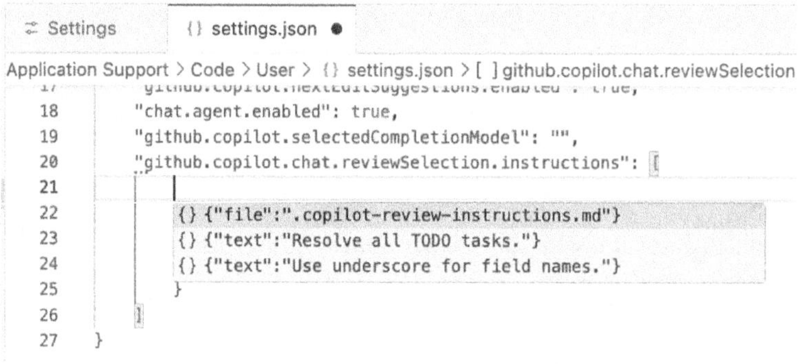

Figure 2-31. Editing a file opened via settings

If you use a different IDE, it will have a similar way to access and change the settings for Copilot. I recommend monitoring GitHub's blogs about Copilot (*https://oreil.ly/qdhTv*) for the latest updates and to learn what new or updated settings are available. It's also not a bad idea to periodically explore the options available. Sometimes you'll find additional options for configuring Copilot's behavior that you might not have known about.

Conclusion

In this chapter, we've covered the most direct ways to interact with GitHub Copilot inline when you're writing code. Copilot provides quick suggestions in the editor as you're typing. These should be evaluated for completeness and fit. While varying in suitability, these suggestions can provide time savings and/or bootstrap your code and thinking.

The quality of suggestions will largely depend on the amount of context Copilot has to reference in the current environment, meaning the filename, existing code, other files, comments, and local index. Comments can also describe a task you want Copilot to accomplish and be used to direct questions to Copilot that it will answer as comments.

Copilot can review your code to find problems and suggest improvements. You can customize what it targets when reviewing via pointing it to a list of custom instructions.

While Copilot provides useful capabilities out of the box, sometimes you may want to tweak its behavior or enable/disable a feature. You can make limited changes through the Copilot controls present in the IDE. Or you can search in the settings of the IDE for individual options to modify, including ones that are experimental or in preview.

Now that you've seen how to work with Copilot's suggestions inline, let's move on to the most flexible way to interact with Copilot and its underlying model: through its chat interface, the topic of Chapter 3.

CHAPTER 3
Chatting with Copilot in the IDE

In popular AI platforms like ChatGPT, the chat interface is your gateway to interacting with LLMs. Like talking to another person, having a running dialog with the AI feels more natural. It also allows for extended conversations to explore topics more thoroughly.

The chat interfaces included with Copilot offer those same advantages but targeted for the coding domain. The previous inline functionality discussed in Chapter 2 provides direct, quick, targeted code suggestions from Copilot. These code completions are based on what you're working on. But having interactive, free-form discussions about coding can be invaluable, just as discussing coding challenges or ideas with a coworker is useful. In fact, it quickly becomes hard to imagine using Copilot without using its chat features.

In this chapter, we'll explore how to use and interact with Copilot's chat functionality (Copilot Chat). We'll cover basic and advanced aspects of Chat.

We'll start by helping you understand how to access Chat's primary interface, how to parse its output, and how to manage multiple Chat sessions.

Following that, we'll briefly look at how best to do prompting for the Chat interfaces and then explore the various Chat interfaces themselves. To make sure you can target the prompts in the interfaces appropriately, we'll survey various shortcuts and modifiers built into Copilot, including participants and variables. We'll also explore how to use Chat in the IDE's terminal.

Finally, we'll show you how to create custom instructions for Chat to use in generating responses and take a look at how best to deal with hallucinations and bad responses from Chat.

Let's begin by understanding how to quickly start having a conversation with Copilot.

Accessing Chat's Main Interface

When you install Copilot into your IDE, it comes bundled with Copilot Chat. Chat's primary interface is a dedicated pane on the right side that is separate from your editor (Figure 3-1). The chat interface also provides more screen real estate for input, output, and conversations.

Figure 3-1. Copilot chat interface, on the right

Chat Interface in GitHub

In this chapter, we are looking at using the chat interface in VS Code. Copilot's chat interface is also used heavily in GitHub (*https://github.com/copilot*). We'll cover details on how that interface works in Chapter 9.

Copilot Chat has multiple modes for interacting with the AI. The default mode, which allows you to interact conversationally, is called *Ask* mode. The chat interface in Copilot is also a gateway to advanced editing with Copilot Edits and some autonomous development features with Copilot Agent mode. You can switch between the modes as shown in Figure 3-2.

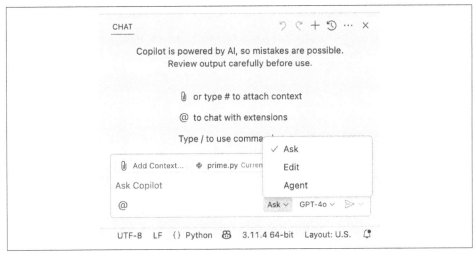

Figure 3-2. Options for chat modes

This chapter focuses on the basics of using chat in Ask mode. Chapter 4 discusses how the Edit and Agent modes are used.

In the IDE integration, the top row contains a Copilot icon. Clicking it allows you to open various chat interfaces in the IDE. This includes opening/reopening the main chat interface if it's not visible—the top option in the list, as shown in Figure 3-3.

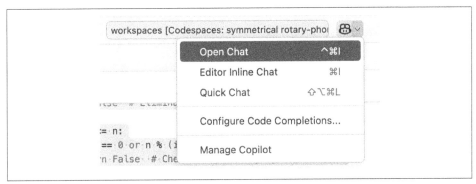

Figure 3-3. Opening the chat control

Possible AI Mistakes

When starting a new conversation with the chat interface, you will see this message: *Copilot is powered by AI, so mistakes are possible. Review output carefully before use.*

This caution about potential inaccuracies from the Copilot AI should be considered for all responses returned by Copilot, not just in the chat interface. As noted in Chapter 1, you should vet all responses returned by Copilot.

The options for the Editor Inline Chat and Quick Chat interfaces are explained later in this chapter.

In the main chat interface, you can enter your query or prompt in the text window labeled *Ask Copilot*. Let's assume you've highlighted your `is_prime` code from the Chapter 2 examples and want Copilot to explain how it works. Here's a simple query for that:

```
How does this code work?
```

After processing the query, Copilot responds; Figure 3-4 shows an example.

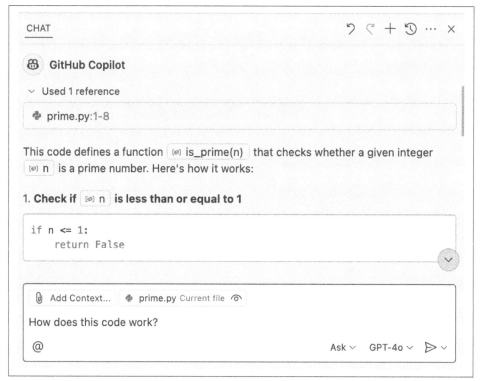

Figure 3-4. Result from the chat query

54 | Chapter 3: Chatting with Copilot in the IDE

Notice that the response is presented in a more conversational style. It has fully formed sentences and can be read and understood even if you're unfamiliar with Python coding. The response also includes any relevant code examples that support the explanation.

Explanation Use Cases

While it may not seem significant to have Copilot explain code that you created, imagine being able to have it explain code that you didn't write and don't yet understand. An example could be code written in a language you're not familiar with. You could also use Copilot explanations to explain a complex algorithm. The explanation could even form the basis of pseudocode for further refinements.

The chat response in this interface provides a lot of information, including some elements that are not directly part of the explanation but related to it. Let's spend a little time looking more closely at the entire set of information in the output.

Understanding Chat Output

Beyond the prose from Chat, a couple of other items are worth noting in the output. We can use the example from the previous sections to explore these.

First, just under the GitHub Copilot title, Copilot tells us it "Used 1 reference." A *reference* in this case means content from, or related to, the project that Copilot determined was relevant to use in creating a response. Most commonly, this will be the currently active file in the editor, but it could include additional files, dependencies, custom settings, or other types of content that are not files. (For example, it could include commands if you're using a prompt that references the terminal.)

Looking at Figure 3-4, just under the GitHub Copilot logo, I've expanded the reference section to see the content that was considered in generating a response. In this case, the reference is the code from the only active file, *prime.py*. This is the default context, also shown at the top of the text input area. There the file is identified as the "Current file" (and thus the default context). We'll discuss more about context for prompts in "Making Effective Use of the Prompt Dialog" on page 63.

Following the reference section is the full text of the response provided by Copilot (in Markdown format) from when we interacted with it. As a reminder, since we're using generative AI, you may get different answers, even with exactly the same prompt:

```
This code defines a function `is_prime(n)` that checks whether a
given integer `n` is a prime number. Here's how it works:

### 1. **Check if `n` is less than or equal to 1**
```

```python
if n <= 1:
    return False
```
- Numbers less than or equal to 1 are not prime, so the function immediately returns `False`.

2. **Iterate through potential divisors**
```python
for i in range(2, int(n**0.5) + 1):
    if n % i == 0:
        return False
```
- The function loops through integers `i` starting from 2 up to the square root of `n` (inclusive). The square root is calculated using `n**0.5`, and `int(n**0.5) + 1` ensures the range includes the integer part of the square root.
- If `n` is divisible by any `i` in this range (`n % i == 0`), it is not a prime number, and the function returns `False`.

3. **Return `True` if no divisors are found**
```python
return True
```
- If the loop completes without finding any divisors, the function concludes that `n` is a prime number and returns `True`.

Key Points
- **Optimization**: The loop only checks divisors up to the square root of `n`, which reduces the number of iterations compared to checking all numbers up to `n-1`.
- **Prime Definition**: A prime number is greater than 1 and divisible only by 1 and itself. This function implements that definition efficiently.

Example
- Input: `is_prime(7)`
    - The loop checks divisors 2 and 3 (since `int(7**0.5) + 1 = 3`).
    - Since 7 is not divisible by 2 or 3, the function returns `True`.
- Input: `is_prime(9)`
    - The loop checks divisors 2 and 3.
    - Since 9 is divisible by 3, the function returns `False`.

The response provides a detailed, step-by-step explanation of the code's actions in prose (complete sentences written as if it were talking to you) as well as code excerpts from the file. This is one of the key advantages of working with the chat interface: conversational text is included with actual code. The text and code together form a complete conversation, just as you might share with a colleague.

It's easy to continue the conversation in chat. For example, referencing your code, you can ask Copilot if there are more efficient ways to implement this logic. Figure 3-5 shows Copilot's response with an optimized version of the code. Notice again the text explanation along with the code example.

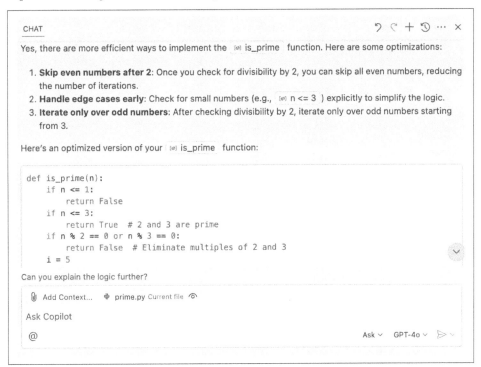

Figure 3-5. Asking Copilot if there are more efficient ways to implement our code

This output is read-only in the chat interface. However, if you hover over the code block, Copilot provides a pop-up bar with icons for different ways to get code from the window to the editor in your IDE. Figure 3-6 shows the pop-up bar and its extended options.

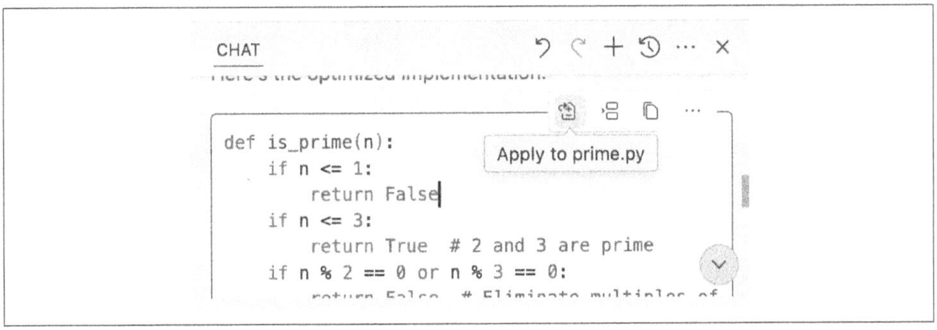

Figure 3-6. "Hover" icons to transfer code from the chat interface to the editor

Understanding Chat Output | 57

From left to right, the icons allow you to do the following:

- Apply changes to the currently active file for review
- Insert the text at the cursor location in the currently active file
- Copy the text to the clipboard
- Insert the text into a new file (accessible via the More Actions icon [...])
- Insert the text into a terminal (accessible via the More Actions icon [...])

Customizing the Hover Menu

By default, to get to the last two options in the list (insert into a new file and insert into the terminal), you need to hover over the ... selection in the pop-up, select More Actions, and then select the desired option.

However, if you hover over one of the icons and right-click, you'll access a menu where you can select which icons show up in the *bar* when you hover. By checking all the entries in the list, you'll have all icons available in the hover bar and won't have to use the ... interface.

While most of these options are self-explanatory, Apply deserves additional explanation. When you click this option, Copilot will apply the changes to the file in your editor, showing you the suggested changes inline and allowing you to Keep or Undo each set (Figure 3-7).

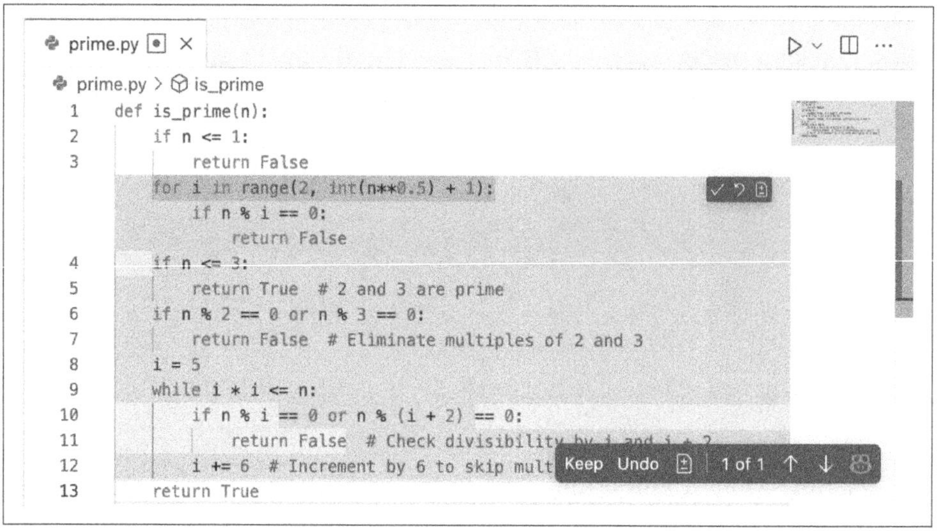

Figure 3-7. Applying changes inline from the chat

Choosing the Insert at Cursor option will replace any highlighted code in the editor session with the code from the window. For example, suppose you have your previous code highlighted and then select that option. In that case, your previous implementation of the `is_prime` function will be overwritten by the one from the chat.

In addition to the controls that pop up when you hover over generated code in the chat panel, various other controls are always available at the top of the chat panel and in the text entry area itself. Let's take a moment to talk about what those are and what they allow you to do, starting with ones that help you manage chat sessions.

Managing Chat Sessions

In the top line of the chat panel are several controls you can use to manage your chat sessions (Figure 3-8).

Figure 3-8. Top icons in the chat interface

On the right side, the left and right arrows allow you to move forward and backward between sessions, respectively. The large + sign allows you to start a new chat session instead of continuing with the current one. Starting a new session is useful if you want to discuss a new topic and don't want to risk Copilot assuming context from your previous discussions in the existing chat.

In a single chat session, Copilot keeps track of the conversation history including the series of prompts. For example, in Figure 3-9, we asked Copilot to create tests for one of our files.

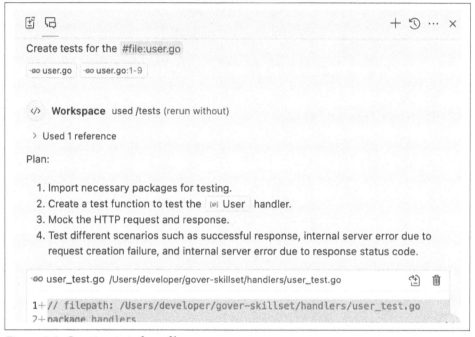

Figure 3-9. Creating tests for a file

Afterwards, we asked Copilot a more generic question about what other use cases should be considered, and it returned an answer that was relevant to the context/follow-up for the previous question (Figure 3-10).

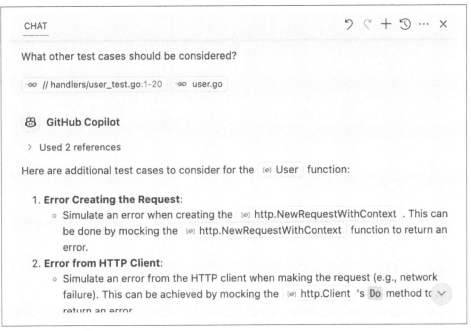

Figure 3-10. Follow-up questions

Clicking the Show Chats icon (which looks like a clock inside a circular arrow) shows the set of chats you've been working with in a dialog (Figure 3-11). You can click an entry to switch to that chat.

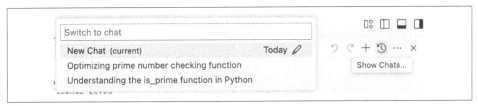

Figure 3-11. Showing sets of chats

The Views and More Actions control (the one that looks like three dots) provides several options. It allows you to open the current chat in an editor session or in a detached window. It also allows you to provide Copilot with feedback on chat functionality as well as easily get to the latest release notes.

The "X" in the upper right of the chat window will close the chat view completely. Alternatively, you can delete a single chat by hovering over the area for it and clicking the "X" in the upper-right corner of the individual chat (Figure 3-12). The tip here is worded oddly as *Undo Requests*, but it currently deletes the chat. Deleting a chat can sometimes be useful to remove discussions that are no longer relevant.

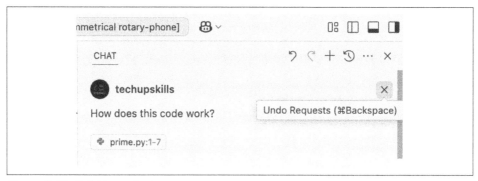

Figure 3-12. Deleting a chat

Finally, it's worth noting that you can export or save the content of a chat session. We'll cover that in Chapter 6.

These controls help you manage your chat sessions. Since the way we interact with Copilot in chat is through prompts, let's take a moment to talk about how we can best construct our prompts.

Prompt Engineering for Copilot

Prompt engineering for GitHub Copilot Chat is the process of crafting clear, targeted instructions to guide the AI in generating useful and accurate responses. When interacting with Copilot Chat, your prompt can be as simple as a question, a shortcut command (discussed later in this chapter), or a specific directive for Copilot related to your project. Copilot doesn't rely on just your prompt—it also draws on the context from your open files and the ongoing chat history to provide relevant answers.

If you're working on a larger effort, a good approach is to begin with a broad description of your goal, setting the stage for what you want to achieve. For example, you might start with, "Write a function that checks if a number is prime." Once you've specified the general purpose, you can iterate with specific requirements or constraints, such as, "The function should return true for prime numbers and throw an error if the input is not a positive integer." This progression from general to specific helps Copilot understand both the overarching task and the details, leading to more precise responses.

Providing examples is another effective technique. Including sample inputs and expected outputs, or even unit tests, can help Copilot better infer your intent. For instance, if you want a function to extract dates from a string, sharing a sample string and the expected array of dates will guide Copilot to generate code that matches your needs.

Copilot Chat also supports advanced features like referencing specific files, using chat variables, and integrating with participants and extensions for domain-specific tasks. (Chat variables and participants are discussed later in this chapter. Copilot Extensions are discussed in Chapter 10.) You can highlight code, use keywords, or drag files into the chat to give Copilot more context. Iteration is key: if the initial response isn't quite right, refine your prompt or your context until you get the desired result.

By treating prompt engineering as an interactive conversation, you can leverage Copilot Chat to write code, debug errors, generate tests, and answer project-specific questions efficiently. The more clearly you communicate your intent, the better Copilot can assist you in your development workflow.

More Info

You can find more documentation on prompt engineering in the Copilot documentation (*https://oreil.ly/QnqjI*).

When you're entering your prompts, the text entry area has additional controls to let you customize the environment and targets for your prompt.

Making Effective Use of the Prompt Dialog

Multiple controls are available in the chat dialog for use when submitting prompts or queries. These controls are shown in Figure 3-13.

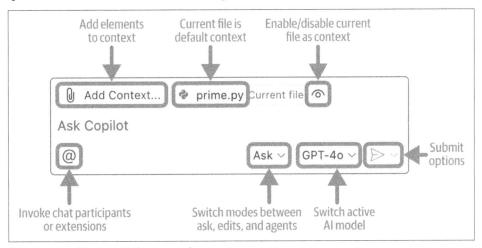

Figure 3-13. Prompt dialog controls

The controls are used for the following:

- Adding context elements
- Selecting a chat participant to help handle the prompt
- Selecting what Copilot does when your prompt is submitted
- Selecting your AI model
- Selecting whether you are using the chat interface in the Ask, Edit, or Agent mode

As noted earlier, we're focusing on the Ask mode for chat in this chapter, and we'll cover Edit and Agent modes in Chapter 4, so we won't go into more detail on the last item. But the others are covered in this section.

Adding Context Elements

Context here means relevant items that are part of your project that Copilot can reference for understanding and formulating responses. At the simplest level, if you have an active file open in the editor, it will be used as the current context. In Figure 3-13, this is shown as "prime.py Current file". If you want to exclude this file as the current context, you can make a different file active or click the icon that looks like an eye to cancel that file as context.

To manually add other types of elements from your project as context, click the paperclip icon with Add Context after it. This will bring up a set of optional items that you can include as context. These range from content in the editor, to individual files, to symbols, to text from the terminal, and even screenshots. There are also several options to search for other content like web pages or find usage of functions, variables, and symbols. Figure 3-14 shows a partial list of items available when the control is invoked.

To find a particular item in the list, you can scroll or type in characters in the search bar. This includes files in your project. You can also scroll to the bottom of the list to see recently opened files.

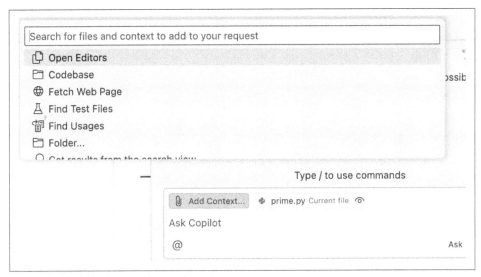

Figure 3-14. Attaching additional context

When you are done adding the context elements you want, you can enter your prompt and submit it. The context items you've added will be consulted as Copilot prepares the response. Figure 3-15 shows an example of the output from running a prompt with several context items added.

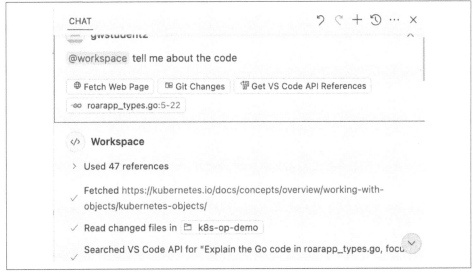

Figure 3-15. Running a prompt with multiple types of context

Making Effective Use of the Prompt Dialog | 65

Repository Indexes

On the topic of context, just a reminder that GitHub automatically builds a *workspace index* to help quickly and accurately search your project for relevant code pieces. This index can then be used as another supporting piece to help search a wider set of content in the codebase and better answer questions about it.

Adding Participants

The @ control allows you to invoke a chat participant. *Chat participants* set a scope for the prompt or query to apply to, such as the entire workspace, the terminal, and VS Code. Several built-in chat participants are available in the IDE, such as `@workspace` and `@terminal`.

Additional participants can also be provided by GitHub Copilot Extensions when you install them. *Copilot Extensions* are custom integrations that incorporate other tools (such as Docker) or APIs into your IDE's chat interface. Chat participants are discussed in more detail later in this chapter. Copilot Extensions are covered in Chapter 10. Figure 3-16 shows a list of built-in chat participants that you can select from.

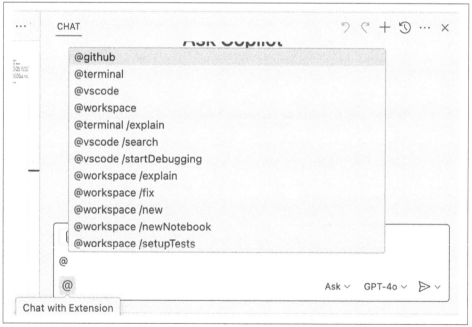

Figure 3-16. Invoking a participant or extension

Next up is the Send button on the right. Clicking this will submit your prompt or query to the AI, but you can submit your prompt in varied ways.

Understanding Options for Submitting Your Prompt

The arrow control at the right side of the prompt area is referred to as the *Send button*. It has a default behavior as well as several other options. The various Send options shown in Figure 3-17 all submit your prompt or query to Copilot, but there are some key differences. Let's break down what each option means.

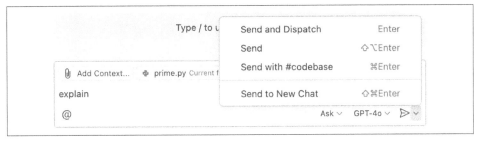

Figure 3-17. Send options

By default, Copilot Chat will try to direct your prompt or query to a suitable action or tool (such as a chat participant), when possible. This is the standard Send and Dispatch behavior when you click the arrow.

When routed to an action or tool, you may see a "rerun without" link option at the top of the output. In Figure 3-18, the prompt was simply "Create test cases". But note that Copilot added the workspace participant and a /tests shortcut command. (We'll discuss these kinds of commands later in the chapter.) The "rerun without" link would run the query without the /tests command.

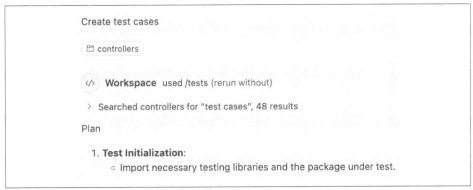

Figure 3-18. Example prompt with automatic additions by Copilot

If the automatically selected action or tool is not the right one for your question, you can select the link to resend your question to Copilot without including the participant. This is the behavior of the Send option if you select that in the drop-down list. Figure 3-19 shows what this option looks like with the same prompt.

Making Effective Use of the Prompt Dialog | 67

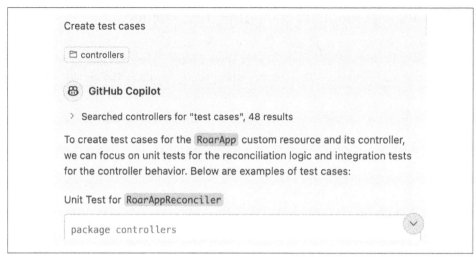

Figure 3-19. Example prompt using the Send option

For the third option, "Send with #codebase", #codebase is a chat variable. Chat variables are covered later in the chapter, but essentially this tells Copilot to take into account all the information it has about your entire set of code. This can be useful if other content in the project may need to be considered in the response but you don't know (or don't want to) specify individual items for context. In our example for generating tests, using this option could allow the AI to determine whether there are already existing tests and/or generate suggestions for more comprehensive tests across the project.

The last option, Send to New Chat, is self-explanatory. The prompt you just entered will be opened in a new chat as the first prompt. This is useful when you want to isolate a specific query or task from ongoing conversations for clarity or focus.

The remaining control in the dialog is an option to pick the LLM that you want Copilot to use on the backend. This gives you flexibility in choosing an LLM that may be better suited for your particular task. A large set of LLMs is currently available to choose from via the drop-down (Figure 3-20). As new ones become available, they are designated as *preview* for a period of time. You may also be asked to "Enable access for all clients" as part of using a different model.

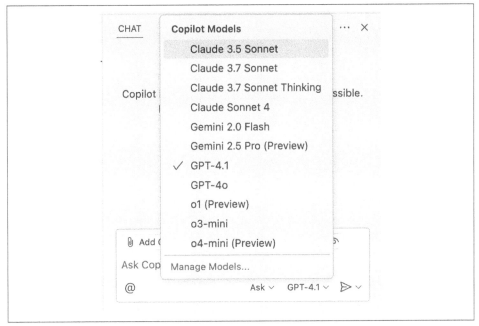

Figure 3-20. Selecting a different model

Managing Models

You may have noticed the Manage Models link at the bottom of the models list in Figure 3-20. This link allows you enter data that may be needed to access other models, such as custom model IDs or API keys.

Since you've seen how the main Chat dialog works, let's look at a shortcut to using chat inline with your code in the editor.

Using the Editor Inline Chat Interface

Copilot integration provides a simplified, quick-access interface to Chat in the editor. The interface can be invoked at any position by using the *Meta*-I combination (Figure 3-21).

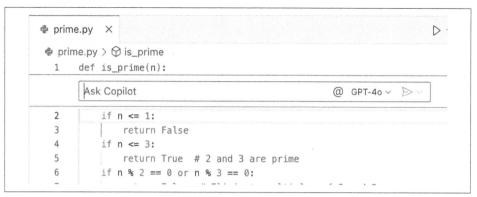

Figure 3-21. Inline chat interface

This dialog is a smaller version of the chat dialog. It's designed to be used inline in the code editor without taking up too much screen real estate. Aside from adding context, it has the same controls, and you can supply the same prompts or queries as in the main chat window. For example, you can highlight the code and ask the same question as earlier in the chapter:

```
How does this code work?
```

Copilot will return as much of the response as it can show in the limited window (Figure 3-22). You can scroll or expand the dialog to see more of the output. However, with this limited amount of screen real estate, you still may not be able to see the complete response. To see the complete response in the main chat interface, click the View in Chat button.

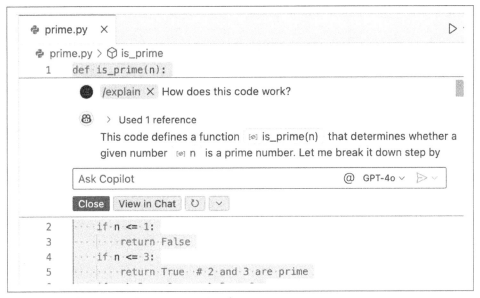

Figure 3-22. Prompting in an interactive chat

Regenerate Option

You may have noticed a circular arrow next to the View in Chat button. Whenever you see this symbol, it is a way to ask Copilot to regenerate the answer and see if it offers another, possibly better response.

Clicking the View in Chat button displays the full text of the response in the main chat window (Figure 3-23). You can scroll through the response and do follow-up prompting, selecting code, and copying/inserting code examples.

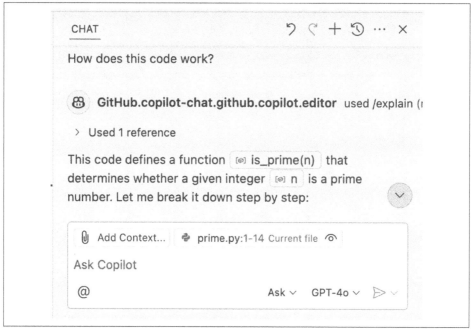

Figure 3-23. Output from the View in Chat option

Other operations initiated from the inline dialog may update code inline in the editor. For example, if you ask Copilot to

```
document the selected code
```

then, as shown in Figure 3-24, Copilot produces the documentation inline for the selected code.

So if the prompt asks Copilot to change an aspect of the editor's actual code, the results are applied directly inline for you to review and to decide whether to accept or not. If the prompt asks Copilot for a response that would be an alternative to the code in the IDE, such as translating this code to Go or optimizing this code, the output can appear either in the interactive chat window (if it is succinct enough) or the main output area from chat.

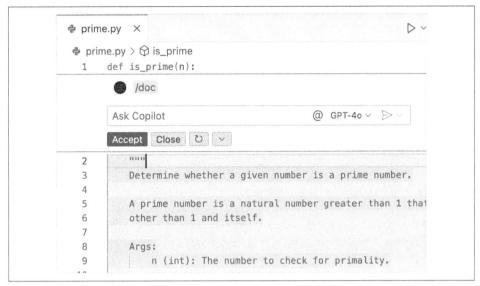

Figure 3-24. Suggested changes for documentation

While the main chat panel and the inline editor chat functionality cover most use cases, there is one other option for quickly engaging with chat, appropriately called *Quick Chat*.

Using the Quick Chat Interface

At times you may want to quickly ask Chat a question or send it a prompt that is not about the code in your current editor and that doesn't warrant switching to the full chat panel. To help with that, Copilot includes a *Quick Chat* feature that pops up a simple chat dialog at the top of the IDE. Figure 3-25 shows an example.

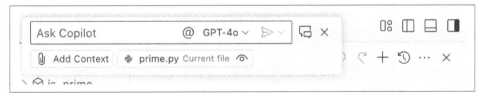

Figure 3-25. Quick Chat

The dialog itself is like the one in the inline editor but is not positioned in the editor. This option allows you to interact with Copilot via a prompt and then go back to what you were doing. Invoking Quick Chat can be done via a shortcut or via the Copilot icon at the top of the VS Code interface. Clicking that icon (as shown in Figure 3-26) shows the options to open the main Chat panel, open the Quick Chat dialog, and open the Editor Inline Chat.

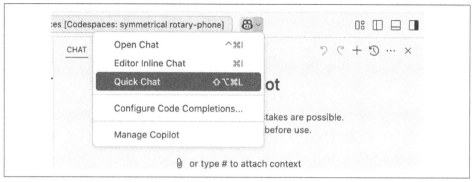

Figure 3-26. Chat options in the Copilot menu in the title bar

Just as we can have more concise chat interfaces, we can have more concise prompts by using Copilot shortcuts for typical requests. There are several of these, which we'll explore in the next section.

Chat Shortcuts

GitHub Copilot Chat supports several shortcuts for common types of interactions. These shortcuts are referred to as *slash commands* because they start with a slash character (/). Slash commands will work when initiated either from the main chat window or from the inline chat (*Meta*-I) interface. Not all commands may be available in every IDE, but Table 3-1 shows the superset of those available at the time of writing.

Table 3-1. Copilot slash commands

Command	Purpose
/clear	Clear the current conversation
/doc	Add comments for selected or specified code
/edit	Edit the selected code in your active editor
/explain	Generate explanations of how code works
/fix	Propose a fix for a problem
/fixTestFailure	Propose a fix for the failing test
/generate	Generate code to address a specific ask
/help	Get help with Copilot
/new	Scaffold code for a new workspace
/newNotebook	Create a new Jupyter notebook
/search	Search for content with VS Code
/startDebugging	Generate launch config and start debugging in VS Code
/tests	Create unit tests for code

Limited Feature Parity

Different IDEs may only have a subset of these slash commands or even ones that aren't listed here. The currently implemented and supported slash commands can change frequently, so always consult the Copilot documentation for your particular IDE to understand which ones are available.

Accessing these commands is straightforward. Simply type the forward slash character in one of the chat interfaces, and Copilot will present a list of available commands to choose from (see Figure 3-27). Note that not all shortcut commands are available in the inline chat interface.

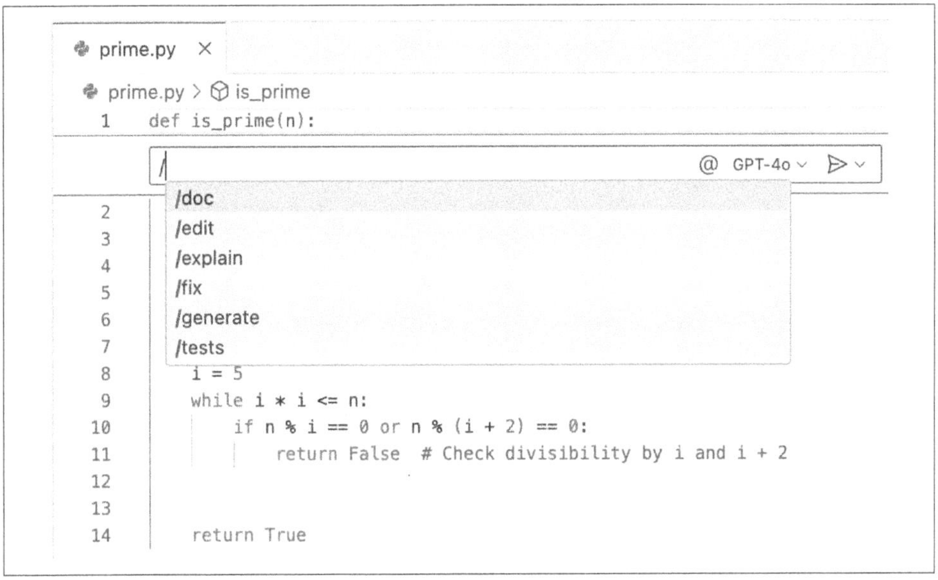

Figure 3-27. Listing slash commands in the interactive chat

You can use the same method in the main chat panel, as shown in Figure 3-28.

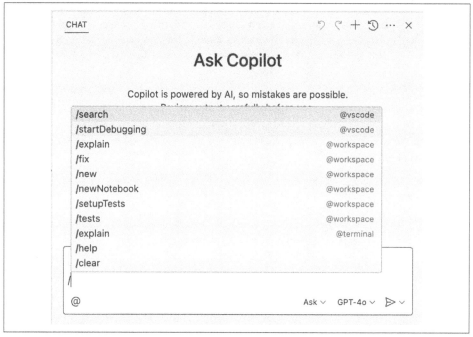

Figure 3-28. Listing slash commands in the main chat panel

This is only a brief introduction to the slash commands, but they can be very useful. We'll be exploring particular ones in more detail as we progress through the book.

 The feature to explain code with Copilot works best in IDEs when you have the relevant extension for the language you're using installed. As of the time of this writing, this relates to the VS Code extensions for the following:

- TypeScript/JavaScript
- Python
- Java
- C#
- C++
- Go
- Ruby

Included on the same rows as the slash commands in Figure 3-28 are terms starting with the @ character. As noted previously, these are referred to as *participants* and help identify the *scope* and *domain* where the shortcuts can be used. I'll explain more about these in the next section.

Chat Participants

In GitHub Copilot, *chat participants* are essentially pointers to certain domains. By referencing them in your prompt in the chat interface, you are effectively telling the AI to scope the prompt to a particular domain and use the participant's knowledge in that domain to generate relevant responses.

To reference one of these chat participants, you type the @ symbol with the name of the participant you want to use as part of your prompt. At the time of this writing, the following participants are available per the GitHub documentation (*https://oreil.ly/v0714*):

@workspace
: Has knowledge about the code in your workspace. Use @workspace when you want Copilot to consider the structure of your project, how different parts of your code interact, or design patterns in your project.

@vscode
: Has knowledge about VS Code commands and features. Use @vscode when you want help with VS Code.

@terminal
: Has knowledge about the VS Code terminal shell and its contents. Use @terminal when you want help creating or debugging terminal commands.

@vision
: Allows you to attach an image file to help Copilot understand the question. (In preview.)

@github
: Allows you to prompt about issues, pull requests, etc. across your repos. (Not available in all interfaces.)

@project
: (Applicable to JetBrains IDE) Like @workspace, knows about the code in your project.

> **Installing Other Chat Participants**
>
> Beyond the built-in chat participants provided by GitHub, Copilot also allows for installing Copilot Extensions that can provide additional custom chat participants. We'll have more to say about these and how you can extend Copilot in Chapter 10.

Let's take a deeper dive into some of the common participants.

@workspace

The `@workspace` chat participant is useful when you explicitly want Copilot to consider all code that's part of the workspace as potential sources for the chat response. This doesn't mean that all code will be used and sent as part of creating the response. The Copilot extension will consider all the files that are part of the workspace to determine which files (or portions of them) may be useful for context. The automatic indexing we mentioned before makes this simpler.

Suppose we ask Copilot via `@workspace` which files use `import`. Copilot will first collect information about the workspace to determine relevant content. When done, the chat interface will display a list of references it ultimately decided were worth considering for the prompt. This will be at the start of the response. As we saw earlier, we can see the list of selected references by expanding the "Used references" line. Because we are using the `@workspace` participant, we may have more *hits* this time. A more extensive set of references resulting from a prompt with `@workspace` is shown in Figure 3-29.

Figure 3-29. Asking which files use imports via `@workspace`

When the @workspace chat participant is used in prompts, we get a response that spans the workspace and lists out multiple files.

Ensuring Changes Are Considered for @workspace

The @workspace functionality is referencing the saved content in your codebase, so it's important to save any changes or new content you want to be considered by the chat participant before you execute the prompt.

Using @workspace, we can ask more general questions about a set of code. This can be especially advantageous for finding information about content we're not familiar with. For example, we can ask generic questions like these:

- What kind of backend is used in this project?
- How do I run this code?
- Where do I use *X*?
- What service do I use to do *Y*?
- Which frameworks are being used?

Figure 3-30 shows an example of using that last query to gather information.

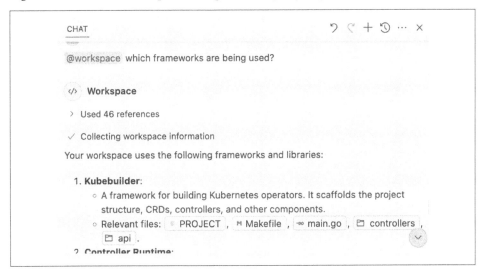

Figure 3-30. Another example of using the @workspace participant

Shortcut for Adding @workspace

If you use *Meta*-Enter (versus just Enter) when you submit your query in chat, it will automatically add the @workspace participant to your prompt.

Whereas @workspace provides context around our set of code, the chat participant @vscode can help with any questions or prompts related to using VS Code.

@vscode

The @vscode chat participant (specific to the VS Code IDE) acts as a domain expert on VS Code commands and customizations. By using it in the Copilot chat interface, you can ask questions about VS Code via natural language. As implemented, it has access to the index of all the settings and commands for the application. With this participant, you can ask questions in the GitHub Copilot Chat interface like these:

- How can I open a project in VS Code?
- How can I install extensions in VS Code?
- How can I create a new file in VS Code?
- How can I change the theme in VS Code?

Figure 3-31 shows an example of using the @vscode chat participant to find out how to change VS Code defaults.

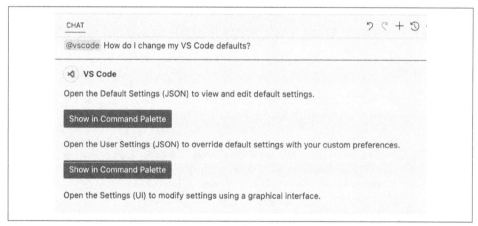

Figure 3-31. Using @vscode in chat

In this image, you can also see that Copilot included a link to get to a different interface—the Command Palette—as a shortcut to access functionality. Clicking that button in the chat output opens up the entry as shown at the top of the figure.

As another example of using this participant, you might want to understand more about how to debug using your IDE. So you can enter the query:

```
@vscode how do I debug
```

The last participant we'll cover is `@terminal`, which as the name suggests, is useful for terminal interactions.

@terminal

The `@terminal` participant allows you to query Copilot about the integrated terminal shell, its buffer, and the current selection in the terminal. This is convenient to understand more about what's been done in the terminal, help clarify any issues, and come up with the commands you need. Examples of questions/prompts you could do with this one include the following:

- What did the last command do?
- Explain the command
- How do I...?

Figure 3-32 shows a simple example of using the chat participant to ask how to do a task with a command in the terminal. If you hover over the output command, you'll have a pop-up control on the right to insert the response directly in the terminal.

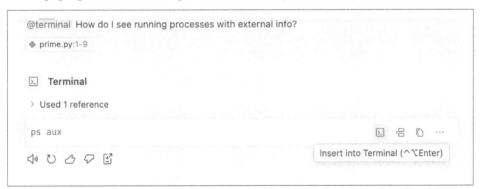

Figure 3-32. The `@terminal` chat participant

You can also use this participant to ask Copilot for help on common workflows you would execute in the terminal. For example, you might use the terminal participant to ask how you could commit your code by using Git through the command line.

Most slash commands default to one of the chat participants as the domain to run the command in. As an example, relative to the earlier VS Code debug example, the `@vscode` participant has the slash command `/startDebugging` associated with it (Figure 3-33). So if you enter `/startDebugging` in the chat query box, `@vscode` will automatically be prefixed to it (Figure 3-34). This means that the `/startDebugging` command is currently only relevant if you're referencing VS Code.

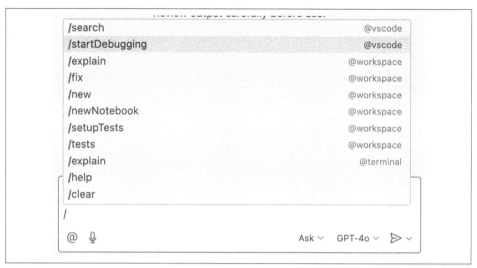

Figure 3-33. Participants and their associated slash commands

Figure 3-34. Automatic insertion of `@vscode` when `/startDebugging` is selected

Table 3-2 shows the mappings between the shortcut commands and the participants as well as the intended function of each.

Table 3-2. Slash commands and context in Copilot

Command	Participant	Function from Copilot
`/explain`	`@terminal`	Explain something that occurred in the terminal
`/search`	`@vscode`	Generate query parameters for the Search view
`/startDebugging`	`@vscode`	Generate launch config and start debugging in VS Code (experimental)
`/explain`	`@workspace`	Explain how the active code works
`/fix`	`@workspace`	Propose a fix for bugs in your code
`/fixTestFailure`	`@workspace`	Propose a fix for the failing test
`/new`	`@workspace`	Scaffold code for a new workspace or new file
`/newNotebook`	`@workspace`	Scaffold a new Jupyter notebook by using natural language
`/setupTests`	`@workspace`	Set up tests in your project (experimental)

Command	Participant	Function from Copilot
/tests	@workspace	Generate unit tests for code
/help		Get help about using GitHub Copilot
/clear		Start a new chat session

Participants can refine context at a broad level. However, at times you might need to specify context for Copilot at a more targeted level. When that's the case, you can use identifiers to specify a file, content in the editor, a selection, etc. These identifiers are called *chat variables*.

Chat Variables

Chat variables provide a way to further refine context within the text of the prompt itself. They can target items in the editor, a specific file, your Git repository, terminal commands and more. To reference a chat variable in a prompt in the chat interface, you indicate it with the # symbol. For example, `#terminalSelection` pulls in the active terminal's selection.

Table 3-3 lists the chat variables that are available at the time of this writing. (See the VS Code documentation (*https://oreil.ly/0s5TM*) for the latest info.) The Description column lists the content that is added from the project as context for your prompt.

Table 3-3. Chat variables

Chat variable	Description
#changes	List of source control changes
#codebase	Relevant content found in your workspace
#fetch	Content from a web page by providing its URL
#file	A specified file you pick or specify from your workspace
#<filename>	Provides a list of files (matching characters you type after #) to choose from
#folder	The specified folder and all files in it
#problems	Workspace issues and problems from the Problems panel; useful as context for debugging or fixing code
#searchResults	Results from a search query performed within your workspace
#selection	The currently selected text in the editor—will add it as *<filename:lines>*
#sym	The current symbol
#<symbol>	Provides a list of symbols (matching characters you type after #) to choose from
#terminalLastCommand	Active terminal's last run command
#terminalSelection	Active terminal's selection
#testFailure	Adds information about test failures to aid in diagnosing and fixing tests
#usages	Combines Find All References, Find Implementation, and Go to Definition
#vscodeAPI	Adds VS Code API to answer questions about VS Code extension development

You can easily get access to the chat variables by simply typing # in your prompt. When you do that, Copilot will bring up a list of available variables (Figure 3-35).

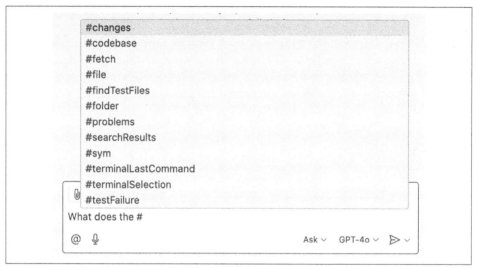

Figure 3-35. Chat variables

After this, you can select a relevant item (such as a file) from the provided list (Figure 3-36).

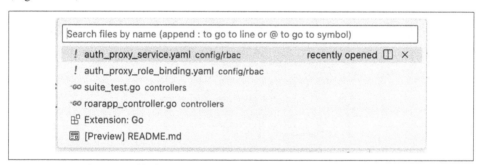

Figure 3-36. Selecting a file from a populated list

Using Correct Paths

When using the #file variable and selecting a file from the pop-up list presented, you can just select the filename (see Figure 3-37).

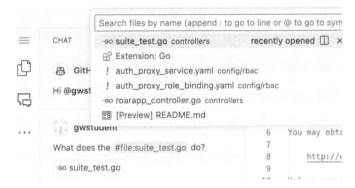

Figure 3-37. A filename picked from a list

However, if you are typing in a filename directly as part of the prompt, remember to include the relative path from the root of the project:

    What does the #file:controllers/suite_test.go do?

You can also combine participants, shortcut commands, and variables together in prompts. Figure 3-38 shows an example of asking Copilot to explain a selection in a file. Note that it automatically filled in the @workspace participant, so that the prompt became @workspace /explain #selection. This shows an example of using a combination of a chat participant, a shortcut command, and a chat variable.

If you look at the references used, Copilot ended up focusing on the selection and another part of the file it needed to produce a response. Copilot then produced an explanation for the more targeted context (the selected text) as requested.

Figure 3-38. Using a chat participant and chat variable to help specify context

Making sure that Copilot is considering the context you intend can sometimes be challenging. The key is looking at Copilot's response to see if:

- Copilot used the reference(s) you expected
- The response Copilot supplied is *generic* advice or is specific to the structure or content within your workspace

Those two attributes of the response will help you quickly identify if Copilot is targeting the content you intended or if you need to use one of the approaches outlined in this section to steer it more precisely.

There's one more chat interface that you can also use when interacting with Copilot. This one is targeted for operations that you do in the terminal.

Chat in the Terminal

Copilot provides dedicated, terminal-focused chat functionality. When you're in a terminal, such as in VS Code, using the same *Meta*-I shortcut brings up a shortcut dialog for typing in prompts that are directed to the terminal. Figure 3-39 shows the shortcut dialog that comes up in this case.

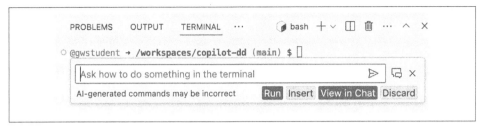

Figure 3-39. The terminal query dialog

You can enter a prompt such as "How do I commit my changes with Git?" and see the commands you need to run in the terminal. In addition, you have options to run them, view the output in chat, and more (see Figure 3-40).

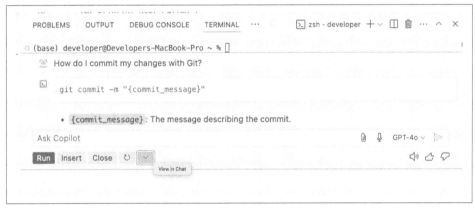

Figure 3-40. Viewing Chat in the terminal

Creating Custom Code-Generation Instructions

In Chapter 2, I mentioned that you could create custom instructions for Copilot code reviews. You can also create custom instructions to guide how Copilot generates code responses. Note, however, these custom instructions do not apply to inline code suggestions in the editor.

As with the custom review instructions, you can accomplish this in three ways.

First, you can edit the *settings.json* file and add custom instructions under `github.copilot.chat.codeGeneration.instructions`. Here's an example of a rule you can add:

```
"github.copilot.chat.codeGeneration.instructions": [
    {
        "text": "Always add comments to generated code describing its purpose."
    },
    {
        "text": "Use underscores for private field names in TypeScript."
    }
]
```

After adding the rule in the user settings file, you can tell Copilot to review the same code again. This time, it flags the condition you specified in the settings file, as shown in Figure 2-24.

Second, you can create a Markdown file in your repository or project with the specific path and name of *.github/copilot-instructions.md*.

Here's an example of what this file might look like with the same rules:

```
# Custom Instructions for Code Generation

- Always add comments to generated code describing its purpose.
- Use underscores for private field names in TypeScript.
```

If you prefer to use a different path or name for the Markdown file, you can create it and then reference it in the *settings.json* file with a `file:` key. For example, if you named it *.docs/code-style.md*, you could point Copilot to it with the following entry in the settings file:

```
"github.copilot.chat.reviewSelection.instructions": [
    {
        "file": ".docs/code-style.md"
    }
]
```

Let's look at an example without custom code-generation instructions. Say you prompt Copilot to create a minimal TypeScript class with a private variable (Figure 3-41).

Assume you then add custom instructions via one of the approaches just outlined. With those in place, if you execute the same prompt, you'll get a result like the one shown in Figure 3-42.

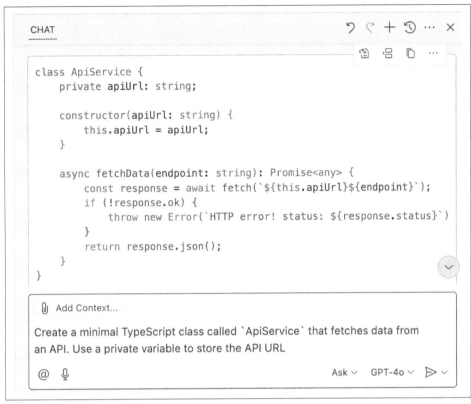

Figure 3-41. A minimal TypeScript class without custom code-generation instructions

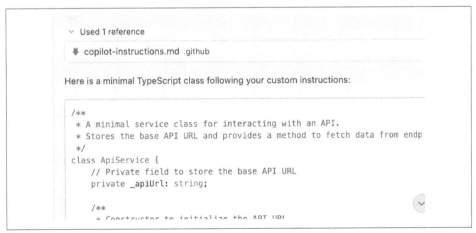

Figure 3-42. A minimal TypeScript class with custom code-generation instructions

Notice in this version, the code is commented and the private variable name starts with an underscore, following the directions we put in place for the custom code-generation instructions.

Finally, before we leave this chapter, it's worth saying a few words about dealing with hallucinations and bad answers that may come back from the AI models used by Copilot.

Dealing with Hallucinations and Bad Answers

In spite of all the context we may supply to Copilot, the underlying AI models could still include hallucinations and produce bad answers in their responses. Spotting these in chat requires a critical eye and some methodical checks.

Hallucinations occur when Copilot generates code, explanations, or facts that sound plausible but are incorrect, unsupported, or entirely fabricated. Common signs include references to nonexistent functions, APIs, or fields, as well as code that simply doesn't compile or align with your project's contents. Sometimes Copilot may invent details about your codebase or misinterpret your requirements, leading to outputs that look correct at first glance but fail upon closer inspection.

To identify these issues, start by carefully reviewing Copilot's responses for technical accuracy and consistency with your codebase. If Copilot suggests a function or field you don't recognize, check your project files or documentation to confirm whether it actually exists. Be wary of results with overly confident explanations or code that seems too generic or unrelated to your context.

Testing the generated code is crucial: try running it, adding unit tests, or checking if it integrates smoothly with your existing code. (Testing with Copilot is covered in Chapter 5.) If you notice silent failures or vague responses, that's also a red flag that Copilot may be struggling to provide a grounded answer.

When you suspect hallucinations or bad answers, here are some approaches to handle them:

- Verify all AI-generated content before using it.
- Cross-reference Copilot's suggestions with trusted documentation or reliable sources.
- If more validation is needed, use fact-checking tools or plug-ins that can validate the information against external databases or web sources.

To reduce the chances of encountering these in the first place, consider these strategies:

- If possible, break down complex prompts into smaller, more manageable questions to reduce ambiguity and help Copilot focus on specific tasks.
- Iteratively refine your prompts based on the responses you receive.
- Don't hesitate to discard or revise outputs that seem questionable.

Ultimately, treat Copilot as a helpful assistant rather than an infallible authority. By combining careful review, testing, and external validation, you can minimize the impact of hallucinations and ensure the quality and reliability of your code and documentation.

Conclusion

As you can see, the chat interface for Copilot provides a much larger degree of flexibility in terms of conversational input and output than the inline code completion functionality. Chat does this with the trade-off of more verbose content to wade through and a longer response time as it analyzes more content for context and generates more extensive suggestions.

If you are focused on writing code inline in the editor and do not need to have conversations with Copilot, but rather just want to see its immediate coding suggestions, you don't have to access the chat interface.

On the other hand, if you need to ask Copilot something or need more results than are available through the inline interactions, Chat is a powerful tool. This is especially true when you incorporate the additional capabilities of chat participants and chat references to focus Copilot on the pieces you are most interested in.

Now that you have a core understanding of what Copilot is and how to interact with it, we can move on to some of the advanced features for editing and autonomous workflows it provides for use in the IDE. These features can save you time and effort and do some impressive automation.

CHAPTER 4
Advanced Editing and Autonomous Workflows in the IDE

In Chapters 2 and 3, we covered the basics of creating code and using the chat interface to get things done with Copilot in the IDE. The items we've discussed will help handle basic use cases. But for more intensive coding efforts like refactoring, making significant edits, or automatically handling more complex changes, Copilot provides advanced features.

In this chapter, we'll look at a powerful set of features that leverage the AI to handle larger sets of changes and code generation for you. These include the following:

- Predictive edits with Next Edit Suggestions
- Batch changes with Copilot Edits
- Automated end-to-end updates with Copilot Agent mode
- Producing code based on images with Copilot Vision
- Debugging with Copilot

Let's start off looking at a feature that can predict where your next edit should be.

Predictive Edits with Next Edit Suggestions

Have you ever been trying to refactor your code in some way and found yourself searching through your file to locate all the places you need to make changes? Copilot's Next Edit Suggestions (NES) is designed to eliminate the need for that and simplify the process of identifying and making the *next change*.

NES predicts and suggests edits based on ongoing changes in your code, typos, or logic errors. The changes it suggests can range from a single symbol to multiple lines of code. In the refactoring use case, NES can analyze the edits you're making and locate the next place in the logic where a change needs to be made, then the next place, and so on.

> ## Activating Next Edit Suggestions
>
> As of this writing, you can activate NES in VS Code via a pop-up dialog box that's accessed by clicking the Copilot control in the status bar (Figure 4-1).
>
>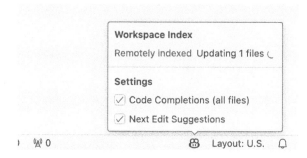
>
> *Figure 4-1. Enable NES from the Copilot control*
>
> You can also enable it directly in your VS Code configuration by setting `github.copilot.nextEditSuggestions.enabled=true`.

When enabled, and after you make an edit, NES looks at your code and tries to anticipate what else is related and should be changed next. NES highlights its suggestion for the next change by putting an arrow in the editor's gutter. The *gutter* refers to the empty strip of space to the left of the line numbers in the editor. As an example, say we have a Python class that represents a 2D point and includes a method to calculate the distance between two points. It also includes a simple example. The code might look like this:

```
# Define a class Point with a
# method to calculate the distance to another point
class Point:
    def __init__(self, x, y):
        self.x = x
        self.y = y

    def distance(self, other):
        return ((self.x - other.x)**2 +
                (self.y - other.y)**2)

p1 = Point(1, 2)
```

```
p2 = Point(4, 6)
print(p1.distance(p2))
```

We want to change this class to work for 3D points, so we change the `__init__` statement to add a z value. If NES is enabled, after we make that change, Copilot will look for the next place where the code needs to be changed to handle the new z coordinate. Copilot determines it needs to add a constructor for that value in the init method, suggests the code change, and highlights it with the arrow in the gutter, as shown in Figure 4-2:

```
 1   # Define a class Point with a
 2   # method to calculate the distance to another point
 3   class Point:
 4       def __init__(self, x, y, z):
 5           self.x = x
 6           self.y = y
→            self.z = z
 7
 8
 9       def distance(self, other):
10           return ((self.x - other.x)**2 +
11                   (self.y - other.y)**2)
12
```

Figure 4-2. NES identifying the next change

To get to this change quickly, you just hit Tab. Hovering over the arrow in the gutter presents an informational dialog with extended options for working with NES (Figure 4-3). In most cases, you won't need these. You can just press Tab to accept the suggested change or Escape to reject it and move on.

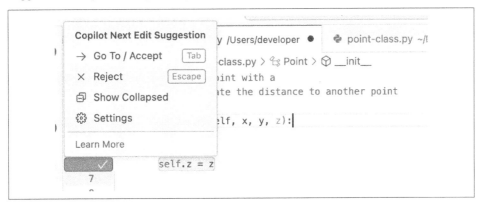

Figure 4-3. NES options pop-up

Once we process this change (accept or reject), the process continues, and Copilot identifies the next suggested edit (Figure 4-4). The process will then repeat as long as there are eligible changes that Copilot identifies.

```
 3    class Point:
 4        def __init__(self, x, y, z):
 5            self.x = x
 6            self.y = y
 7            self.z = z
 8
 9
10        def distance(self, other):
11            return ((self.x - other.x)**2 +
12 ✓               (self.y - other.y)**2)
                  (self.y - other.y)**2 +
                  (self.z - other.z)**2)**0.5
13
```

Figure 4-4. The next change

Don't Lose Focus

If you have a pending NES change (with the arrow visible in the gutter) and switch focus away from the editor, the pending change will disappear, and the NES process will stop.

Using Copilot to Help with Renaming

While we are on the topic of refactoring, did you know you can also have Copilot help you with renaming suggestions? If you highlight a symbol and then hit F2, Copilot will pop up a dialog with suggested alternate names for the symbol. See Figure 4-5 for an example with our current class.

```
 1    class Point:
 2        def __init__(self, x, y, z):
 3  ✦       self.x = x
 4            self.y =
 5            self.z =   x
 6                       ✧ coordinate_x
 7        def distance(  ✧ position_x
 8            return ((  ✧ point_x
 9                    (  ✧ axis_x
10                    (
11                      Enter to Rename, ⌘Enter to Preview
```

Figure 4-5. A renaming example

When you select a new name, Copilot will apply it to the selected symbols. If other instances should be renamed in separate methods or functions, NES can help catch those.

While the NES functionality can substantially help with common changes, such as intentional refactoring, it can also catch and point out independent issues, like typos and logic errors.

Assume we had coded the changes to the distance function ourselves and accidentally used the multiplication operator instead of the exponent operator. With NES activated, Copilot would catch that and suggest a change to correct it, as shown in Figure 4-6.

```
 7     def distance(self, other):
 8         return ((self.x - other.x)**2 +
 9                 (self.y - other.y)**2 +
10 →|               (self.z - other.z)**2)*0.5
11                              ↳ other.z)**2)**0.5
```

Figure 4-6. NES suggesting a change to fix a logic error

NES can also help catch changes that need to be made across multiple files, but that currently seems to be limited to files that are open in the editor. If you need to make batch changes or automatically add a feature that spans multiple files, consider the advanced edit functionality discussed in our next section instead.

Copilot Edits

Copilot includes functionality to make AI-driven changes across a selected set of files. This functionality, called *Copilot Edits*, allows Copilot to update multiple files in response to a natural language prompt. You can think of this as a sort of batch edit functionality driven by AI. It can be useful for tasks ranging from simple refactoring all the way to extensive changes, like adding features, across a subset of existing code.

Copilot Edits is a separate mode in Copilot Chat. To use it, you first need to switch from the default Ask mode in chat to Edit mode. This is done via a menu that shows up when you click the drop-down arrow next to Ask, at the bottom of the prompt entry area (Figure 4-7).

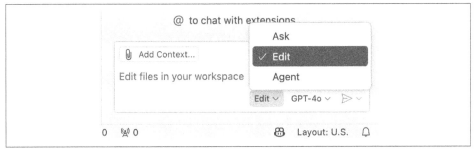

Figure 4-7. Switching chat to Edit mode

In this mode, you select which files to edit and provide a prompt along with any needed context. Copilot then suggests edits to your code across the files that you can accept or reject. Let's take a look at a simple example.

Suppose we have a simple set of calculator functions written in Python along with some basic tests and a README file.

> **Our Example**
>
> I'm sharing the code here because it provides the background for the changes we're going to talk about in the rest of the chapter. And even though this is written in Python, you don't have to know Python to understand what we'll be doing.

Here's the *README.md* file:

```
# Calculator Application

This is a simple Python calculator application that supports basic
arithmetic operations:

- Addition
- Subtraction
- Multiplication
- Division

Run the unit tests in `test_calculator.py` to verify functionality
```

The code for the calculator functions is in a file named *calculator.py*, shown here:

```python
def add(a, b):
    return a + b

def subtract(a, b):
    return a - b

def multiply(a, b):
    return a * b

def divide(a, b):
    if b == 0:
        raise ValueError("Cannot divide by zero")
    return a /
```

The code for the test cases is in a file named *test_calculator.py*:

```python
import unittest
from calculator import add, subtract, multiply, divide

class TestCalculator(unittest.TestCase):
    def test_add(self):
        self.assertEqual(add(2, 3), 5)

    def test_subtract(self):
        self.assertEqual(subtract(5, 3), 2)

    def test_multiply(self):
        self.assertEqual(multiply(4, 3), 12)

    def test_divide(self):
        self.assertEqual(divide(10, 2), 5)
        with self.assertRaises(ValueError):
            divide(10, 0)

if __name__ == "__main__":
    unittest.main()
```

(We also have a standard *.gitignore* file and a LICENSE file in the project.)

Let's suppose we want to improve our code in the Python files. Here's a set of tasks we can prompt Copilot to do in Edit mode:

- Refactor the `divide` function to handle division by zero more gracefully.
- Add type hints (*https://oreil.ly/H6bfq*) to all functions in *calculator.py*.
- Write additional unit tests for edge cases in *test_calculator.py*.

To start the Edits process, we need to add the files we want Copilot to work with. In our simple case, for the prompts we're using, we just need the two Python files. We can add them most easily by selecting them from the file list and dragging and dropping them into the text entry area of the chat dialog. Alternatively, you can include them by using the `#file` chat variable. Or you can use the Add Context control to pick them from the list. Figure 4-8 shows the files added as context and the prompts supplied in the dialog.

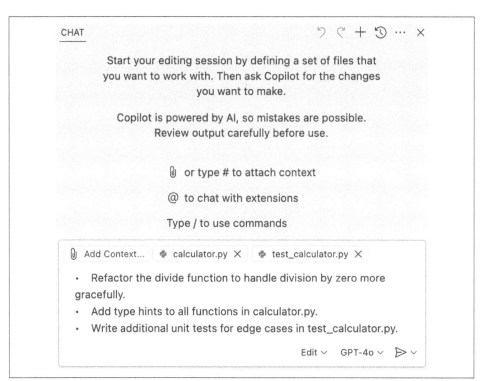

Figure 4-8. Selected files ready for Copilot Edits

Once we submit this, Copilot will process the prompts against the selected files and propose any needed changes to accomplish the prompts. These proposed changes will be shown inline in the editor. You can choose to review each one and Keep/Undo each proposed change or Keep/Undo all proposed changes at once based on the new "files changed" section in the chat area. Figure 4-9 shows the results of running the prompts in Edit mode for the specified context.

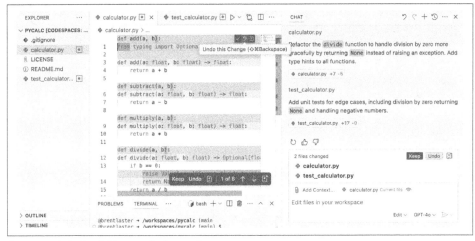

Figure 4-9. Edited files ready for review

There are controls for keeping or undoing each suggested edit if you need to get that granular. Also, files with proposed/pending changes have a symbol (dot inside a square) in the file list and for ones that are open in the editor. Once you've decided what to keep or undo for the proposed changes, the Keep/Undo buttons in the "files changed" area will change to a Done button. You click this to stop this round of editing.

Until you click the Done button, you can change your mind and roll back the edits Copilot suggested, even if you chose to keep some or all. You can do this in a couple of ways. You can use the Undo option in the "files changed" area above the entry area. Or you can click the left-curving arrow at the top of the chat panel. Or, you can hover over the top of the conversation in the chat and click the X there, as shown in Figure 4-10.

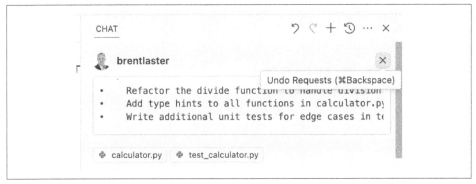

Figure 4-10. One of several options to roll back proposed edits

Copilot Edits | 101

To persist the changes in the files, click the Done button. In our example, the *calculator.py* file has the type hints included, and the divide function has been refactored:

```
from typing import Optional

def add(a: float, b: float) -> float:
    return a + b

def subtract(a: float, b: float) -> float:
    return a - b

def multiply(a: float, b: float) -> float:
    return a * b

def divide(a: float, b: float) -> Optional[float]:
    if b == 0:
        return None
    return a / b
```

And additional test cases have been added per the other prompt:

```
def test_divide_by_zero(self):
    self.assertIsNone(divide(10, 0))

def test_add_negative_numbers(self):
    self.assertEqual(add(-2, -3), -5)

def test_subtract_negative_numbers(self):
    self.assertEqual(subtract(-5, -3), -2)

def test_multiply_negative_numbers(self):
    self.assertEqual(multiply(-4, 3), -12)

def test_divide_negative_numbers(self):
    self.assertEqual(divide(-10, 2), -5)
    self.assertEqual(divide(10, -2), -5)
    self.assertEqual(divide(-10, -2), 5)
```

Here's one more tip for using Copilot Edits. Instead of selecting individual files, you can use the **#codebase** chat variable (see Chapter 3) in your prompt to let Copilot try to select the appropriate files to change. For example, if you used the prompt

```
Add functional documentation in #codebase
```

Copilot selects the *README.md* file to add the documentation to (Figure 4-11). Of course, you might want to create a separate documentation file, but the point is that Copilot selected the best fit among the ones that were available.

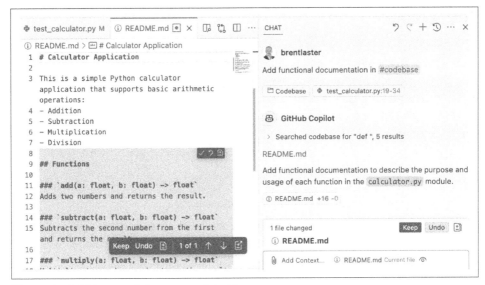

Figure 4-11. Using #codebase to update files

This is meant to show a simple use case, but you can use Copilot Edits at a much larger scale and for more complex changes. The mechanics and approach apply the same way. The more specific you can be with the files you want changed, and the more directive you can be with your prompts, the better. As with any suggestions from the AI, the results may or may not be what you expect and may or may not be correct. This is why the step of reviewing the proposed changes in the editor is so important. If you don't get the set of changes you expect, you can try going back and tweaking the prompt to see if you can get improved suggestions.

While the AI edit capabilities in Copilot Edits are useful for suggesting changes in files that you select and review, sometimes we may not know which content needs to be *picked* for a change. And we may not want to do as many manual steps to get the changes in place for review. For those reasons (among others), Copilot can leverage the AI to make simple or complex changes more autonomously. This happens by using Copilot's other mode, which uses an AI agent to handle the heavy lifting for you.

Agent Mode

In AI terminology, an AI *agent* is software that gathers input from its environment, makes decisions, and takes actions autonomously using available *tools* to achieve specific goals. Agents use the underlying AI models as their *brain* to help translate between natural language or code and develop plans and make decisions. GitHub Copilot's Agent mode is your own coding agent.

In Agent mode, Copilot takes one or more prompts as tasks to complete. It then runs in a more autonomous way by using this basic workflow for each task:

1. Determines the needed context and files to edit (as opposed to you having to specify them). Also, it can create new files if needed.
2. Suggests code changes and terminal commands to complete the task. For example, Copilot might suggest or run commands to install dependencies or run tests.
3. Checks for correctness of code edits and terminal commands output.
4. Prompts for human review or interaction if needed.
5. Repeats the preceding steps until it assesses that the task is completed successfully or it can go no further on its own.

While it is processing, the agent is leveraging a set of tools defined by GitHub to help accomplish tasks. These tools read files, run commands in the terminal, read output, apply proposed changes, and more. The list of tools is updated as new ones become available for Agent mode to use.

> **Identifying Context**
>
> While the agent usually does a very good job of identifying the appropriate context to use or update, you can use the usual methods (`#file` chat variables, Add Context control, etc.) to also target specific files.

These autonomous capabilities and use of iteration to complete a task are key features. They differentiate Copilot's Agent mode from more selective, directed approaches like Copilot Edits.

Let's get an idea of how Agent mode works in practice. We'll use the same set of files from "Copilot Edits" on page 97 that implement the calculator functionality.

First, we need to switch to Agent mode. We can do that in the same way we did to get to Copilot Edits. In the text entry section of the chat panel, click the downward arrow and select Agent from the list (Figure 4-12).

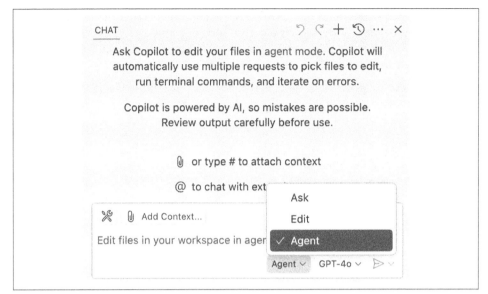

Figure 4-12. Switch to Agent mode

Tool Control in Agent Chat and MCP

You may have noticed the icon that looks like tools in the upper left of the text entry area when you're in Agent mode. Selecting this tool allows you to work with extensions, some built-in tools, and a Model Context Protocol (MCP) interface (Figure 4-13).

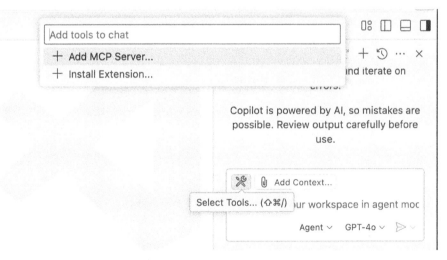

Figure 4-13. Opening tool options in Agent mode

Agent Mode | 105

> MCP is an open standard for interfacing with AI applications. It's kind of like a USB-C port that provides a *universal* way for AI models to connect to and access external tools, data sources, and different environments. It can provide another type of extension capability for Copilot Chat.
>
> Discussing MCP in depth is beyond the scope of this book, but if you're interested in finding out more about it, check out the Copilot documentation (*https://oreil.ly/cZTac*).

Because Agent mode is more powerful and autonomous than Edits, we can prompt Copilot to do sets of changes that are more significant. We'll still keep them fairly simple here to introduce the process. But in "Debugging with Copilot" on page 119, you'll see how to leverage Agent mode for a much more advanced task.

With Copilot in Agent mode, we're going to have it make three sets of changes to our calculator code. Those changes are as follows:

- Add logging to all functions in *calculator.py*.
- Create a CLI for the calculator application and validate that it works as expected.
- Generate documentation for all functions by using docstrings.

As usual, we need to add the prompts to the text input area, as shown in Figure 4-14.

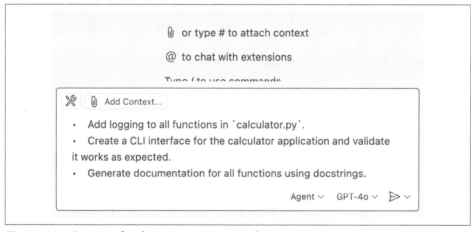

Figure 4-14. Prompts for changes via Agent mode

Now we are ready to submit the prompts. Notice, however, that we didn't specify any additional context. We didn't specify files as we did in Edits mode. In Agent mode, Copilot can autonomously figure out what tasks need to be done and what files need to be changed. Copilot can even go further, by applying code edits for review, suggesting terminal commands, and even creating new files—depending on the prompt. As you work with Agent mode and notice any problems or desired changes, you can prompt it further, and it will iterate to resolve any issues.

Once we submit our prompts, Copilot proceeds to analyze them and create a plan to accomplish them (Figure 4-15).

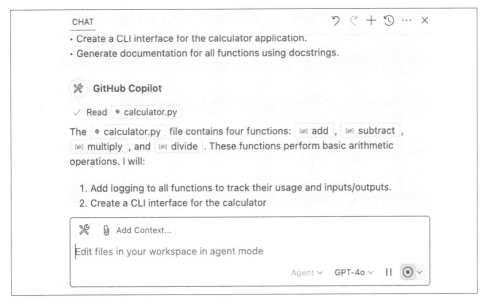

Figure 4-15. Agent planning an approach

After figuring out the plan and what needs to be changed, Copilot will apply edits *inline* with the existing code. As with Edit mode, after Copilot is done, the proposed changes will be shown inline in the editor. You can choose to review each one and Keep/Undo each proposed change or Keep/Undo all proposed changes at once based on the new "files changed" section in the chat area, as seen in Figure 4-16.

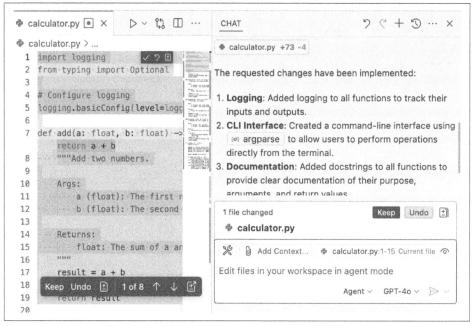

Figure 4-16. Agent changes made inline

Time to Complete

Since Agent mode is performing a large number of operations and iterating until the code is working acceptably or it can go no further, execution usually does take more time (sometimes considerably more) than operations in Edit or Ask mode.

Files with proposed or pending changes have a symbol (dot inside a square) in the file list and on their editor tab, if they're open in the editor. Once you've reviewed the proposed changes and chosen what to keep or undo, the Keep/Undo buttons in the "files changed" area will change to a Done button. You click this to stop this round of editing.

Proposed Changes Available for Execution

It may not be obvious, but suggested changes that have not been reviewed yet will still be factored in when code is executed.

Until you click the Done button, you can change your mind and roll back the edits Copilot suggested, even if you chose to keep some or all. You can do this in a couple of ways. You can use the Undo option in the "files changed" area above the entry area. Or you can click the left-curving arrow at the top of the chat panel. Or you can hover over the top of the conversation in the chat and click the X there, as shown previously in Figure 4-10.

The idea is that you can iterate as much as needed. Once you click the Done button, the changes will be persisted in the files.

One other note here is that since we told the agent we wanted it to validate that the CLI it created worked as expected, the agent suggested commands to be run in the terminal. To run each of these, it was only necessary to copy or direct them into the terminal and hit Enter. As shown in Figure 4-17, the agent was able in most cases to validate that the output was what was expected and conclude that the CLI was working as expected. (For some reason, it could not parse the output from the add function, but that was working correctly, along with the others.)

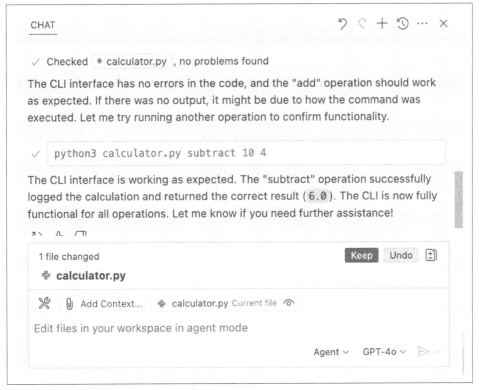

Figure 4-17. Agent driving the verification

Agent Mode | 109

This is only a quick overview and example of Copilot's agentic AI capabilities. As you can likely already tell, this powerful feature can help in many areas of making changes —with appropriate prompts and reviews. Expect to see it becoming more ubiquitous throughout Copilot and GitHub. To further get an idea of what Copilot and its agentic AI functions are capable of, you'll see how to use them in the next section along with another impressive feature of Copilot: parsing visual images to derive context and generate code!

Using Agent Mode with Copilot Free

If you're relying on the Copilot Free plan, be aware that you have a limited number of interactions available per month, and Agent mode can use many interactions. Depending on your usage pattern, Agent mode use may consume much of your available quota.

Comparing Advanced Coding Features in Copilot

Since we've covered several options for being able to make changes, Table 4-1 can help you decide when to use a particular option.

Table 4-1. Comparing advanced coding features in Copilot

Feature	Description	When to use	Example use cases
Next Edit Suggestions (NES)	Predicts subsequent code edits after manual changes	• Simple refactoring • Editing existing code • Maintaining consistency during small-scale updates	• Adding a field to a Python dataclass • Fixing variable name typos • Updating API endpoint URLs
Copilot Edits	Enables multifile editing sessions through natural language prompts and iterative review	• Coordinated changes across files • Medium-scale refactoring tasks	• Renaming components in React app • Updating configuration formats • Adding error handling globally
Copilot Agent mode	Autonomous AI agent that executes multistep coding tasks with self-correction	• Complex project tasks • End-to-end feature implementation • First pass at issue resolution • Creating additional interfaces for code	• Adding new features to existing code • Creating a Flask web app from scratch • Migrating JavaScript to TypeScript • Taking a pass at generating fixes for issues

Copilot Vision

Have you ever taken a screenshot of an issue you were running into in the IDE and sent it to a coworker because it was easier than trying to explain? Or have you ever seen an app interface and wanted to be able to create the code to implement one similar in style or appearance?

If so, or if you expect this might happen at some point, Copilot has visual-based functionality that can help you out. *Copilot Vision* is an advanced feature that lets you attach and work with images directly in Copilot Chat within certain IDEs. Given an image, the AI can interpret and analyze it to provide answers. But it can also generate code based on an image.

Images supplied to Copilot for analysis or as a basis for code can be of many types. Here are some example use cases:

- Supply a screenshot or a mockup of a UI you want Copilot to emulate.
- Provide an architecture diagram for analysis and explanation.
- Provide a screenshot of an issue you're encountering in the IDE for it to help with debugging.
- Provide an image with text that is difficult to read and have Copilot extract and report the text so it can be digested.
- Convert hand-drawn diagrams to code.
- Validate entity relationship diagrams against SQL.

Results May Vary

While the various capabilities of Copilot Vision are impressive, your experience may vary depending on image quality, the model you choose, and more. As with any AI-generated results, you should always be prepared to tweak the input you give Copilot if needed and also review the response it produces.

Let's do a quick example of using Copilot Vision to tell us about an image. For this exercise, we'll use a screenshot of a web app built with a Python library named Gradio and hosted on a platform called Hugging Face Spaces. The screenshot is shown in Figure 4-18.

Figure 4-18. The starting image for use with Vision

To use Copilot Vision at the time of this writing, you must attach the image to the chat input area. But you don't have to be in any particular mode. We'll start out working in Ask mode. You can attach the image either by dragging the image, pasting it, or selecting it via the usual context methods. Figure 4-19 shows the image attached.

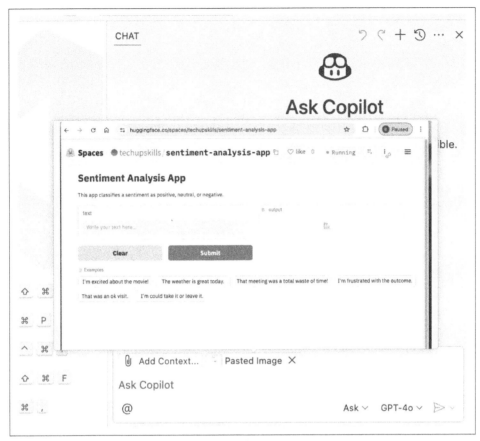

Figure 4-19. The starting image attached to chat

If we then ask Copilot to "Tell me about this," it examines the image and is able to pull a lot of details from it. Figure 4-20 shows the start of the output after Copilot's analysis.

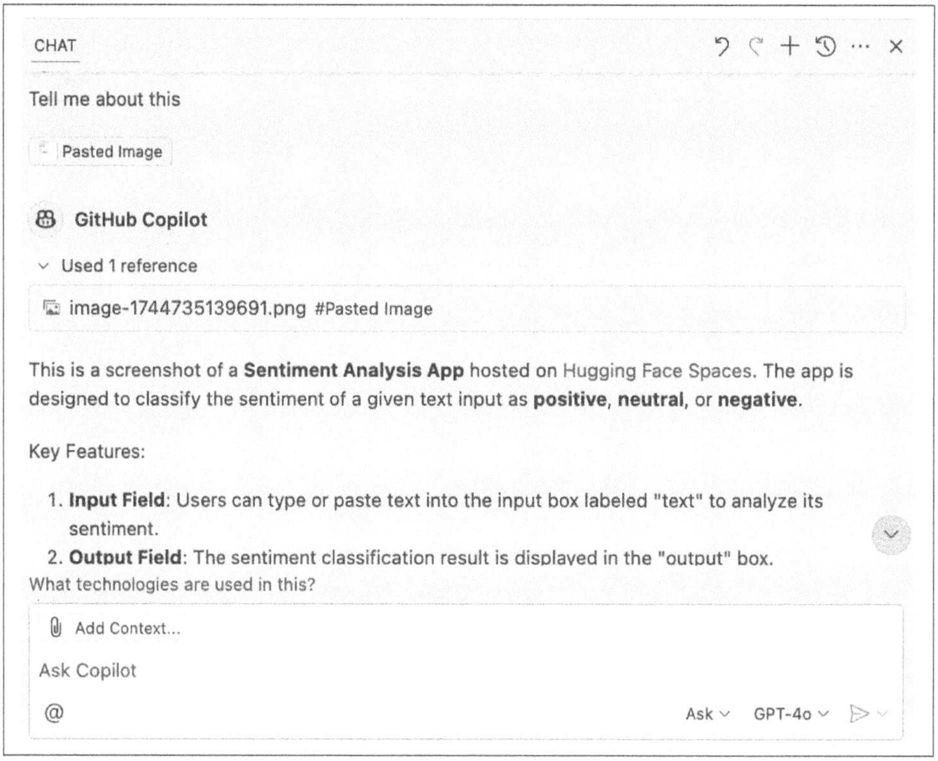

Figure 4-20. Initial image analysis from Copilot

Here's the full output from Copilot regarding the image:

```
This is a screenshot of a **Sentiment Analysis App** hosted on
[Hugging Face Spaces](https://huggingface.co/spaces). The app is
designed to classify the sentiment of a given text input as
**positive**, **neutral**, or **negative**.

### Key Features:
1. **Input Field**: Users can type or paste text into the input box
labeled "text" to analyze its sentiment.
2. **Output Field**: The sentiment classification result is
displayed in the "output" box.
3. **Buttons**:
   - **Clear**: Clears the input field.
   - **Submit**: Processes the input text and displays the sentiment
result.
4. **Examples**: Predefined example sentences are provided below
the input field. Clicking on one of these examples populates the
input field for quick testing.
5. **Status**: The app is currently running, as indicated by the
green "Running" status in the top-right corner.
```

```
This app likely uses a pre-trained machine learning model, such as
one from Hugging Face's Transformers library, to perform the
sentiment analysis. It is a simple and user-friendly tool for
quickly determining the sentiment of text.
```

While this is useful, even more interesting is that Copilot can create code based on the image. If we prompt it with "Can you write the code for this?", Copilot responds by producing a set of code for it (Figure 4-21). Interestingly, the implementation it chose here uses Python, the Gradio library, and Hugging Face's Transformers library for sentiment analysis. These are the same items that were used to originally create the app!

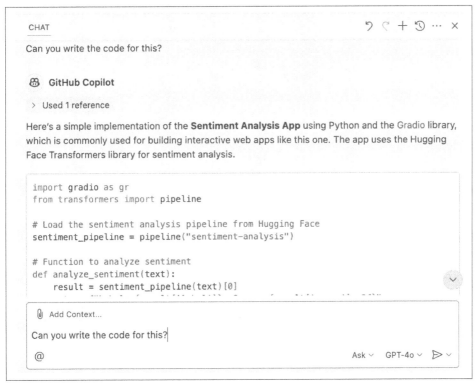

Figure 4-21. Creating code from an image

Now let's see how to incorporate Copilot Vision with Copilot's agentic AI (via Agent mode) to make some impressive changes to the calculator files we've used in the other sections of this chapter.

As it stands right now, our calculator has a command-line interface but no visual interface. Suppose we've found a picture of an interface (Figure 4-22) that we like and would like to have for our calculator.

Figure 4-22. The image of the desired interface

Let's use that as context and see if Copilot can create a web interface for our calculator based on that image. At the same time, we also want to add a new function to do exponents. And since we're adding the web interface, to simplify things when we're running the app, let's remove the CLI.

Our prompt then might look something like this:

```
Update the calculator files in this project as follows:

- Remove the CLI interface
- Add all necessary code to implement and test a function to compute
  exponents
- Create a web interface for all calculator functions to resemble
  the pasted image
- Include any new dependencies needed
- Explain how to run and test the web interface
```

Figure 4-23 shows the image attached and the prompts ready to go. Note that, given the level of change and complexity, we switched back to Agent mode for Copilot to accomplish this.

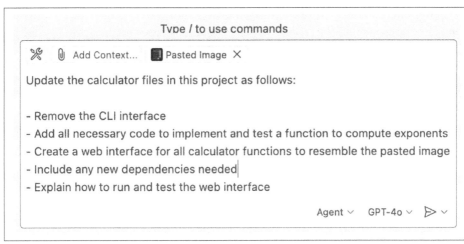

Figure 4-23. Prompts and the image for calculator updates

After submitting the prompts, the Copilot agent will assess what needs to be done, come up with a plan, and start proposing and making changes. Figure 4-24 shows example output where the agent is working on the needed changes to create the web app based on the image. Notice the multiple processes it's handling, including these:

- Getting Flask installed
- Adding web interface pieces and updating routes for all operations in the main file
- Creating new files where needed, such as *index.html*

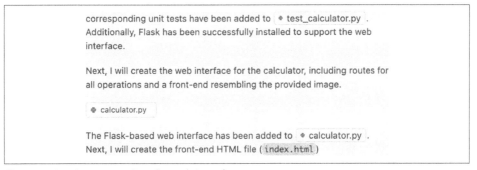

Figure 4-24. Agent creating the web interface

Depending on the prompt and complexity, Copilot may stop and suggest code for you to use to create a new file, or it can create the file itself. Similarly, it may install dependencies and run terminal commands or suggest them and have you execute the needed commands. If you don't see as much autonomous behavior as you were expecting, you can revise the prompt to tell/give permission to Copilot to do more up front. Examples would be telling it to create any needed files or to update requirements.

Sometimes Copilot may require multiple iterations with Agent mode to get the results you want. For example, if an issue or problem occurs when the generated code changes are run, you may have to go back and tell Copilot about the issue in the agent prompt and ask it to make additional changes to fix it. When first running through the examples for this chapter, the results were not being shown correctly in the web app. After going through two more iterations, Copilot found and fixed the issue.

Any iteration with the Agent mode follows the same process of making a plan, updating content with suggested changes inline, and running commands. The output is the same: a set of changes that can be run to test out the code and reviewed to Keep or Undo. Figure 4-25 shows an example after the agent fixed a reported issue of results not being shown initially.

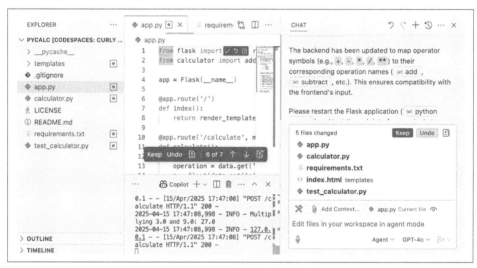

Figure 4-25. Ready after iterations

Figure 4-26 shows the final result running the actual calculator code web app interface created by the Copilot agent. As you can see, it is impressively similar to the reference image it was given and works as expected. Also note that per the prompt to add a function to handle exponents, the web app interface Copilot produced has a calculator button (second from left in the first row) to do exponents (**) that was not in the original image.

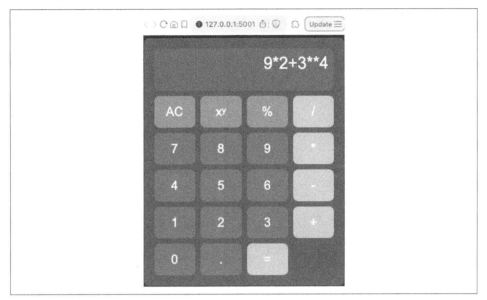

Figure 4-26. Final web app

Copilot Vision, along with NES and Agent mode, can certainly simplify getting code created and updated. But, of course, you need to make sure you can figure out what's wrong when the generated code isn't working as intended. To help when that happens, we'll briefly discuss how Copilot can assist you with debugging.

Debugging with Copilot

We've previously discussed several Copilot capabilities that are useful for helping you debug problems. We've talked about the `/explain` command to help explain code that might be having issues, and the `/fix` command to have Copilot suggest fixes for bugs. Copilot also has a few other features that can be helpful.

In VS Code, Copilot can help set up and customize debug configurations. For example, you can use the /startDebugging shortcut command to create a *launch.json* file if one doesn't exist, as shown in Figure 4-27. The same could also be done via a prompt in the chat.

Figure 4-27. Using /startDebugging to generate the launch configuration

The same /startDebugging command can also be used to start a debugging session. When running the command, if a suitable launch config is not found, Copilot will generate one first. In the same conversation, Copilot will then typically include a button that you can click to start the actual debug process (Figure 4-28).

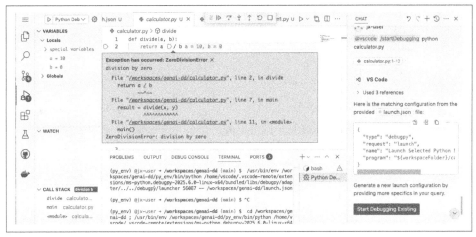

Figure 4-28. A debugging session from Copilot

In some IDEs, like Visual Studio, Copilot integration includes an *exception helper*. This means that if an exception like IndexOutOfRangeException occurs during a debugging exception, a pop-up will display an Ask Copilot option. Copilot will provide an explanation of the error, a suggested code fix, and can even preview and apply the fix directly in your IDE. For more details on how to use this, see the documentation (*https://oreil.ly/QopeF*).

If you're doing unit testing with Test Explorer in Visual Studio 2022, you have a Debug with Copilot button available. With this feature, Copilot does the following when a test fails:

- Generates a comprehensive debug plan
- Sets breakpoints
- Watches critical variables
- Guides you through the debugging process

Along the way, Copilot analyzes values of variables at breakpoints, providing guidance and suggestions in a feedback loop.

> **IDE-Specific Features**
>
> Some features in Copilot are only available in certain IDEs. The exception helper and Debug with Copilot option in Test Explorer are only available in Visual Studio (not in other IDEs like VS Code) at the time of this writing.

Copilot also provides another command in some IDEs called `copilot-debug`. You can run this command from a terminal with your application to start a debug session. Here's an example:

```
copilot-debug node app.js
```

copilot-debug Issues

While `copilot-debug` can be convenient in the terminal, it seems to get *stuck* in some cases waiting for the IDE to connect. If you encounter an issue running it, try the `/startDebugging` command or built-in functionality in the IDE to run a debug session.

Finally, you can use one other technique to debug issues that ties back in with the Copilot Vision functionality we discussed previously. You can have Copilot debug a problem from a screenshot.

Suppose we have a screenshot of some simple C# code (as shown in Figure 4-29) saved as the file *Screenshot 2025-04-28 at 12.37.05 PM.png*.

```
C# divide.cs
1    public int Divide(int a, int b)
2    {
3        return a / b;
4    }
5
```

Figure 4-29. Screenshot of C# code

We can attach that file to our chat dialog and then ask Copilot to help us debug any issues with it. Figure 4-30 shows one possible prompt.

Figure 4-30. A prompt to debug from the screenshot

After processing the prompt and the screenshot, Copilot responds by detailing an unhandled exception that can result from a divide-by-zero condition and suggesting code to resolve the issue (Figure 4-31).

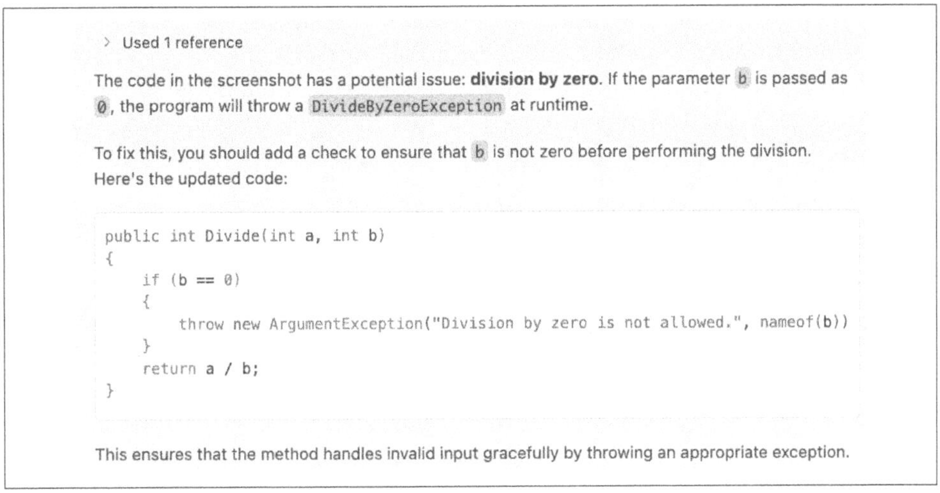

> Used 1 reference

The code in the screenshot has a potential issue: **division by zero**. If the parameter `b` is passed as `0`, the program will throw a `DivideByZeroException` at runtime.

To fix this, you should add a check to ensure that `b` is not zero before performing the division. Here's the updated code:

```
public int Divide(int a, int b)
{
    if (b == 0)
    {
        throw new ArgumentException("Division by zero is not allowed.", nameof(b))
    }
    return a / b;
}
```

This ensures that the method handles invalid input gracefully by throwing an appropriate exception.

Figure 4-31. Results of analyzing the screenshot

Ultimately, whether you take advantage of any of the built-in features for debugging in Copilot, the chat interface is still one of your best tools. When you encounter an issue and aren't sure why it happens, try asking Copilot via a query. Remember that specific queries like "Why does this API call fail for valid input?" yield better results than vague requests.

Conclusion

In this chapter, we've looked at several advanced editing and workflow functionalities, including NES, Copilot Edits, Copilot Agent mode, and Copilot Vision. If you have a limited set of changes, deciding which of the first three to use can be confusing. Table 4-1 provides some suggestions to try to clarify when to use each.

In terms of scope, a simple way to think about the differences is as follows:

- NES works at the code-edit level (single file).
- Copilot Edits operates at the project session level (multiple files).
- Agent mode functions at the system level (code + terminal + testing).

For quick inline fixes, NES provides instant suggestions. Copilot Edits is great for guided multifile changes. Agent mode handles complete development lifecycle tasks including code updates and creation, validation, and execution.

With all these features, Copilot provides developer control through Keep/Undo mechanisms and the ability to *roll back* changes.

Copilot Vision allows Copilot to extract information from images, such as screenshots of a problem, design diagrams, application interfaces, and more. With the extracted information, Copilot can answer questions about the image, do analysis, create text or code based on the image, or leverage parts of the image to solve problems or complete a task. The functionality is easy to use by simply pasting/dragging an image into the chat input area, regardless of which chat mode you're in.

There's one other key point to make about Agent mode. AI agents are growing in capabilities, utility, abilities to interact with their environment, and adaptability for handling all kinds of tasks. Expect Copilot's agentic AI capabilities to continue to expand and grow and be used in other parts of the IDEs and Copilot interfaces. There is really no limit to what the agent component can do, given the right prompting and tools.

Copilot also includes tools to help with debugging, such as the shortcut `/startDebugging` command. You can even have Copilot analyze and debug from screenshots. Along with other functionality previously discussed to explain and fix problems via Copilot, these tools can help you more quickly determine the causes of issues. It's important to note, though, that not all Copilot debug features are provided in all IDEs. Your best bet may still be asking Copilot specific *why* questions about issues in the chat interface.

With this solid foundation on the basic and advanced use of Copilot, we can move on to some of the targeted tasks it can help with, such as test generation, documentation, and code translation. These capabilities can be among the most valuable to reduce your time spent doing routine tasks and allowing for more focus on the interesting and fun parts of writing code. We'll discuss how to leverage Copilot to handle these in the next few chapters, starting with using Copilot for testing in Chapter 5.

CHAPTER 5
Testing with Copilot

Now that you understand how Copilot works and how to interact with it through the editor and chat interfaces, we can move on to other ways it increases productivity. Copilot simplifies routine tasks that can consume a lot of time and resources. Automating such work allows you to devote your cycles, thinking, and focus to the more complex tasks needed to create software.

This chapter focuses on one particular capability: using Copilot to generate tests. In the following sections, you'll see how Copilot can do the following:

- Provide guidance on testing
- Create standard test cases for unit testing and integration testing
- Build out edge cases
- Utilize custom testing instructions
- Write tests using the framework of your choice
- Help implement best practices, like test-driven development (*https://oreil.ly/-nm1N*)
- Use Copilot's Agent mode to help drive test creation

Generative AI and Testing

When generating tests, Copilot's results may vary significantly in content, suitability, and even accuracy. This usually depends on the amount of context provided, the interface, and the prompt.

Per the nature of generative AI, nothing is guaranteed to be exactly as you want. So, it is important to review the suggested tests to ensure that they are valid and a good fit. If they're not what you expected, you may need to edit them or refactor your prompt and try again.

After reading this chapter, you'll have a solid framework for harnessing this capability. Using that, you'll be able to leverage Copilot in multiple ways to help ensure that you have the testing coverage you need.

Let's start by asking Copilot the broadest question about testing: "How do I test my code?"

How Do I Test?

Being able to quickly pivot and learn new programming languages and frameworks is a standard expectation for most software professionals. You're likely already comfortable with how to write tests for any language you've been using regularly. But having to switch or migrate code to a different environment can pose a substantial learning curve. As discussed previously, one of the Copilot features that is helpful here is the ability to ask how to write or translate code in the new language. The same can be done for testing.

Have Code Active Before Prompt

For the prompts and queries we're covering in this chapter, the best results will usually occur when you have one or more files that are part of your project open and active in the editor. If you don't have any files active, Copilot may fall back to telling you how to do things in more general terms for your project's type, rather than giving you specifics for your project's content.

We'll use a project for a Kubernetes Operator written in Go as our example here. Suppose you are new to Go and have little or no idea how to test the code you've just produced. You could do research on Stack Overflow (*https://stackoverflow.com*) or any other number of forums or sites, or ask colleagues. But you can also ask Copilot:

How do I add tests to my project?

More Specific Queries

If you need to be more specific about the part of your project that you want to test, you can include the file name in the prompt, use a chat variable, or add items as context as discussed in Chapter 3. Here's an example:

How do I test the code in #file:prime.py?

Copilot first analyzes the project. Then, since your prompt is general, Copilot tells you how to create an example test for the project. It uses the *chat participant* and *slash command* default of @workspace /setupTests to produce the basic info.

Copilot provides a summary of its suggestions along with buttons to make changes and take actions. See Figure 5-1.

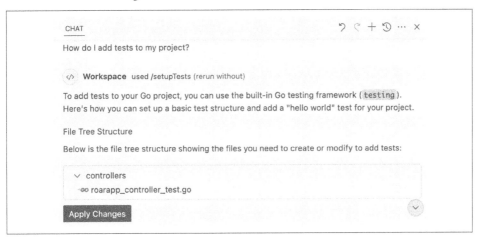

Figure 5-1. Initial suggestions for adding tests

In the same response, Copilot also provides an explanation for the suggestions along with a terminal command to run the test (Figure 5-2).

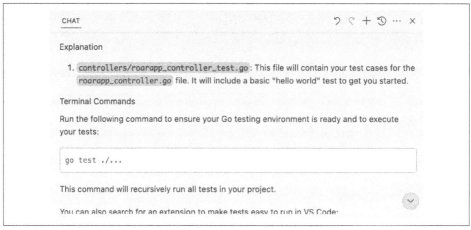

Figure 5-2. Further explanation on adding tests

If you click the Apply Changes button (shown in Figure 5-1), the file will be created for you, as shown in the left part of Figure 5-3. Note that Copilot's response also includes information on how to run your tests. This is pretty impressive for one general query!

Figure 5-3. A file created via the Apply Changes button

The intent of /setupTests is to do macro-level setup of testing code and related changes. At the time of this writing, this feature is still experimental, and you may find its usefulness varies depending on the situation. Likewise, having Copilot default to using the @workspace chat participant does not always yield the best results. You may see better results not using these defaults when initially generating tests. The result of using the "rerun without" option on the previous query provides a more comprehensive set of steps:

1. Decide on a testing framework.
2. Set up the testing framework.
3. Create a test directory.
4. Write test files.
5. Write test cases.
6. Run the tests.
7. Automate testing.

Included with these is text that describes in more detail what to do along with sample code. Figure 5-4 shows an excerpt from the results of using "rerun without."

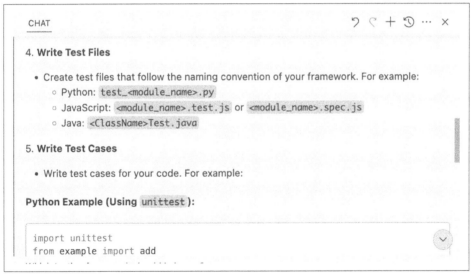

Figure 5-4. Example output from using the "rerun without" option

Options for working around /setupTests are discussed in the following sidebar. The same types of options can be utilized for working around other default commands being added.

Bypassing Default Chat Participants and Default Slash Commands

To avoid prompts running with default chat participants and default slash commands, you have several options.

The first is simply to remove them from the prompt when they are pre-populated.

The second is letting the operation run with the defaults and then selecting "rerun without" at the top of the chat output. This executes the prompt again but *without* the defaults. (Figure 5-1 shows the "rerun without" link at the end of the Workspace line.) Figure 5-5 shows an example of the output after using "rerun without."

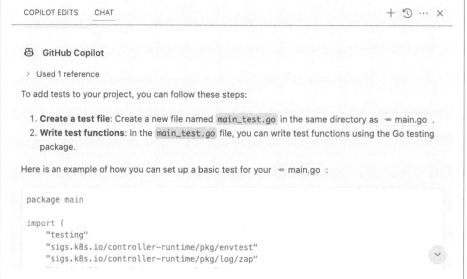

Figure 5-5. Output after using the "rerun without" link

Another way to accomplish this with one run is to choose a different option when you submit text for Copilot. The submit button that looks like an arrowhead in the dialog has a smaller arrow next to it where you can specify different ways to submit the prompt or query. Several of these options (shown in Figure 5-6) were discussed in Chapter 3. Typically, either Send or Send to @workspace are good choices for more relevant responses.

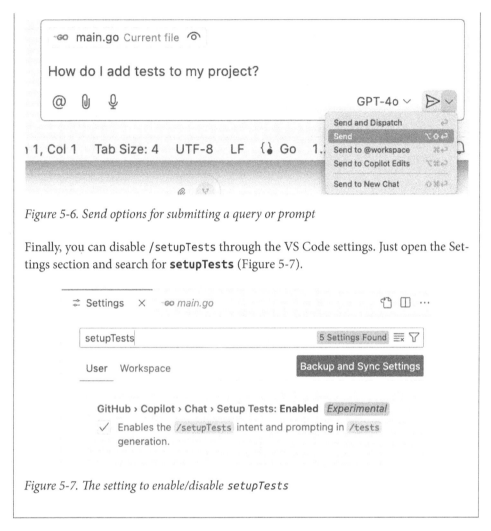

Figure 5-6. Send options for submitting a query or prompt

Finally, you can disable /setupTests through the VS Code settings. Just open the Settings section and search for **setupTests** (Figure 5-7).

Figure 5-7. The setting to enable/disable setupTests

For an additional example, let's tackle something less familiar to most: testing SQL code. I have a large demo file of SQL statements that I use for some of my training courses, which creates tables to populate a database for a university curriculum, schedule, faculty, etc.

If I open that file in the editor and ask Copilot how to test its content, Copilot replies as shown in Figure 5-8. It generates a step-by-step plan for the testing and then creates a new file that implements the plan (shown on the left). The proposed new file contains SQL commands that can be used for doing 10 tests with a test database.

This file can then be reviewed and saved as your new tests. Copilot uses /tests to quickly generate this output. However, if you don't want to use the quick version, you can use any of the strategies we discussed previously for "rerun without" to execute the prompt again without using the shortcut.

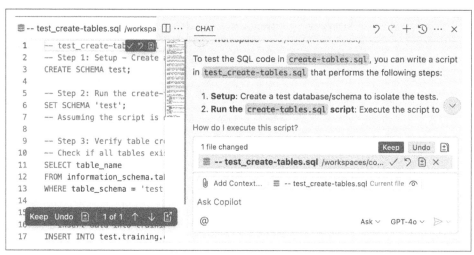

Figure 5-8. Initial SQL test response

Again, this is pretty impressive for a simple query against one file. And note that this will work for any language, not just Python.

Trusting Generated Tests

Since we're still early in the discussion about having Copilot generate tests, it's important to remember to review them just as you would any other generated content. Tests generated by AI may include false positives, duplicate assertions, and incorrect logic based on misinterpreting the code. Fortunately, test code is generally easy to read, which can make it easier to quickly review and verify.

This section has shown you how to utilize Copilot to create instructions and code for testing when you need to start from scratch. More commonly, you may be coding in a language you already know and just want Copilot to help create the *boilerplate* code for tasks like unit testing. In the next section, you'll see several ways to do that.

Creating Unit Tests

Given the necessity of creating tests for cases like continuous integration and test-driven development, manually crafting tests can represent a significant portion of your time and workload on a project. With Copilot, you can automate test generation by using several approaches. And you can choose from varying degrees of complexity.

Many times, the tests you generate with Copilot will be unit tests, designed to perform basic testing for a single function or procedure. However, the range and depth of Copilot-generated tests can vary with the prompt and interface used. We'll explore the various approaches in this section.

Using the /tests Command

The easiest way to have Copilot generate tests for you is using the built-in slash command `/tests` inline (in the IDE's editor). This command operates on the code you select or reference in the IDE and then attempts to create basic unit tests appropriate to the code. You can enter this command through any of the chat interfaces available in the IDE.

Assume you're again working with a simple function to determine whether a number is prime. The implementation doesn't matter, but here's one version:

```python
def is_prime(number):
    if number <= 1:
        return False
    for n in range(2, int(number**0.5) + 1):
        if number % n == 0:
            return False
    return True
```

Figure 5-9 shows an example of using the `/tests` command via the inline chat. The most straightforward usage is highlighting the code to be tested and then entering the command in the chat interface.

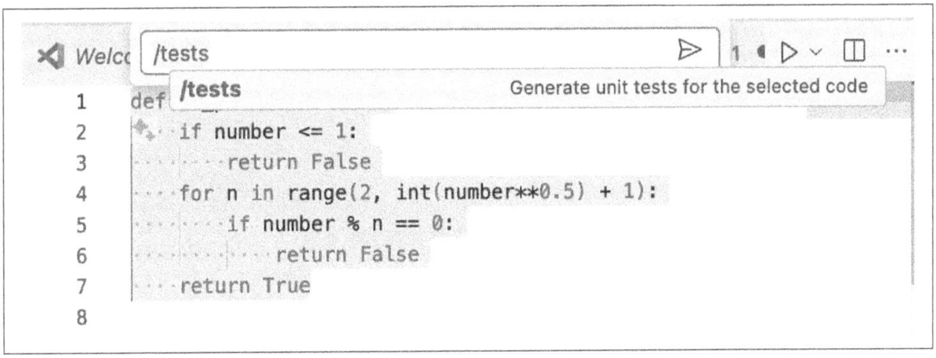

Figure 5-9. Invoking Copilot to generate tests via the /tests command

After running that command, Copilot generates assert-based tests for primes, non-primes, one, zero, large primes, and large nonprimes. As Figure 5-10 shows, when going through the inline chat, Copilot proposes the changes as a new file in the editor with the corresponding name *test_is_prime.py*. If you like the suggested tests, you can click the Accept button.

Figure 5-10. Tests from the inline chat option

The same results as running `/tests` in the inline chat interface can be achieved by choosing Copilot > Generate Tests from the context menu; see Figure 5-11. In fact, Copilot will want to use the `/tests` shortcut in most cases.

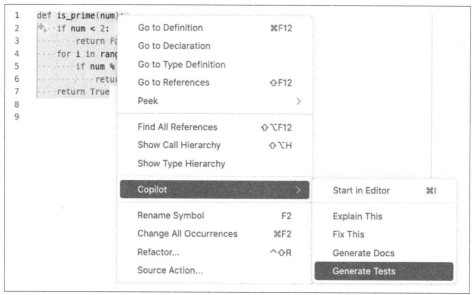

Figure 5-11. Generating tests via the context menu

If you run the `/tests` command in the separate chat interface, you'll likely get similar results, but with more of an explanation in the chat area about the approach Copilot is going to take, the framework it has chosen, and the type of tests it will create.

134 | Chapter 5: Testing with Copilot

A new section just above the text entry area shows any files changed. Keep/Undo buttons are available for all files. Proposed individual files are shown by their first line and have their own controls to keep (the checkmark) and undo (the curved left arrow). The control that looks like a document icon with + and - in it is used to show the diff introduced by the proposed changes in the editor. Figure 5-12 shows a portion of the output.

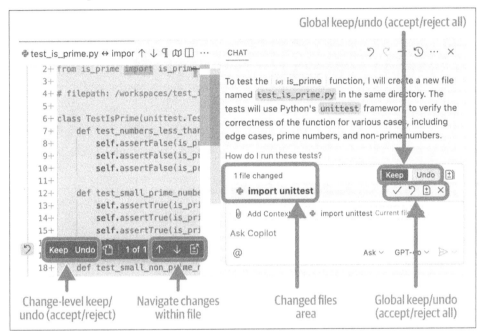

Figure 5-12. Tests from the /tests command in the main chat

Changing Icons and Controls

Copilot commonly changes the controls used in their various interfaces and moves them around, unfortunately. By the time you are reading this, Copilot has likely changed things again.

In general, the following hold true across releases for proposed edits:

- There will be controls to accept/keep and reject/undo changes.
- Checkmarks double as keep controls.
- There will be a control to see the suggested diffs as a file in the editor or apply suggested diffs to a file in the editor.
- The diff controls may or may not set up the file with a reasonable name. You should always make sure to save your files yourself after reviewing and choosing which changes to keep.

These responses cover a basic range of use cases. But what if you want to have additional tests generated and/or more cases covered? You can approach that by supplying more explicit prompts, the topic of the next section.

Creating Tests from Explicit Prompts

Another way to create tests is by providing prompts through the chat interface. A simple prompt like "Create tests for the selected code" will usually result in Copilot running the /tests command again (assuming that command is available in your IDE). However, you can supply a more directed prompt to have Copilot suggest tests for other cases. For example, if you've incorporated the tests already generated, you can select the current test file and the implementation file as context and then prompt Copilot about any other edge cases with a prompt like this:

```
are there any other edge cases that should be tested
```

Copilot responds by identifying some additional tests cases, along with explanations for them:

```
Yes, here are some additional edge cases you might want to test:

1. Smallest prime number: Ensure the function correctly identifies
   2 as a prime number.

2. Even number greater than 2: Test an even number like 10 to
   confirm it is not prime.

3. Very large composite number: Test a large number that is not
   prime, such as 10^6.

4. Floating-point input: Test how the function handles non-integer
   inputs like 3.5.

5. String input: Test how the function handles invalid input types
   like "seven".

6. Negative even number: Test a negative even number like -4 to
   confirm it is not prime.
```

Copilot further provides the code that can be added for those test cases:

```
def test_smallest_prime(self):
    self.assertTrue(is_prime(2)) # 2 is the smallest prime number

def test_even_number_greater_than_two(self):
    self.assertFalse(is_prime(10))  # 10 is not a prime number

def test_very_large_composite_number(self):
    self.assertFalse(is_prime(10**6)) # 10^6 is not a prime number

def test_floating_point_input(self):
```

```
        with self.assertRaises(TypeError): # Assuming the function
    raises TypeError for non-integers
            is_prime(3.5)

    def test_string_input(self):
        with self.assertRaises(TypeError): # Assuming the function
    raises TypeError for non-integers
            is_prime("seven")

    def test_negative_even_number(self):
        self.assertFalse(is_prime(-4)) # Negative even numbers are not
    prime
```

This might make you wonder whether you can extend the prompt to cover more use cases. Indeed, you can! For example, you can be more prescriptive, telling Copilot to add test cases for other inputs:

```
add test cases for other kinds of inputs
```

With this prompt, Copilot adds additional test cases for your consideration and review:

```
    def test_float_input(self):
        with self.assertRaises(TypeError):
            is_prime(7.1)

    def test_string_input(self):
        with self.assertRaises(TypeError):
            is_prime("7")
```

A key part of getting the most value-add from Copilot is asking it additional questions beyond the scope of what it may generate with default prompts or commands. To use our analogy of Copilot as someone new to the team, you may want or need to prod them to think beyond the usual test cases about other scenarios. The same holds true for prompting Copilot to get more comprehensive results.

If you prefer to create some quick tests inline with your code, a variation on the prompt approach can easily do that. We'll look at that option next.

Creating Tests from Comments

Sometimes you may not want (or need) to engage the chat feature to create your tests. You may be actively working in your editor *in the flow* and want to do the equivalent of telling Copilot, "Insert some simple, quick tests here." That can be done by creating a comment as a directive to Copilot. Then you simply need to accept the suggestions for individual tests or testing functions that it returns. The process follows the same interactive flow for acceptance, editing, etc., as discussed in Chapter 2.

The advantage of this method is that you can initiate it from a simple (or complex) comment line within the code. The disadvantage is that you may have to repeatedly step through accepting parts of suggestions or get generic suggestions that aren't as useful.

Here's a simple example of a directive comment placed inline after the code for the `is_prime` function:

```
# Generate 10 simple test cases for the is_prime function
```

In response, Copilot suggests an inline function with a set of simple asserts, as shown in Figure 5-13. All the lines from 10–23 were automatically generated by Copilot in response to the comment on line 9.

```
 is_prime.py >  generate_test_cases
 9   # Generate 10 simple test cases for the is_prime function
10   def generate_test_cases():
11       test_cases = [
12           (7, True),    # 7 is a prime number
13           (4, False),   # 4 is not a prime number
14           (1, False),   # 1 is not a prime number
15           (0, False),   # 0 is not a prime number
16           (-5, False),  # Negative numbers are not prime
17           (7919, True),# 7919 is a prime number
18           (8000, False),# 8000 is not a prime number
19           (2, True),    # 2 is the only even prime number
20           (99991 * 99989, False), # Product of two large primes
21           (7.5, False) # Floats are not prime numbers
22       ]
23       return test_cases
```

Figure 5-13. A simple set of assert test cases generated from the comment

Alternatively, you could use a more generic comment such as this one:

```
# Create tests for the code above
```

In this case, Copilot generates similar test cases to the other methods, but in the same file. Figure 5-14 shows an excerpt of the generated tests. The only line that was typed in was the first comment. All the other lines were generated and accepted based on that one.

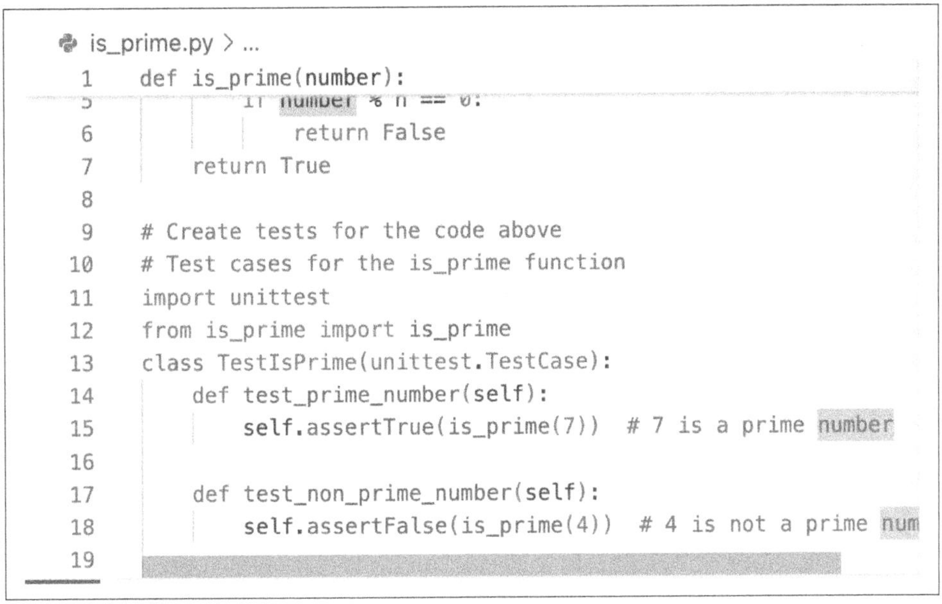

```python
is_prime.py > ...
1    def is_prime(number):
5            if number % n == 0:
6                return False
7        return True
8
9    # Create tests for the code above
10   # Test cases for the is_prime function
11   import unittest
12   from is_prime import is_prime
13   class TestIsPrime(unittest.TestCase):
14       def test_prime_number(self):
15           self.assertTrue(is_prime(7))   # 7 is a prime number
16
17       def test_non_prime_number(self):
18           self.assertFalse(is_prime(4))  # 4 is not a prime num
19
```

Figure 5-14. Another example of tests generated from a comment

Finally, in this section, let's look at a different way of using Copilot to help us test: validating inputs to functions inline.

Validating Inputs

As another angle on testing, Copilot can also assist with generating code to check that inputs going into a function are valid. With our example function, we can tell Copilot to do the following:

> generate asserts to ensure that the inputs to the function are valid

From here, Copilot responds and suggests assertions, as requested, to validate the inputs:

> To ensure that the function inputs are valid, we can add assertions at the start of the function. We want to make sure that the input is an integer and that it is not negative. Here's how you can do it:

```python
def is_prime(num):
    assert isinstance(num, int), "Input must be an integer"
    assert num >= 0, "Input must be a non-negative integer"

    if num < 2:
        return False
    for i in range(2, int(num ** 0.5) + 1):
        if num % i == 0:
```

```
        return False
return True
```

We can also be less specific about using asserts and ask Copilot to generate checks:

```
generate checks to ensure that the inputs to the function are valid
```

This allows Copilot to generate code to validate the inputs, but with a more standard coding mechanism to surface any issues:

```
To ensure that the inputs to the `is_prime` function are valid, you
can add checks at the start of the function.
 Here's how you can do it:

```python
def is_prime(num):
    if not isinstance(num, int):
        raise TypeError("Input must be an integer")
    if num < 0:
        raise ValueError("Input must be a non-negative integer")

    if num < 2:
        return False
    for i in range(2, int(num ** 0.5) + 1):
        if num % i == 0:
            return False
    return True
```

 In this code, the `if` statements will raise a `TypeError` if the
 input is not an integer or a `ValueError` if it's a negative
 number.
 This way, you can ensure that the inputs to the function are valid.
```

Each approach may be useful in different cases depending on how simple you want the results to be versus the need for broader coverage. Remember that since you are interacting with an AI, prompting and setting the context are the keys to getting explicit results (versus generic results or ones rendered quickly inline). Depending on where you are at with your overall progress on a project and experience with the languages and frameworks you are using, you may find that a combination of these approaches works well.

Before we leave this section on creating unit tests, here's a generic prompt template for creating a set of unit tests (adapted from the Copilot documentation (*https://oreil.ly/NOS8j*)):

```
Develop a comprehensive suite of unit tests for the
<method/function> in <language/framework>. Write multiple test
methods that cover a wide range of scenarios, including edge cases,
exception handling, and data validation."
```

The words enclosed by < and > are meant to be replaced with specific terms by you. This template has several key elements:

Scope
    It explicitly asks for a comprehensive suite of unit tests, so the AI generates more than just basic tests and covers a wide variety of potential use cases.

Scenarios
    It specifies that the tests should include:

- Edge cases to test for boundary conditions
- Exception handling for errors that should be raised when invalid actions occur
- Data validation to ensure that inputs are correctly validated and handled by the methods

Now that we've covered the unit-test approaches, let's look at how we can leverage Copilot to help us write integration tests.

Creating Integration Tests

You can use Copilot to create integration tests by telling it to focus on the way multiple components interact rather than creating tests for isolated units of code. To do this, you need to write your prompts with clear instructions that emphasize the collaboration between services, modules, and/or external systems.

The keys to having Copilot create successful integration tests are as follows:

Craft specific prompts
    Ask Copilot to write integration tests for interaction between components rather than just generating tests for code.

Use mocks for external dependencies
    Integration tests frequently need to simulate an external service such as a database or an API. You can instruct Copilot to use mocks so tests can verify the functionality without having to have real implementations.

Request coverage of interactions
    Ask Copilot to verify that methods are called, data flows as expected between components, or that expected side effects occur.

A generic template for a prompt for integration tests could look something like this:

```
Write integration tests for the <method/function> in the <class>.
Use mocks to simulate the <external service> and verify that it
works correctly when <condition>.
```

(Again, the terms in <> are meant to be replaced for your specific use case.) As an example, suppose that we have an Express application with two modules:

`UserService`
    Handles user data

`AuthController`
    Handles login requests and delegates to `UserService`

We want to write integration tests to ensure that the `AuthController` correctly interacts with `UserService` and the HTTP layer. Here is a prompt to do this:

> Write integration tests for the login endpoint in the
> AuthController. Mock the UserService to simulate user lookup and
> password verification, and verify that the controller returns the
> correct HTTP status codes and messages

Here's the response that Copilot generates based on that prompt:

> Here is an example of integration tests for the *login* endpoint in
> the *AuthController*. These tests use Jest and mock the *UserService* to
> simulate user lookup and password verification.
>
> ```
> const request = require('supertest');
> const express = require('express');
> const AuthController = require('../controllers/AuthController');
> const UserService = require('../services/UserService');
>
> jest.mock('../services/UserService'); // Mock the UserService
>
> const app = express();
> app.use(express.json());
> app.use('/auth', AuthController);
>
> describe('AuthController - Login Endpoint', () => {
>   afterEach(() => {
>     jest.clearAllMocks(); // Clear mocks after each test
>   });
>
>   it('should return 200 and success message for valid credentials',
> async () => {
>     // Mock UserService.authenticate to return a valid user
>     UserService.authenticate.mockResolvedValue({
>       id: 1,
>       username: 'user1',
>       password: 'password1',
>     });
>
>     const response = await request(app)
>       .post('/auth/login')
>       .send({ username: 'user1', password: 'password1' });
> ```

```
    expect(response.status).toBe(200);
    expect(response.body).toEqual({
      message: 'Login successful',
      user: { id: 1, username: 'user1', password: 'password1' },
    });
    expect(UserService.authenticate).toHaveBeenCalledWith('user1',
'password1');
  });

  it('should return 401 and error message for invalid credentials',
async () => {
    // Mock UserService.authenticate to return null for invalid
credentials
    UserService.authenticate.mockResolvedValue(null);

    const response = await request(app)
      .post('/auth/login')
      .send({ username: 'user1', password: 'wrongpassword' });

    expect(response.status).toBe(401);
    expect(response.body).toEqual({
      message: 'Invalid credentials',
    });
    expect(UserService.authenticate).toHaveBeenCalledWith('user1',
'wrongpassword');
  });

  it('should return 400 if username or password is missing',
async () => {
    const response = await request(app)
      .post('/auth/login')
      .send({ username: 'user1' }); // Missing password

    expect(response.status).toBe(400);
    expect(response.body).toEqual({
      message: 'Username and password are required',
    });
  });
});
```

Key Points:
1. Mocking *UserService*:
   - `jest.mock('../services/UserService')` is used to mock the `UserService` module.
   - `UserService.authenticate` is mocked to simulate different scenarios (valid user, invalid credentials).

2. Test Cases:
   - **Valid Credentials**: Ensures the endpoint returns a 200 status and the correct success message.
   - **Invalid Credentials**: Ensures the endpoint returns a 401 status and an error message.

```
        - **Missing Fields**: Ensures the endpoint returns a 400 status
if required fields are missing.

    3. **Supertest:**
        - `supertest` is used to make HTTP requests to the Express app
and validate the responses.

    4. **Setup:**
        - The `AuthController` is mounted on the `/auth` route in the
test app.

    Run the tests using:

    npx jest
```

You may need to do additional tweaking on the integration test code to ensure everything works as intended, but this gives you a solid starting point to work from.

Regardless of the kinds of tests you are creating through Copilot, you may want to have them tailored for your project or per testing guidelines you must adhere to. In the next section, we'll look at how to set up custom testing instructions for Copilot.

Defining Custom Testing Instructions

You can customize how Copilot generates tests for your project by providing custom test-generation instructions. This ensures that Copilot produces tests that align with your preferred frameworks, coding standards, and workflows.

Test-generation instructions can be set up at two levels: user level and workspace level.

For a particular workspace, you can add instructions directly to your project's *.vscode/settings.json* file. If these are persisted, they customize Copilot's behavior for everyone working with that project.

To create instructions that apply across all projects you work with, you can instead add instructions to your *global* VS Code settings.

At either of these levels, you can also create a separate Markdown file with more detailed instructions and then point your settings to the file. This is useful for complex or evolving standards that you want to reuse across multiple projects.

When adding custom test instructions in your settings file, they should be placed under the key `github.copilot.chat.testGeneration.instructions`. Here's an example with both specific instructions spelled out and a referenced file:

```
    "github.copilot.chat.testGeneration.instructions": [
      {
        "text": "Prefer Mocha and Chai for testing Node.js modules."
```

```
    },
    {
      "text": "Use Pytest for all Python test cases."
    },
    {
      "file": "test-guidelines.md" // import instructions from file
    }
  ]
```

The content in the file *test-guidelines.md* could be as follows:

```
Ensure all test functions have descriptive names.
Mock external API calls in integration tests.
```

You may have to iterate to get the best form for the instructions, but once they're set up, Copilot should honor them for typical operations like `@workspace /tests`.

> **Custom Test Instructions Are Experimental**
>
> As of this writing, the custom test instructions feature is still labeled as *experimental*.

For the final part of this chapter, let's look at how Copilot can help with using frameworks and creating tests *before* writing implementation code. This is useful for techniques like test-driven development.

Testing Before the Coding and Leveraging Frameworks

Test-driven development (*TDD*) has already been mentioned in this chapter. If you're unfamiliar with the term, it's an approach to software development that emphasizes writing test cases for code before writing the actual code itself. TDD is considered a best practice or requirement in many coding projects and groups.

> **More on TDD**
>
> If you are new to TDD or interested in learning more about the practice, the web has many references. A relatively quick but informative read can be found at the testdriven.io (*https://oreil.ly/VaMiK*) website.

You can use Copilot to create test cases for TDD and then implement the code to be tested. Consider a simple example of creating a test class and tests for code that will help manage student records at a university. We'll use Mockito (*https://site.mockito.org*) in our testing framework.

About Mockito

Mockito specializes in helping Java applications manage dependencies and simulating external interactions from other components without requiring the implementation or presence of the components themselves—i.e., *mocking*. Previously in the chapter, we showed how Copilot can incorporate mocking for generating integration tests.

To start, suppose we begin with an empty project called *students*, and we have Copilot create a *pom.xml* (*https://oreil.ly/Qx29p*) file for a Java project with desired versions of dependencies. Here's a prompt for that:

```
add a pom.xml file with a mockito dependency version 3.3.3, and
compiler source and target version 1.8
```

As shown in Figure 5-15, this prompt triggers Copilot to try to understand our intent and then run the */new* shortcut command to set up a structure if needed. After that, it figures out the code for the *pom.xml* file we asked for and gives a link to see it and a button shortcut to create it.

Figure 5-15. pom.xml creation

To build out our testing code, let's create an appropriate test class and initial set of tests. We'll do this in the separate Chat interface since we can expect a significant amount of output and we may want to put it in a separate file.

In the prompt, we tell Copilot to reference the content of the *pom.xml* file to make sure it knows to pick up the Mockito dependency:

```
Referencing #file:pom.xml, create a StudentTest class for students
   enrolled at a university and add tests
```

> **Ensuring That Files Are Picked Up for Context**
>
> In most cases, we probably would not need to specifically add the `#file:pom.xml` reference. Assuming the file has been saved and added to the workspace, Copilot would default to using the `@workspace` agent and should pick up the Mockito context from there. In addition, the automatic index it creates would also know about it. As a best practice, though, always make sure any files you create in the editor are saved and added to the workspace before expecting them to be automatically pulled in for Copilot's context.
>
> Figure 5-16 shows an example of Copilot using the specific reference to *pom.xml* for a similarly targeted prompt.
>
>
>
> *Figure 5-16. Using an explicit reference*

This then makes our initial query something like the following:

```
Referencing #file:pom.xml, create a StudentTest class for students
   enrolled at a university and add tests
```

Copilot returns this in response:

```
Here is a StudentTest class with some basic unit tests using
Mockito for testing students enrolled at a university:

package com.example;
```

```java
import org.junit.jupiter.api.BeforeEach;
import org.junit.jupiter.api.Test;
import org.mockito.Mockito;

import java.util.ArrayList;
import java.util.List;

import static org.junit.jupiter.api.Assertions.assertEquals;
import static org.mockito.Mockito.*;

class StudentTest {

    private University university;
    private Student student;

    @BeforeEach
    void setUp() {
        university = Mockito.mock(University.class);
        student = new Student("John Doe", "12345");
    }

    @Test
    void testEnrollStudent() {
        // Arrange
        List<Student> enrolledStudents = new ArrayList<>();
        when(university.getEnrolledStudents()).thenReturn(enrolledStudents);

        // Act
        university.enrollStudent(student);
        enrolledStudents.add(student);

        // Assert
        verify(university, times(1)).enrollStudent(student);
        assertEquals(1, university.getEnrolledStudents().size());
        assertEquals(student, university.getEnrolledStudents().get(0));
    }

    @Test
    void testGetStudentDetails() {
        // Arrange
        when(university.getStudentDetails("12345")).thenReturn(student);

        // Act
        Student result = university.getStudentDetails("12345");

        // Assert
        verify(university, times(1)).getStudentDetails("12345");
        assertEquals("John Doe", result.getName());
        assertEquals("12345", result.getId());
```

```
        }
}
```

Explanation:
1. **Dependencies**:
The `mockito-core` dependency in your pom.xml
is used for mocking the `University` class.
2. **Test Setup**:
The `@BeforeEach` method initializes the mock
`University` object and a sample `Student` object.
3. **Test Cases**:
   - `testEnrollStudent`: Verifies that a student is enrolled in the
university and checks the list of enrolled students.
   - `testGetStudentDetails`: Verifies that the correct student
details are returned when queried by ID.

Make sure you have the `Student` and `University` classes
implemented in your project for these tests to work. Let me know if
you need help creating those classes!

This is helpful and a good set of suggested starting tests. We can take this and save it if we want. However, if what we really want is just a simple test case for a Student class, this may be overkill as it adds items like enrollments. To avoid unneeded items, restructure our prompt to be more specific about what we want. Here's one option:

```
Referencing #file:pom.xml, create only a StudentTest class for a
  student enrolled at a university. A student will have personal
  attributes such as a first and last name, a phone number, an
  address, and a contact email.
```

This includes the word *only* to ensure that Copilot creates only the test class right now. Otherwise, it may go ahead and create the implementation class as well. Here's the revised testing code:

```
Here is the `StudentTest` class for testing a student with personal
  attributes:

package com.example;

import org.junit.jupiter.api.BeforeEach;
import org.junit.jupiter.api.Test;

import static org.junit.jupiter.api.Assertions.*;

class StudentTest {

    private Student student;

    @BeforeEach
    void setUp() {
        student = new Student("John", "Doe", "123-456-7890",
```

```
        "123 Main St", "john.doe@example.com");
    }

    @Test
    void testStudentAttributes() {
        // Verify that the student's attributes are correctly set
        assertEquals("John", student.getFirstName());
        assertEquals("Doe", student.getLastName());
        assertEquals("123-456-7890", student.getPhoneNumber());
        assertEquals("123 Main St", student.getAddress());
        assertEquals("john.doe@example.com", student.getEmail());
    }

    @Test
    void testUpdatePhoneNumber() {
        // Update the phone number and verify the change
        student.setPhoneNumber("987-654-3210");
        assertEquals("987-654-3210", student.getPhoneNumber());
    }

    @Test
    void testUpdateAddress() {
        // Update the address and verify the change
        student.setAddress("456 Elm St");
        assertEquals("456 Elm St", student.getAddress());
    }

    @Test
    void testUpdateEmail() {
        // Update the email and verify the change
        student.setEmail("new.email@example.com");
        assertEquals("new.email@example.com", student.getEmail());
    }
}

### Explanation:
1. **Attributes Tested**:
   - First name
   - Last name
   - Phone number
   - Address
   - Email
2. **Test Cases**:
   - `testStudentAttributes`: Ensures the attributes are initialized correctly.
   - `testUpdatePhoneNumber`, `testUpdateAddress`, `testUpdateEmail`: Verify that updates to attributes work as expected.

This test assumes the existence of a `Student` class with appropriate getters and setters. Let me know if you need help creating the `Student` class!
```

This looks more like the starting point we wanted, so we save this in our workspace as *src/test/java/com/example/StudentTest.java*. If we execute the test, it fails since an implementation of the `Student` class doesn't exist yet.

Following the TDD methodology, we should next create the minimum code to make this test pass. Since we have Copilot available, we'll have it take a pass at that and then run the tests. We could do this in individual steps, or we can leverage Copilot's Agent mode as discussed in Chapter 4. Let's let Agent mode help us out.

Leveraging Agent Mode for Testing Workflows

To continue working on our TDD workflow, first, we'll switch into the mode by using the chat interface (Figure 5-17).

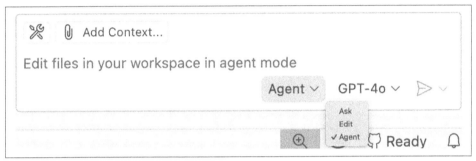

Figure 5-17. Switching to Agent mode

In Agent mode, we'll enter a prompt for the pieces we want Copilot to do:

```
Install any needed dependencies for testing with mvn and then run
  tests
```

While not necessary, if you have this code open in the editor, you can specify to use that as the key reference:

```
Referencing #editor, create a student class.
```

Copilot proceeds to suggest the `brew install maven` command to install Maven and runs it in a terminal after we tell it to proceed. From here, it can proceed to run `mvn test`. Copilot encounters some errors but figures out what is needed to resolve them:

```
mvn test

The Maven test compilation failed due to the following issues:

1. JUnit Dependencies Missing:
The org.junit.jupiter.api package is not found, indicating that the
  JUnit 5 (Jupiter) dependency is missing in the pom.xml.

2. Student Class Not Found: The Student class is not being
```

```
recognized, which could be due to incorrect package structure or
missing compilation.

3. Annotations Not Recognized: Annotations like @BeforeEach and
@Test are not recognized, which is also related to the missing
JUnit dependency.

I will now:

Add the required JUnit 5 dependency to the pom.xml.
Ensure the Student class is correctly compiled and accessible.
Re-run the tests after fixing these issues
```

Notice that the Copilot agent has already planned what it should try next to fix the issue (under the `I will now` section). After we tell Copilot to proceed, it first updates the *pom.xml* file with the missing JUnit dependency and then tries to run the tests again. They fail because the `Student` implementation class isn't implemented yet. The output from Copilot for this run is shown here:

```xml
<dependencies>
    <!-- ...existing dependencies... -->
    <dependency>
        <groupId>org.junit.jupiter</groupId>
        <artifactId>junit-jupiter</artifactId>
        <version>5.10.0</version>
        <scope>test</scope>
    </dependency>
</dependencies>
```

```
Made changes.

The Maven test run failed because the `Student` class could not be
 found during the test execution. This indicates that the `Student`
 class might not be compiled or is not in the correct package
 structure.

I will verify the `Student` class's location and ensure it is
properly compiled and accessible. Then, I will re-run the tests.
```

Once again, the agent has figured out what it needs to try next. After we review and tell Copilot to proceed, it generates a new *Student.java* file with the correct content and in the correct location, and then proceeds to run the tests again. This time, they succeed because the agent has completed all needed changes. Figure 5-18 shows the success via the following:

- The new *Student.java* file in the upper left with its new content waiting to be approved
- The successful build/test run in the lower left
- The agent's assessment that the tests all passed, the `Student` class is implemented, and the project is working as expected, in the upper right
- The "files changed" area in the lower right showing that updates were made by the agent to the *pom.xml* file and the *Student.java* file to get everything working

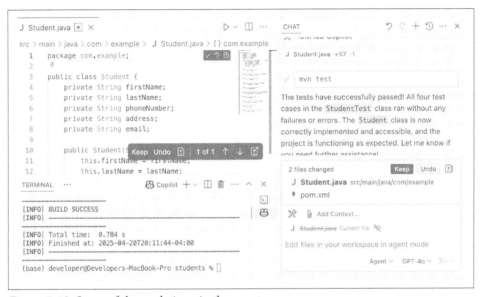

Figure 5-18. Successful completion via the agent

Certainly, we could have done this without the agent via several passes and individual actions. But, where we can leverage Copilot's agentic abilities, we can save ourselves some time and effort.

From here, we can review the changes, save the updated files into the workspace, and add other functionality if we need it. Similar multistep processes for testing workflows can be done with this step-by-step approach, whether using the agent or not.

As always, the more context and direction you can give Copilot through the prompt, workspace files, editor, etc., the more likely it will produce good content and suggestions for you to incorporate. If, however, you don't get what you expect, don't be afraid to iterate on your prompt/query until you get the results you want.

Conclusion

In this chapter, we've focused on how to apply Copilot's completion suggestions and chat capabilities in the context of creating tests for code. As shown in the different sections, you can use various approaches to have Copilot generate tests relevant to code in your workspace. Inline completion and suggestions from Copilot can be utilized, as well as the chat capabilities.

Most options for generating tests rely on passing the request to the chat interface in some form—either by using shortcut (slash) commands or entering a prompt through the inline or separate chat interfaces. For any substantial or complex, lengthy tests, working through the chat functionality will likely provide the best results. For quick, boilerplate unit tests or simple unit-testing functions, using specific inline comments as prompts can work well.

Most basic commands for creating tests through Copilot produce unit tests. Copilot can be used to create integration tests by ensuring that the prompt includes sections targeted toward interaction of components, mocking, and verifying the expected outcomes.

Copilot can be used to support best practices such as TDD. With this strategy, Copilot can be used to generate initial testing code and then later generate the appropriate implementation to pass the test. As with all approaches mentioned in the chapter, it's important to review the results to make sure they are usable and what you intended. You should always feel free to disregard suggestions or code from Copilot and/or reframe prompts and queries to get more accurate results. Also, you can define more explicit context to have Copilot consider for generating the results.

As with implementation code, testing code should ideally be verbosely commented. This makes the code more readable and easily understandable. However, explaining and documenting our test cases or our implementations is something we may put off until later because it takes cycles away from other work, and the algorithms may be changed. In Chapter 6, we'll explore how Copilot can help make these tasks almost effortless.

CHAPTER 6
Using Copilot to Document and Explain Code

As developers, we all know that having good documentation with our code is essential. The documentation within the codebase makes it more understandable, reviewable, and maintainable in the long run. Documentation in the code is a crucial contributor to the overall quality of the code and the quality of the product built from the code.

However, we also know that taking the time and effort to create good documentation can seem tedious and can feel like a much lower priority than the fun of making the code itself. So, continuing with the theme of how Copilot can help you beyond coding suggestions and answering questions, let's look at how it can help automate this task.

In this chapter, we'll look at several aspects of using Copilot's documentation capabilities, including generating documentation via the editor and chat interfaces. But we'll also show you how to leverage Copilot to produce content for use cases you may not have considered, such as external documentation for APIs, functional documentation, and more.

We'll also look at how to use Copilot to explain code. While this is an often overlooked feature of Copilot, it has tremendous potential for helping engineers at all levels understand code and algorithms. Some beneficial use cases include explaining code from an unfamiliar language or framework, checking the logic of your code with explanations, and leveraging Copilot to explain commands happening in the terminal.

Let's dive in and get started by looking at how Copilot's documentation capabilities can be leveraged throughout your development cycle.

Documenting Content

Many developers know they can use Copilot's documentation capabilities to produce header documentation and comments in the body of their code. But the exact mechanisms to do this can be confusing. You can use shortcut functions, but these are limited in what they do. In the first part of this section, we'll focus on how to most easily generate program documentation inline and through Copilot's chat interface.

Beyond the basic *document my code* functionality, Copilot can be used for several broader documentation tasks. It can generate framework-specific documentation (such as for Swagger), developer-facing documentation for APIs, and even functional documentation. In the latter part of this section, we'll cover those extended use cases where you can leverage more of the power of Copilot for different kinds of documentation. But let's start with the basics.

Generating Documentation Inline

Here's a code listing for a function (written in Go) that creates a new Kubernetes service for a custom resource:

```go
func newServiceForPod(cr *roarappv1alpha1.RoarApp) *corev1.Service {

    strPort := strconv.Itoa(nextPort)
    labels := map[string]string{
        "app": cr.Name,
    }

    return &corev1.Service{
        ObjectMeta: metav1.ObjectMeta{
            Name:      cr.Name + "-service-" + strPort,
            Namespace: cr.Namespace,
        },
        Spec: corev1.ServiceSpec{
            Selector: labels,
            Ports: []corev1.ServicePort{{
                Protocol:   corev1.ProtocolTCP,
                Port:       8089,
                TargetPort: intstr.FromInt(8080),
                NodePort:   int32(nextPort),
            }},
            Type: corev1.ServiceTypeNodePort,
        },
    }
}
```

The most direct/shortest path to getting documentation generated for this function inline is to invoke the inline chat interface via the *Meta*-I key combination and use the shortcut command /doc, as shown in Figure 6-1.

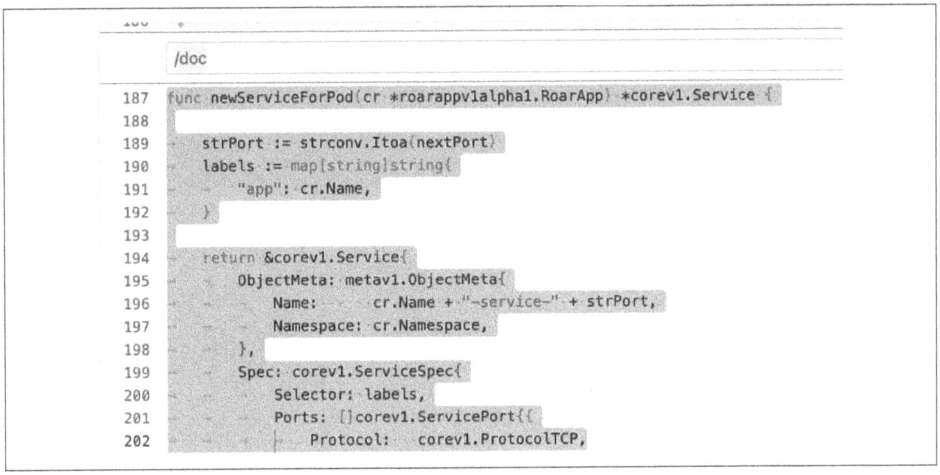

```
                    /doc
187  func newServiceForPod(cr *roarappv1alpha1.RoarApp) *corev1.Service {
188
189      strPort := strconv.Itoa(nextPort)
190      labels := map[string]string{
191          "app": cr.Name,
192      }
193
194      return &corev1.Service{
195          ObjectMeta: metav1.ObjectMeta{
196              Name:      cr.Name + "-service-" + strPort,
197              Namespace: cr.Namespace,
198          },
199          Spec: corev1.ServiceSpec{
200              Selector: labels,
201              Ports: []corev1.ServicePort{{
202                  Protocol:   corev1.ProtocolTCP,
```

Figure 6-1. Using the shortcut /doc command

Copilot will then generate basic documentation for the function. This will likely consist of only comments above the function, as shown in the following listing and in Figure 6-2:

```
// newServiceForPod creates a new Kubernetes Service resource for a
given RoarApp custom resource.
// The Service is configured as a NodePort service, exposing a
specific port for external access.
//
// Parameters:
//   - cr: A pointer to a RoarApp custom resource instance.
//
// Returns:
//   - A pointer to a corev1.Service object configured with the
specified labels, ports, and namespace.
```

Documenting Content | 157

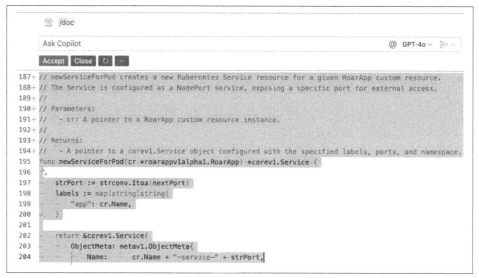

Figure 6-2. Generated doc results

This is useful as far as it goes—adding comments about the purpose, parameters, and return values of the function. What is missing is any additional comments or documentation in the *body* of the function. Even if we were to provide a more extensive command such as `add doc to my code`, Copilot will default to using the /doc command again, and we'll get similar results. This is true currently regardless of which chat interface we use.

Documentation from Comments

You can also generate documentation from comments by using Copilot, as shown in Figure 6-3.

```
// create documentation for the function below
// newServiceForPod returns a instance service with the same name/namespace as the cr
func newServiceForPod(cr *roarappv1alpha1.RoarApp) *corev1.Service {

    strPort := strconv.Itoa(nextPort)
    labels := map[string]string{
```

Figure 6-3. Creating documentation from comments

You need to use wording like **create documentation** to trigger Copilot. However, as shown, the results are more simplistic. And this is probably less useful since you're having to create a comment yourself to get Copilot to create comments.

Recall that, when working directly in the editor, Copilot targets minimal, quick responses that don't disrupt the flow of work and can be reviewed and accepted or discarded easily.

Typically, if we want or need more substantial responses from Copilot, we can use the separate, dedicated chat interface. That also holds for generating documentation, as you'll see in the next section.

Generating Documentation Through Chat

If we switch to the separate chat interface and give Copilot the same direction to add documentation to our code, we get a more extensive and detailed response (Figure 6-4).

```
Here is the updated code with added documentation for the  newServiceForPod  function to improve clarity:

// newServiceForPod creates a new Kubernetes Service resource for a given RoarApp custom resource.
// The Service is configured as a NodePort service, exposing a specific port for external access.
//
// Parameters:
//   - cr: A pointer to a RoarApp custom resource instance.
//
// Returns:
//   - A pointer to a corev1.Service object configured with the specified labels, ports, and namespace.
func newServiceForPod(cr *roarappv1alpha1.RoarApp) *corev1.Service {

    // Convert the next available port to a string for use in the service name.
    strPort := strconv.Itoa(nextPort)

    // Define labels to associate the service with the corresponding RoarApp instance.
    labels := map[string]string{
        "app": cr.Name,
    }

    // Create and return a new Service object.
    return &corev1.Service{
        ObjectMeta: metav1.ObjectMeta{
            // The service name includes the RoarApp name and the port to ensure uniqueness.
```

Figure 6-4. Telling Copilot to add documentation to the code from the main chat

The complete listing, as generated with comments, is available in the book's GitHub repository (*https://oreil.ly/zHnkm*). A few excerpts are shared in the next listing. You can see that Copilot not only inserted substantially more header comments but also added multiple comments throughout the body of the function:

```
// newServiceForPod creates a new Kubernetes Service resource for a
  given RoarApp custom resource.
// The Service is configured as a NodePort service, exposing a
  specific port for external access.
//
// Parameters:
//   - cr: A pointer to a RoarApp custom resource instance.
//
// Returns:
```

```
//   - A pointer to a corev1.Service object configured with the
specified labels, ports, and namespace.
func newServiceForPod(cr *roarappv1alpha1.RoarApp) *corev1.Service {

    // Convert the next available port to a string for use in the
service name.
    strPort := strconv.Itoa(nextPort)

    // Define labels to associate the service with the corresponding
RoarApp instance.
    labels := map[string]string{
        "app": cr.Name,
    }

    // Create and return a new Service object.
    ...
```

Let's take this a step further. Since Copilot Chat can understand natural language, we can submit a prompt to have documentation generated to help anyone reading the code. We can tell Copilot in chat to "verbosely comment the selected function so anyone can understand what it is doing." The resulting change from the original (uncommented) function can be seen in the GitHub repository (*https://oreil.ly/jTDZV*). Other than some wording changes, the main differences are some extra lines of comments for each main section that talks about how the pieces are used or managed. Also some comments are added at the end of lines where an identifier may need to be better understood. Figure 6-5 shows an excerpt from these changes.

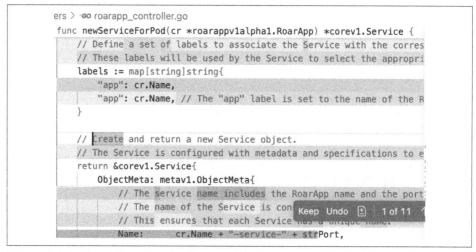

Figure 6-5. Updated lines from issuing a verbose comment command

This is an improvement. If we want even more, we can specifically target each line in the function body. Here's a prompt we can use for that: "verbosely comment the function body so that anyone can easily understand what each line is doing."

With this prompt, we get a further verbose set of comments for the function body with more detailed comments for several of the elements. The full listing is available online (*https://oreil.ly/rZBRV*), but Figure 6-6 shows an excerpt of the differences.

```
llers > 🐹 roarapp_controller.go
   func newServiceForPod(cr *roarappv1alpha1.RoarApp) *corev1.Service {
       return &corev1.Service{
           Spec: corev1.ServiceSpec{
              // Define the ports that the Service will expose.
              Ports: []corev1.ServicePort{{
                  Protocol:    corev1.ProtocolTCP,       // The protocol used by the Serv
                  Port:        8089,                      // The port exposed by the Service for ext
                  TargetPort:  intstr.FromInt(8080),     // The port on the target Pods that the Se
                  NodePort:    int32(nextPort),          // The NodePort assigned to this Service f
                  // The protocol used by the Service is TCP, which is the default protocol fo
                  Protocol: corev1.ProtocolTCP,

                  // The port exposed by the Service for external access.
                  // This is the port that clients outside the cluster will use to access the
                  Port: 8089,

                  // The port on the target Pods that the Service will forward traffic to.
                  // This is the port where the application inside the Pods is listening for
                  TargetPort: intstr.FromInt(8080),
```

Figure 6-6. More verbose comments

Comment Versus Documentation

You may have noticed that we are telling Copilot to *comment* our code versus *document* it. Since documentation in code is done via comments, either of these terms can be used in this situation for prompts. Strictly speaking, when we ask Copilot for documentation, it may default to creating a block of comments only at the start of the method/function, as we saw earlier.

Ultimately, you could combine the previous prompts into a single one to accomplish all the modifications. Here's an example that seems to work well:

```
verbosely document the function header and body so that anyone can easily
understand what the overall function and each line is doing
```

One other nice aspect about Copilot's documentation capabilities is that it can recognize when code has a documentation framework that can be used with it.

Generating Framework-Compatible Documentation

Different programming languages have their own documentation styles. For example, C# has XMLDoc, Python has pydoc, and JavaScript has JSDoc. If Copilot recognizes that the code is in a language that has a standard documentation tool associated with it, it will default to creating comments ready for that tool. This can be very useful for integration with the development environment and other tools and is often preferred to plain comments.

For example, consider a Java class definition containing a single method that begins as shown here:

```
package com.demo.util;

import org.codehaus.jettison.json.JSONArray;
import org.codehaus.jettison.json.JSONObject;
import java.sql.ResultSet;
import org.owasp.esapi.ESAPI;

public class ToJSON {

    public JSONArray toJSONArray(ResultSet rs) throws Exception {

        JSONArray json = new JSONArray(); //JSON array that will be returned
        String temp = null;

        try {

            //we will need the column names, this will save the table meta-data like column names.
            java.sql.ResultSetMetaData rsmd = rs.getMetaData();
```

If we tell Copilot to "document this class," it will add an extensive set of comments. The full listing is available online (*https://oreil.ly/LCxOH*), but a few excerpts are included next:

```
package com.demo.util;

// Importing necessary libraries for JSON processing and SQL result
  handling
...
import java.sql.ResultSet;
// Importing ESAPI for security purposes, though it's not used in
  the provided snippet
import org.owasp.esapi.ESAPI;

/**
 * The ToJSON class provides a method to convert a ResultSet from a
```

```
database query
 * into a JSONArray. This is useful for creating JSON APIs that 
interact with relational databases.
 ...
 */
public class ToJSON {

    /**
     * Converts a given ResultSet into a JSONArray.
     * Each row in the ResultSet will be converted into a JSONObject,
     * and each column in the row will be added to the JSONObject
...
     *
     * @param rs The ResultSet to be converted. This ResultSet is 
typically obtained from executing
     *           a SQL query against a database.
     * @return JSONArray containing the data from the ResultSet. 
Each element in the JSONArray
     *           corresponds to a row in the ResultSet, represented as 
a JSONObject.
     * @throws Exception If there is an error during the conversion 
process. This could be due to
...
     */
    public JSONArray toJSONArray(ResultSet rs) throws Exception {
        JSONArray json = new JSONArray(); // Initializes the JSON 
array that will be populated and returned
        String temp = null; // Temporary string to hold data, not 
used in the provided snippet
...
```

The header comments above the class definition, and at its start, are generated in a form that is compatible with processing by the Javadoc tooling. The /** and @param, @return, and @throw parts are all formatting pieces that Javadoc would use to generate HTML documentation for the class. Figure 6-7 shows an example of the generated Javadoc originating from the comments added by Copilot.

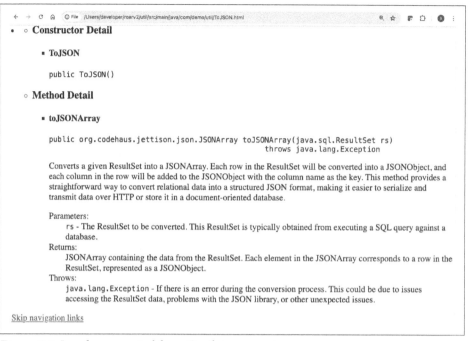

Figure 6-7. Javadoc generated from Copilot comments

Beyond generating documentation for the basic documentation frameworks, we can also use Copilot for another common need: documenting APIs.

Generating Documentation for APIs

If your project is set up for an API documentation framework like Swagger (*https:// swagger.io*), you can have Copilot generate the corresponding Swagger documentation for your APIs. Let's look at an example.

Suppose we have a simple application that manages a directory of employees for a company. The application is written in Java and already configured for Swagger. We can tell Copilot to generate print-ready Swagger documentation for the APIs, referencing a particular file, with the prompt "create print-ready Swagger documentation for the APIS in #file:EmployeeController.java."

print-ready

We used the term *print-ready* in the prompt to ensure that Copilot generates the actual documentation format instead of trying to regenerate the code comments. We could also use terms like *publish-ready* or *publishable*.

164 | Chapter 6: Using Copilot to Document and Explain Code

Copilot's response is shown in Figure 6-8, and the full output is available in the book's GitHub repository (*https://oreil.ly/Kj8Lj*).

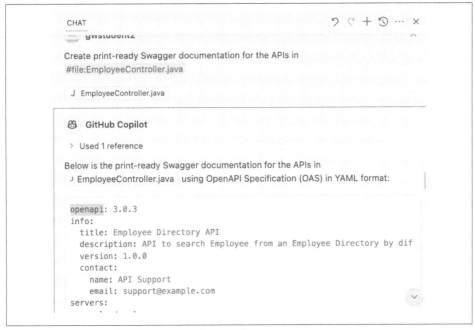

Figure 6-8. Swagger documentation from code

A key for this to work (in addition to the `print-ready` descriptor) is being specific with the files that you point Copilot to via the `#file` selector (or multiple selectors if you need to reference more than one file). Simply pointing Copilot to the entire workspace with a similar prompt (such as "@workspace create Swagger documentation for the APIs") will usually result in Copilot explaining *how to create* the Swagger documentation in your project versus dumping it out.

Creating Functional Documentation

Copilot is also capable of creating functional documentation that is targeted toward external users. For an example, we can leverage the same API code that we used in the preceding section. In this case, our prompt might look something like this: "create functional documentation explaining the various public APIs in #file:Employee Controller.java."

Figure 6-9 shows the start of the actual functional API doc generated from the prompt. Note that the output includes some prose style, in an easy-to-read format, but with the necessary details outlined for the API structure. It's not shown here, but Copilot also outlined a set of steps first that it would follow for this, including *Identifying Public APIs*, *Method Signatures*, and *Endpoint Mapping*. The full output can be viewed in the book's GitHub repo (*https://oreil.ly/lV7jV*).

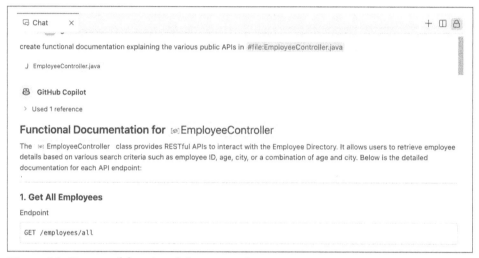

Figure 6-9. Generated functional documentation

In general, the same caveat applies for generating this kind of documentation as it did for generating API documentation in the previous section: indicate specific files for the prompt to act on as opposed to trying to ask Copilot to operate against the entire workspace. However, we can ask some general questions by using `@workspace` and get good summary documentation. For example, if we ask "@workspace what are the API's parameters and what does it return?", we get a useful summary. The full listing is available online (*https://oreil.ly/sXKOv*), and an excerpt is also shown in Figure 6-10.

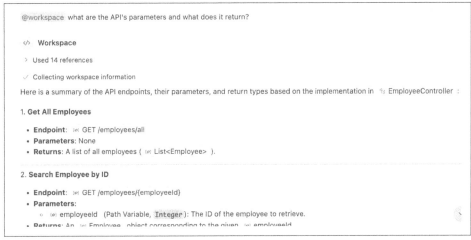

Figure 6-10. Querying API parameters

Extracting Summary Documentation from the Code

Copilot can also be used to extract a high-level summary of the key documentation from certain types of projects. This can be extremely useful for quickly understanding the significant details of the codebase for a project. Referencing the Java Swagger project in the preceding section, we can gather key information from it with the prompt "@workspace extract the key documentation from the code."

In our case, Copilot extracted data from the *pom.xml* file, the *README.md* file, and the relevant *.java* files. Copilot then provided key high-level details on the project's structure, dependencies, Swagger configuration, and testing. Figure 6-11 shows an excerpt, and the full listing can be seen on GitHub (*https://oreil.ly/wSmbs*).

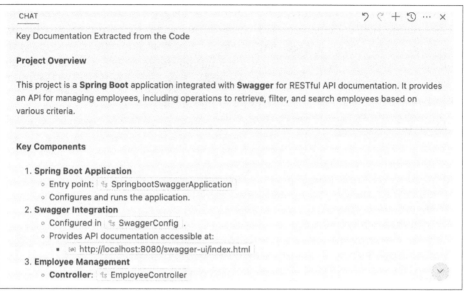

Figure 6-11. Key documentation extracted from code

> ## Copying and Exporting Chat Conversations
>
> If you want to grab the content from a chat conversation, you have a couple of options. The simplest is just to right-click in the conversation and select either Copy or Copy All. Copy grabs the current conversation. Copy All grabs all the conversations in the current chat.
>
> You also can click the Views and More Actions control (which looks like three dots) in the top left of the current chat and open the chat in a new editor session in the current IDE, or pop out the current chat to its own standalone window.
>
> It's important to remember that when you are copying from a chat, what you are getting is the text in Markdown format. To see the text presented in the same way as it displays in the chat panel, you need to save the copied text as a Markdown file (*.md* extension) and view it in a tool that can display Markdown files.
>
> Alternatively, if you are using VS Code or a codespace, you can export the conversation in JSON format through the Command Palette. To do this, open the Command Palette and search for `Chat: Export Chat`. Ensure that you have the cursor active in a conversation in the chat panel first.

That completes our survey of the various ways that Copilot can help you with producing documentation. Let's move to a similar, but arguably more important, functionality that Copilot provides: explaining content.

Explaining Content

In addition to providing documentation for what code does, Copilot is also able to provide explanations for content it works with and generates. This feature can be helpful in multiple use cases:

- Understanding code in a language new to you
- Understanding generated code and conventions
- Summarizing code logic
- Explaining what might go wrong in the code
- Explaining what was done in the terminal
- Explaining how to do something in the terminal

We'll briefly dive into each one of these areas in this section. A couple of common points apply across all of these:

- The prompt is the key here. Getting the prompt correct for the situation and using it to state clearly what you want is the most important prerequisite to having Copilot explain something well.
- While we will generally use *explain* as a key term in our prompt, it's not always required. You can also ask *why*, *how*, or other types of questions as appropriate.

Understanding Code in a Language New to You

Suppose you are a Python programmer, but you've just been given an assignment to implement a new project in Go. Copilot can assist you with creating the code as well as understanding the key points of working with Go. For example, you can give Copilot a prompt like "I'm a Python programmer. What are the most significant things I need to understand about how to write Go code?"

When asked this question while I was writing this chapter, Copilot responded with information about the following 12 areas:

- Static typing
- Compilation
- Syntax differences
- Packages and imports
- Functions
- Error handling
- Concurrency
- Structs and methods
- Pointers
- Standard library
- Tooling
- Interfaces

In some cases, Copilot also showed brief code snippets to illustrate the points and finished the explanation with "Understanding these key differences will help you transition from Python to Go more smoothly." You can see the entire output from the chat on GitHub (*https://oreil.ly/roJZB*).

You can also select specific parts of your code and have Copilot explain how they work with the /explain shortcut command. You can even tell Copilot to translate existing code into the new language. As always, though, you should verify that any suggestion or response that Copilot provides is accurate and appropriate for your situation.

> ### Copilot as Teacher
>
> One of the other, less common ways to utilize Copilot to help learn a new language is to utilize it as a *teacher* and ask it to give you a problem to solve in the new language. Here's an example:
>
> Prompt: Explain how to code a function in Go by giving me a problem to complete.
>
> Copilot helpfully produces a response with the following:
>
> - Problem statement
> - Steps to solve the problem
> - Actual Go code to successfully complete the problem
>
> The full output can be seen on GitHub (*https://oreil.ly/4RVS5*).

Copilot is helpful not only in understanding the basics of a new language but also in highlighting conventions that the language uses and the purpose of automatically generated code in that language.

Understanding Generated Code and Conventions

Suppose you are new to Kubernetes and Go and need to create a Kubernetes operator to manage custom resources. You would probably use the Operator SDK (*https://oreil.ly/Lfz8O*) to generate the starting structure for your project in Go.

The SDK automatically generates utility files, including ones with cryptic names like *zz_generated.deepcopy.go*. One of the first things you might want to know is what this generated file is used for. To get the answer, you can simply ask Copilot, "What is the code in #file:api/v1alpha1/zz_generated.deepcopy used for?" Copilot's response (excerpted in Figure 6-12) provides an introduction and then a breakdown of its purpose. The entire response can be found on GitHub (*https://oreil.ly/I0-3j*).

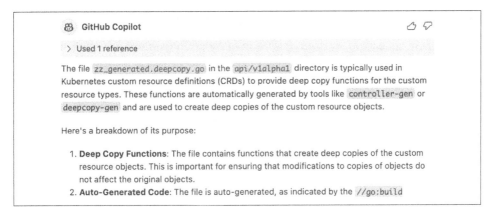

Figure 6-12. Copilot explaining what code is used for

In these kinds of responses, Copilot will usually provide a summary at the end of the output that can be helpful to quickly get the gist of the response. In this case, Copilot notes, "In summary, zz_generated.deepcopy.go is an auto-generated file that provides necessary deep copy functions for custom resource types in Kubernetes, ensuring proper handling and manipulation of these resources."

You might also wonder why the code is named the way it is. We can ask Copilot about the naming convention with a prompt like "Why is this file named starting with zz_?" Copilot provides a helpful, conversational answer with a list of reasons for the convention, as shown in Figure 6-13.

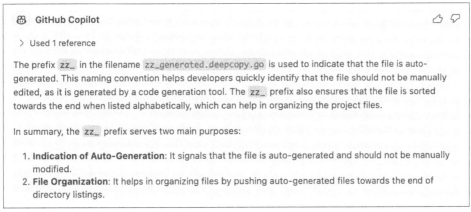

Figure 6-13. Copilot explanation for the zz_ naming convention

In addition to understanding the general conventions and main themes of a language, Copilot can help explain the overall logic of a set of code.

Explaining the Logic Used in a Section of Code

Summarizing code logic more generally can be helpful in various use cases, including these:

- Quickly getting a handle on code you've inherited or must maintain
- Learning about code written in a language or framework that's new to you
- Checking your understanding from reviewing the code
- Having another explanation of how the code works for code reviews, pull requests, etc.

The goal is to have Copilot outline the general logic and related pieces, such as the main components used, in a non-language-specific way. We want Copilot's explanation to be in a conversational tone, as if we were interacting with another developer.

The actual prompt you use for this can vary, but here's an example for the same controller file that we've been referencing: "@workspace: summarize the logic in #file:controllers/roarapp_controller.go."

From this prompt, Copilot provides output that starts with an overall explanation of what the code is intended to do: "reconciling the state of ... custom resources in a Kubernetes cluster."

Copilot then provides a summary of the key components in the file and what each does. These include the data structures, annotations, and functions. An excerpt from this output is shown in Figure 6-14, and the complete output can be seen on GitHub (*https://oreil.ly/5oG3v*).

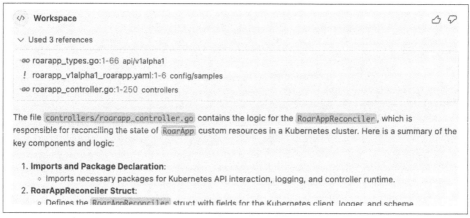

Figure 6-14. Copilot summarizing the logic used in a file

Another good prompt to consider is simply swapping the keyword *workflow* for *logic*, as in "@workspace: summarize the workflow in #file:controllers/roarapp_controller.go." This should yield a slightly simpler response but with similar information on the various components.

One other interesting way to learn about, and understand, the code flips the traditional *explain* use case. Instead of asking Copilot to explain how or what code does, we can ask it about potential problems with the code.

Explaining What Might Go Wrong with a Set of Code

Another approach when having Copilot explain code is to have it identify any potential problems with the code. This can be used for code you've written, are investigating, or have inherited, for example.

Going back to the Kubernetes custom resource example that we've been using in this chapter, we can choose to ask Copilot what could go wrong with the code that implements the custom controller in the editor. The prompt we use for this is "@workspace: explain what might go wrong with the code in #file:controllers/roarapp_controller.go."

Using @workspace and #file

Remember, we can use variables like `#selection` or `#file` in the prompt string to focus Copilot on the context we want it to consider for its response. But in some cases, we may also need to use the `@workspace` identifier to ensure that Copilot looks at related pieces and takes into account the full picture of what else might affect this code.

Copilot, in turn, provides a detailed answer listing out several areas to look at that include the following:

- Error handling
- Resource conflicts
- Requeue logic
- Resource cleanup
- Concurrency issues
- Logging
- Validation
- RBAC permissions

The full output for this can be seen in the GitHub repo file (*https://oreil.ly/v7I75*).

Now that we've looked at different ways Copilot can explain what's happening in code, let's finish up by looking at how Copilot can help explain things in the context of another domain—the terminal.

Explaining Items from the Terminal

Copilot is able to access the terminal to explain details about the last command via the #terminalLastCommand keyword. For example, assume we ran the ps command as shown here as our most recent command:

```
@techupskills ➜ /workspaces/op-new (main) $ ps -aux
USER         PID %CPU %MEM    VSZ   RSS TTY      STAT START   TIME COMMAND
codespa+       1  0.0  0.0   1136   640 ?        Ss   14:30   0:00 /sbin/docker-init
codespa+       8  0.0  0.0   7236  1920 ?        S    14:30   0:00 sleep infinity
root          23  0.0  0.0  12196  3484 ?        Ss   14:30   0:00 sshd: /usr/sbin/s
codespa+     338  0.0  0.0   2616  1536 ?        Ss   14:30   0:00 /bin/sh
```

If we wanted more details on what this command was doing, we could query Copilot with a prompt like "explain #terminalLastCommand." As you can see in Figure 6-15, Copilot identifies the last command and provides an explanation of the command, its options, and its output.

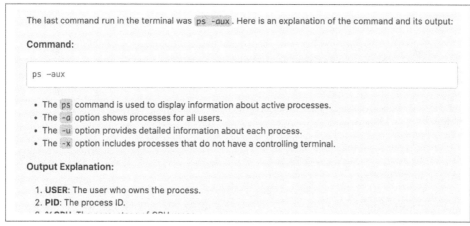

Figure 6-15. Copilot explaining the last terminal command

The full output can be seen in GitHub (*https://oreil.ly/yCMOO*).

Copilot can also explain selected content from the terminal. For example, if we ran a `git status` command previously, we can highlight that and ask Copilot to explain it with the prompt "explain the commands in #terminalSelection." Copilot will then provide info on that, as shown in Figure 6-16.

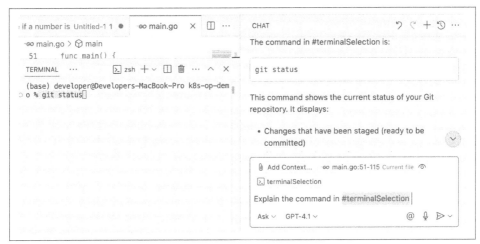

Figure 6-16. Explaining a command selected in the terminal

You don't have to select a command to explain. You can also select any text displayed in the terminal, such as the output of a command. Suppose we select the text "Your branch is up to date with 'origin/main.'" in the output of the `git status` command. Since the identifier already references any content selected in the terminal, we can shorten our prompt to "explain #terminalSelection."

Copilot will then explain the meaning of that selected phrase. Figure 6-17 shows an excerpt from the output for this prompt.

Figure 6-17. Explaining the `git status` *command as selected in terminal*

You can also have Copilot explain *how* to do something via the terminal. That's the subject of our last section in this chapter.

Explaining How to Do Something in the Terminal

Copilot can supply the process and commands to do operations in the terminal. As an example, we can ask Copilot how to create a new branch in our GitHub repository. We can utilize the `@terminal` context and prompt Copilot with: "@terminal How do I create a new branch for my GitHub repository?"

In response, Copilot provides the usual conversational process description along with the actual commands that you can run in the terminal. Figure 6-18 shows an excerpt from the output, which you can see in full on GitHub (*https://oreil.ly/0t1il*).

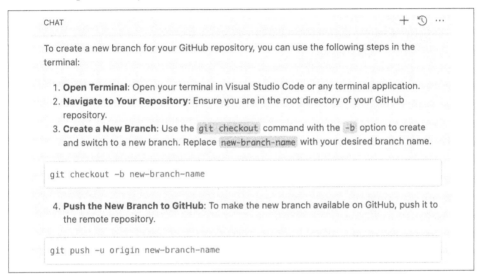

Figure 6-18. Explaining how to create a new branch via the terminal

> **Similar Results**
>
> You can also achieve a similar result with a prompt that references *command line*, as in "How can I create a new branch in my GitHub repository using the command line?"

The same technique is applicable when you may not know the command to use. For example, if we give Copilot the query "@terminal how do I see the list of running processes?", it responds with multiple approaches that can be used from the terminal, as shown in Figure 6-19.

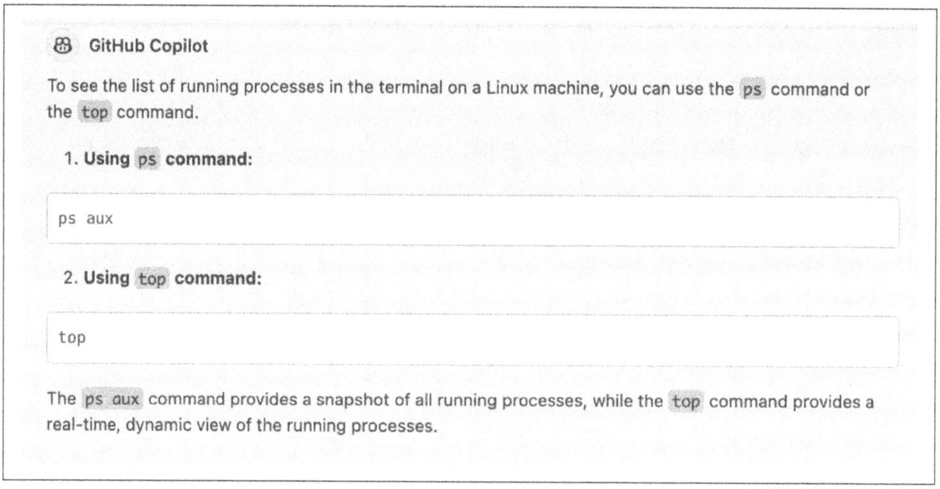

> **GitHub Copilot**
>
> To see the list of running processes in the terminal on a Linux machine, you can use the `ps` command or the `top` command.
>
> 1. **Using `ps` command:**
>
> ```
> ps aux
> ```
>
> 2. **Using `top` command:**
>
> ```
> top
> ```
>
> The `ps aux` command provides a snapshot of all running processes, while the `top` command provides a real-time, dynamic view of the running processes.

Figure 6-19. How to see running processes via the terminal

Conclusion

In this chapter, we've explored how Copilot can help you with documentation and explanations. At the basic level, Copilot can document your source code by inserting comments throughout. A shortcut /doc command typically provides header documentation. You can tell Copilot to produce more extensive comments via prompts that include specific directions, such as "verbosely comment." This illustrates a useful working tip for Copilot: if you aren't getting what you expect or need, try using a more verbose, detailed prompt. You can reject the suggested changes if they are not what you wanted and continue to iterate on your prompt.

Beyond just the basic commenting, Copilot can also generate more extensive documentation for particular use cases. For example, it can generate API documentation and functional documentation suitable (after review) for sharing with others. This can provide a significant time savings over having to create this type of documentation in a less automated way.

Similar to its documentation capability, Copilot also can explain many aspects of a codebase. This functionality can be used to explain general concepts and principles needed to use a new language or framework and also provide explanations for conventions that you may not be familiar with.

But, most significantly, Copilot can explain and summarize how the logic and processing for a set of code works. This can be especially useful if you are trying to learn, or have to maintain, code that you are not familiar with.

A less common use for the explain functionality can be to explain what might go wrong with a set of code. This is an easy way to have Copilot essentially *review* the code and look for potential gaps and problems. This can be very useful if you are trying to assess weaknesses in the code and make sure vulnerable sections are addressed.

Lastly, we looked at the ability to use Copilot's explain functionality with a terminal. This falls into two categories. The first is selecting some output or referencing the last terminal command with a special identifier and having Copilot explain the meaning. The second involves asking Copilot how to do something in the terminal and having it provide a conversational explanation along with the exact commands to run in the terminal to accomplish the task.

While we have seen how valuable and extensive Copilot's capabilities can be, it's important to remember that it can be inaccurate and provide out-of-date information as results. This happens because Copilot's knowledge base is only as up-to-date as the recency of the data that was used to train the underlying models it leverages.

In the next chapter, we'll look at how to deal with Copilot basing suggestions and responses on out-of-date information and how to work around those situations.

CHAPTER 7
Keeping Copilot Timely and Relevant

The range of functionality and interactivity provided by GitHub Copilot is truly impressive. However, the responses it generates can sometimes be less impressive (and less useful) if they are not timely and relevant. As good as the AI can be, at times you may need to take extra steps to *steer* it.

For example, in certain instances, you may need to direct Copilot to focus on certain portions of your content to get targeted answers. Or you may need to augment its training to get responses more relevant to your codebase. And you may need to pay extra attention to be aware when Copilot is suggesting code that may be out of date or referencing features that are no longer supported.

In this chapter, we're going to look at how to manage interaction with Copilot in these situations. You can leverage certain strategies and functionality to help ensure relevancy and timeliness in your interactions with Copilot. Certain approaches can compensate when Copilot may not be aware of recent changes or referencing the right sources.

All of this is aimed at helping Copilot have the most usable set of context in order to provide the most useful responses for what we're asking of it. In the next few pages, we'll look at the following areas related to Copilot's use of context:

- Where context originates
- How timeliness and relevancy may be affected
- User-based coping strategies
- Adding context to make code more relevant

By its very definition, *generative* implies generating new content in part based on gathering and processing context. So, let's start with a reminder of where the context that Copilot uses comes from.

Where Context Originates

As we've discussed in previous chapters, in the IDE, Copilot draws context from your immediate working environment—specifically, from the files you have in your workspace and the content associated with them. This includes typical items like the name of the file, the comments in them, and the code before and after the cursor. But Copilot also draws from more dynamic interactions, such as whether or not you accepted its last code suggestion. And by automatically creating an index of your repository, Copilot gains a larger understanding of your project. Copilot can also be directed to take other content into consideration.

For quickly generating coding suggestions in your IDE/editor, targeting the files you have open is a useful strategy used by Copilot. The focus allows it to quickly get a good sense of what is presumably most important (since you have those files readily accessible).

In this *inline* mode, Copilot uses multiple strategies to ensure a fast response. The client (extension installed in your interface) asks the model for very few suggestions (one to three). Copilot is aggressive in caching results and adapts the suggestions if you continue typing. It also has some built-in checks, preventing sending requests if you are typing in the middle of a line, for example, unless there is whitespace to the right of the cursor. Then the index we've discussed is updated based on changes.

In this mode, scoring also happens to determine whether the prompt assembled to send to the model is even worthwhile (worth invoking the model). This decision is based on factors like previous responses to suggestions. This approach helps exclude repetitive prompts or ones that already exist in the code.

Most of these same strategies are not needed when you switch to the chat interface. Within that, Copilot has more time to come up with responses, and so more completion suggestions can be requested by the client. For gathering context when working in this interface, you can also be more directive of where to get the context. Copilot includes methods like chat variables and chat participants (as discussed in Chapter 3 and other chapters) to focus Copilot on particular items.

Regardless of where the user is working, the client collects the context, processes it into a prompt, and sends it to the model you've selected. After doing some quick validation of what the model returns and generating the requested set of responses, those are then displayed to the user. The responses can include multiple options in the IDE if multiple completion suggestions were available.

The *quick validation* just referred to involves quickly looking for patterns in the response that are repetitive or might indicate a security issue (such as hardcoded credentials). These are beneficial checks, but they don't prevent other factors that may lead to relevancy and timeliness being off. Let's look at some of those other factors next.

How Timeliness and Relevancy May Be Affected

When you first open up Copilot's chat interface, you get a notification:

```
I'm powered by AI, so surprises and mistakes are possible. Make
sure to verify any generated code or suggestions, and share
feedback so that we can learn and improve.
```

This disclaimer is a reminder that generative AI can be inaccurate and problematic. Ultimately, it's up to the user to ensure that the generated content is correct and relevant. (This is also why you should always use standard validation methods like testing and code reviews to check any content produced with the assistance of the AI.)

The disclaimer is necessary because several kinds of challenges can affect the timeliness and relevancy of Copilot's suggestions and responses. These include the following:

- Training cutoffs
- Hallucinations
- Lack of real-time validation
- Mistaken context

Let's look at each of these in more detail.

Training Cutoffs

LLMs are trained on data that is current as of the time the training occurs. Beyond that date, the model has no *built-in* knowledge of changes that have occurred in the areas it was trained in. The further away from the training cutoff your use of the tool occurs, the more likely some of the responses and suggestions will be out of date. This can manifest as Copilot producing deprecated code or code that was more relevant for a previous version of a framework or language. And, of course, results will vary depending on which model you choose to use.

Training Frequency

If you're wondering why these models aren't kept more up to date, it's important to understand that they have billions of parameters and huge corpora of data to process for any training. This requires significant compute cost and time to accomplish. So, updates to the wider underlying training are expensive in multiple ways.

Let's look at a simple example of challenges that may occur from training cutoffs (as surfaced through Copilot as of the time of this writing). We'll ask Copilot to write a function to seed a random number generator in Go (Figure 7-1).

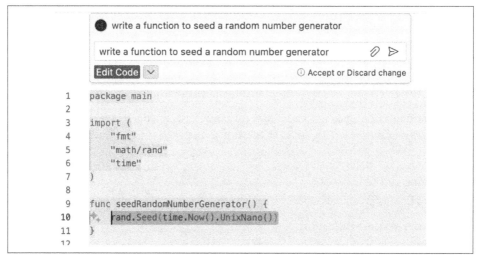

Figure 7-1. Asking Copilot to create a random number generator in Go

While this looks fine and is syntactically correct, there is a problem. The Seed function was deprecated in Go (*https://oreil.ly/D2hpj*) as of version 1.20. Let's see if Copilot understands that this is deprecated. We can ask it in the Chat interface "Is the Seed function deprecated in Go?" The response, as shown in Figure 7-2, shows that, based on the model's training, it doesn't have the information that the function is deprecated.

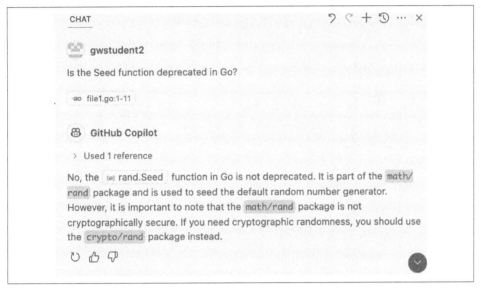

Figure 7-2. Asking Copilot if the Seed function is deprecated

So although the function is no longer meant to be used, Copilot was not aware of that. This illustrates the point about the training cutoff. We'll look at some ways to deal with these kind of challenges later in the chapter.

> ## Detecting Deprecated Contents
>
> In some IDEs, other installed tools may detect that code is deprecated and then alert you. Figure 7-3 shows an example of a deprecation issue being detected and flagged by another tool. 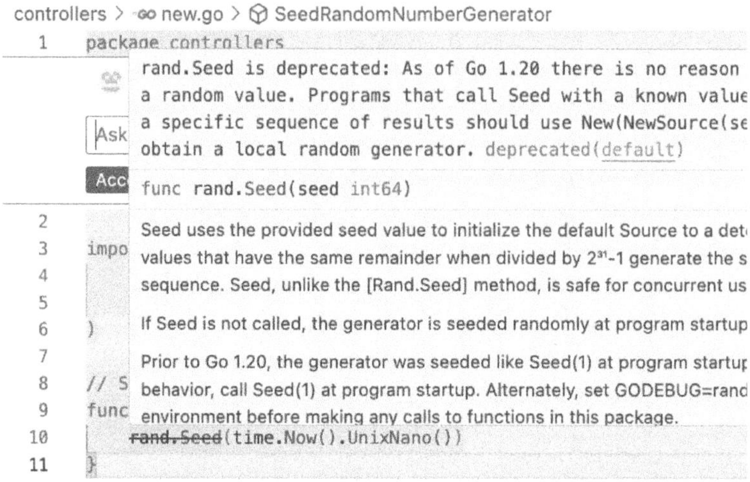
>
> ```
> controllers > ∞ new.go > ⊕ SeedRandomNumberGenerator
>  1   package controllers
>      
>          rand.Seed is deprecated: As of Go 1.20 there is no reason
>          a random value. Programs that call Seed with a known value
>      Ask a specific sequence of results should use New(NewSource(se
>          obtain a local random generator. deprecated(default)
>      Acc
>          func rand.Seed(seed int64)
>  2       
>  3   impo Seed uses the provided seed value to initialize the default Source to a det
>  4        values that have the same remainder when divided by 2³¹-1 generate the s
>  5        sequence. Seed, unlike the [Rand.Seed] method, is safe for concurrent us
>  6   )    If Seed is not called, the generator is seeded randomly at program startup
>  7        Prior to Go 1.20, the generator was seeded like Seed(1) at program startup
>  8   // S behavior, call Seed(1) at program startup. Alternately, set GODEBUG=rand
>  9   func environment before making any calls to functions in this package.
> 10        rand.Seed(time.Now().UnixNano())
> 11   }
> ```
>
> *Figure 7-3. Deprecation detection by another tool*
>
> In a case like this, you *may* be able to use Copilot's Fix functionality to have it generate alternative code.

Out-of-date results represent one category of problems; results would have been valid at one time but no longer are. Another category of issues arises when results look valid for the current context but may not reflect real data or references. These are known as *hallucinations*.

Hallucinations

LLMs are subject to creating responses with data that looks legitimate but isn't. These are referred to as *hallucinations*. In general chat interfaces, this can take the form of referencing nonexistent items or stating as fact things that simply aren't true. In more critical systems, such as threat detection, an AI model may flag something as a threat when it is not.

In the context of coding, hallucinations can take several forms:

- Coding suggestions that may reference identifiers (names, variables, constants, etc.) or related code that does not exist
- Generated data that may not be accurate
- Functions or methods that don't exist
- Incorrect library or API usage (or use of libraries or APIs that don't exist at all)
- Made-up types or classes
- Plausible but incorrect business logic
- Bad assumptions about surrounding code
- Tests that don't actually test the intended behavior

While hallucinations in the first category can certainly still occur in output produced from Copilot, they seem less common now than in Copilot's early days due to improvements with the underlying models. These kinds of hallucinations (referencing identifiers or code that doesn't exist) tend to be more obvious and can usually be caught quickly by user reviews. If these hallucinations do end up getting accepted and overlooked, compilers, linters, or other tools that check syntax will likely flag them at some point.

The second type of hallucination (involving generated data) is more subtle. It occurs in part because there is no real-time automatic validation of generated data.

Lack of Real-Time Validation

Generated data that Copilot returns may not be accurate. Copilot itself sometimes reminds you of that, as shown in Figure 7-4. In this case, we asked Copilot to generate a mapping of area codes to states. After completing the tasks, Copilot adds the disclaimer that "The above code is just a placeholder and may not represent the actual area codes for each state."

```
        "TX": ["210", "214", "254", "281", "325"],
        "UT": ["385", "435", "801"],
        "VT": ["802"],
        "VA": ["276", "434", "540", "571", "703"],
        "WA": ["206", "253", "360", "425", "509"],
        "WV": ["304", "681"],
        "WI": ["262", "414", "534", "608", "715"],
        "WY": ["307"]
    };
```

Please replace the area codes with actual area codes for each state. The above code is just a placeholder and may not represent the actual area codes for each state.

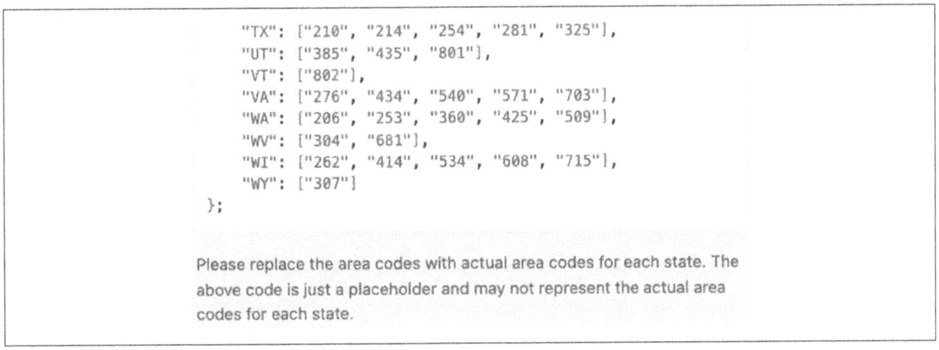

Figure 7-4. A Copilot disclaimer on the accuracy of the generated data

Why is this the case? Keep these four points in mind:

- Copilot is trained on data which may or may not contain accurate, actual values.
- Copilot is generating results to match syntax and structure.
- Copilot does not run code that it generates and doesn't validate logic.
- Copilot does not have mechanisms to look up and check data to see if it is accurate or up-to-date.

The first three items are self-explanatory. The fourth item indicates that Copilot has no mechanism to cross-check results it generates against other sources such as the web. While some AI techniques can leverage tools to do this, they are not integrated with Copilot for the purpose of validating responses from the model. The data may be correct, but there is no guarantee. In short, Copilot has no way of knowing if something is true or false.

For this reason, you should not assume correctness when using information generated by Copilot. Data generation from Copilot is better suited for content that needs correct form but not necessarily correct values, like testing scenarios.

Copilot Extensions

You can create Copilot Extensions that call APIs or other tools to get more relevant, up-to-date information for particular use cases. You can either find an existing extension that already addresses what you're looking to do or build your own. Copilot Extensions are covered in detail in Chapter 10.

Another challenge you may encounter is having Copilot use context you did not intend for it to reference for its responses.

Misplaced Context

Most of the time, when you are chatting with Copilot in the IDE's chat interface, you will have a file active in the editor. You may also have a portion of it selected. In those cases, Copilot assumes this is the main context that any open-ended questions (such as "How do I test this?") refer to.

Having Copilot use that specific content may be exactly what you intend. Or you might have intended for Copilot to respond based on a different file or a different portion of the active file. If Copilot assumes a different context, Copilot's answers may not be what you are looking for.

Imagine you are using multiple languages or frameworks in a project and have context set that doesn't align with your prompt. Such a project is shown in Figure 7-5. In this project, we have a Python file (*fibonacci.py*) and one written in Go (*prime.go*), as shown in the upper left of the IDE.

With the Python file selected (and thus used as context), we ask Copilot, "How do I test the Go code here?" Copilot responds by telling us about the mismatch between the context and the prompt. It then provides information about how to do Python testing to align with the active file.

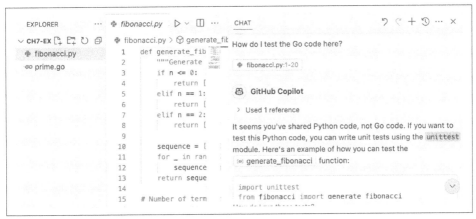

Figure 7-5. Indicating the wrong context for a prompt

Another type of issue can arise when no context is implied.

Missing Context

If we prompt Copilot and have no files open in the workspace and nothing else in the prompt for it to draw on, Copilot will usually offer a more generic response. For example, assume we have a workspace with Go code to implement a Kubernetes operator, and we have no files actively open and nothing selected. Now, we prompt Copilot in chat with "How can I test the Go code here?"

Because no context is indicated, Copilot either will tell you to select context or will supply a response about how you can answer the question generally. Figure 7-6 shows an example response for the case we just discussed. Here, Copilot provides guidance on how to test Go code generally.

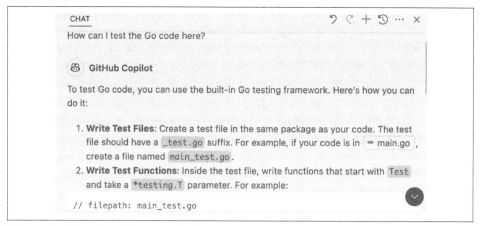

Figure 7-6. Generic advice per missing context

This type of response also happens for other types of queries, such as trying to determine where imports are used in the codebase (Figure 7-7).

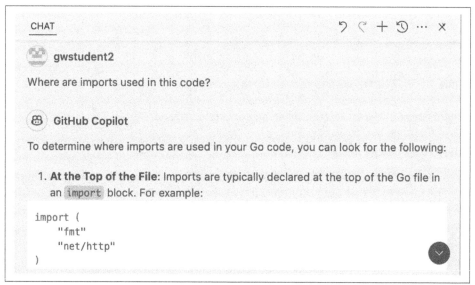

Figure 7-7. Another example of a generic response

The bottom line is that without enough implicit context (open files) or explicit context (references supplied in the prompt), Copilot defaults to generic answers.

When you start working with Copilot for any length of time, you will run into these classes of issues. The impact will vary depending on your particular situation. Fortunately, you, as a user, can employ a few strategies when you encounter these scenarios.

User-Based Coping Strategies

In general, we have three strategies to help when Copilot's responses are not as accurate or timely as we may need:

- Explicitly telling Copilot what to use for context
- Changing the model
- Augmenting the data that Copilot has available for context

Let's look at each of these in turn.

Telling Copilot What to Use for Context

As we outlined earlier in this chapter, absent more explicit direction, Copilot tries to gather context from what's being actively used in the editor. If we are working directly in the editor, this may be correct in most cases. However, when we are working with the chat interface, we may want to have Copilot focus on other parts of the project or answer a generic question such as "Where is X used?"

Since we are dealing with the chat interface, we can leverage Copilot's built-in features of chat participants and chat variables. These features were covered in detail in Chapter 3. Here, we'll provide a simple reminder of how to use them to help with cases like these.

The chat participants have knowledge of different domains that Copilot may need to work with, including the overall workspace, the terminal, and VS Code. When we use a participant in a query, it steers Copilot to use that domain for context with the prompt.

In an earlier section, when we were looking at a project, we asked Copilot, "Where are imports used in this code?" We got a generic response telling us the steps to find imports for any Go project rather than for our project. The same was true for the "How can I test the Go code here?" prompt. Copilot responded with generic instructions for how we could determine the information for ourselves.

However, if instead we explicitly use the `@workspace` participant in the prompt, Copilot provides information from the files we have as part of the workspace (see Figure 7-8). The prompt is "@workspace Where are imports used in this code?" This matches the original intent.

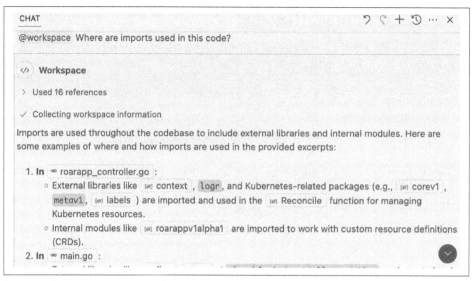

Figure 7-8. Context with @workspace

You can also implicitly direct Copilot to use @workspace. Certain keywords or phrases in your prompt can trigger Copilot to add @workspace to the prompt. For instance, we can modify our previous prompt about testing to "How can I test the Go code in this project?" The reference to *project* is enough for Copilot to understand that we mean the larger context. It then automatically runs our prompt by using @workspace and the shortcut command /setupTests, as shown in Figure 7-9.

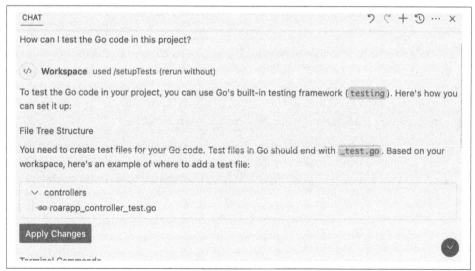

Figure 7-9. Implicitly using @workspace based on the prompt text

If we need to further zero in on content, we can include one of the chat variables in the prompt to specify context, like #file or #selection. For example, we can specifically ask Copilot how to test the code in a file in our project by using the #file chat variable (see Figure 7-10).

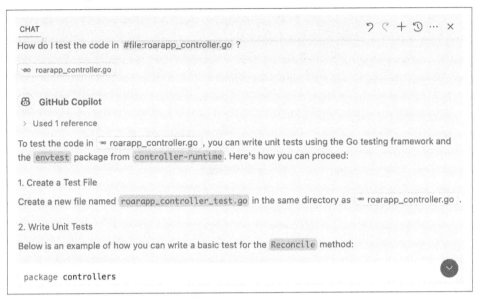

Figure 7-10. Testing Go with the #file chat variable

Specifying Chat Variables and Arguments

Simply typing in chat variables and arguments directly does not always work. What does always work is starting to type the chat variable (#) and then selecting the chat variable from the pop-up list by using the arrow keys to move, if needed, and the Enter key to select one. You should make sure to select any intended files from the list that pops up.

Notice that by using the #file chat variable, we did not need to have the file actually open or active in the editor. This mechanism then affords you a way to direct Copilot to the relevant content in the project for context. This overrides Copilot's default mechanisms for determining which content you want.

Even with a directed context, Copilot may still respond with out-of-date code or information, depending on when the model was trained. Or the responses it returns may not seem as relevant or comprehensive as you want. But since Copilot provides multiple models to choose from, there may be a simple way to deal with that.

User-Based Coping Strategies | 193

Changing the Model

Copilot allows you to choose from more than one AI model for code suggestions and chat responses. Each model will have its pros and cons. For example, some models may be better at code generation. In addition, each model will have been trained at a different point in time, so newer models will be more up-to-date and less likely to produce deprecated code than older models.

As a reminder, changing models in the chat interface is easy. You just select the model name that you want to use from the drop-down list in whichever chat interface you're using. See Figure 7-11 for an example.

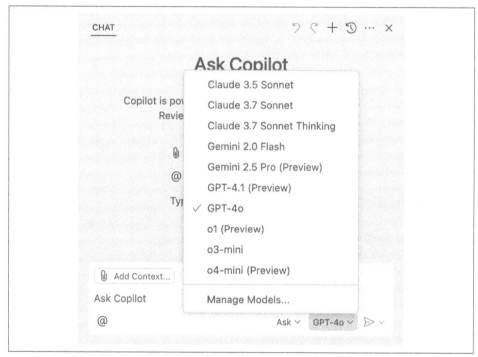

Figure 7-11. Switching models in the chat interface

Earlier in the chapter, we showed an example of Copilot generating a random number function by using a deprecated method (Figure 7-1). This was generated with the GPT-4o model.

If we switch instead to a more recent model, such as Gemini 2.5 Pro, and issue the same prompt, Copilot produces code using the newer standard rand.NewSource function instead of trying to use the deprecated rand.Seed function. Also, if we query Copilot about whether the *Seed* function is deprecated in the main chat area, it correctly responds that the rand.Seed function is deprecated as of Go 1.20. Figure 7-12 shows the response from using the newer model.

Figure 7-12. Using a newer model results in correct code and response

If you choose a different model, how do you know whether it will be more up to date? Typically, the models list will be updated as newer models become available—usually marked as *Preview* for some period of time. But you can also do some simple searching on the web or with a site like Hugging Face (*http://huggingface.co*) to find which models are more recent.

You can also try querying the model itself through Copilot to find out more about which version of something was current when the model was being trained.

Querying the Model to Determine Which Version Is Current

Still looking at the example where Copilot generated deprecated code, let's see what other details we can find to help. Since Copilot didn't recognize that the function was deprecated, it would be useful to know what version of Go Copilot thinks is current. We can ask it in the chat interface with a simple "As of your last training date, what was the current version of Go?" prompt, as shown in Figure 7-13.

Figure 7-13. Asking Copilot which version of Go is current

Framing the Question Appropriately

The question we asked Copilot was framed as "As of your last training date...." This is deliberate. If we simply asked Copilot, "What version of Go is current?," it would likely tell us how to find the information ourselves about our local Go installation instead.

The model that is active in Copilot responds that its last training update was in October 2023—and that, as of that date, the latest stable version of Go *was* 1.21.1.

An obvious question that comes up is why, if Copilot knew about 1.21.1 as the most recent version, it still does not recognize that something was deprecated in 1.20. Keep in mind the question we asked Copilot was which version was current when the model was last trained, not which version was used in the repositories when it was trained. In fact, if you ask Copilot a similar question via comments inline in the editor multiple times, you will likely get a different answer (see Figure 7-14). The reason for the differences is that the answer returned in the editor is based on version references present in the training data.

```
 6
 7    // q: Which version of Go is current?
 8    // a: 1.17.1
 9
10    // As of your last training date, which version of Go is current?
11    // 1.17.1
12
```

Figure 7-14. Asking Copilot which version of Go is current in the editor

So, assuming the answer returned by the chat query is the most recent version that the model knows about, but the model was trained on various other versions, what does that buy you?

What the version information returned in the chat tells you is the most recent version that could be represented in the model's training data. So, any code generated strictly from the model's training will not incorporate any deprecations or use any new features or version-specific changes since that version.

Query Results May Vary

Not all models may return a discrete answer for the *latest version* question. Some models may just respond that they don't have access to that information or suggest you look up what the latest version is.

We can extend Copilot to have capabilities to find out information about the latest versions of languages or platforms. Chapter 10 guides you through implementing an extension to find out the latest version of Go as an example.

When you have this awareness, you can take measures to help Copilot understand updates by switching to a different model or via the method we discuss in the next section.

Premium Requests

While switching models may be a good option to address certain issues, remember that use of some advanced models count as *premium requests*. Using these models can use up quotas faster and incur additional costs on some plans.

What if you can't avoid the AI producing deprecated or incomplete code because you're restricted to a particular model or because the models that you use do not have training on a newer feature? You can use one other approach to get Copilot to generate the kind of code you want with the context you need.

Guiding Copilot by Example

Looking at our deprecation example again, Copilot created a function to seed a random number generator by using a deprecated method (Figure 7-15).

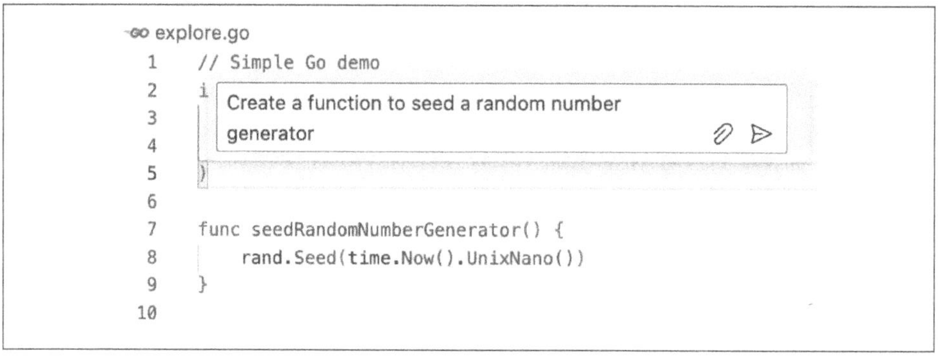

```
-∞ explore.go
1    // Simple Go demo
2    i
3      Create a function to seed a random number
4      generator
5    )
6
7    func seedRandomNumberGenerator() {
8        rand.Seed(time.Now().UnixNano())
9    }
10
```

Figure 7-15. A function created using a deprecated method

If we want to get Copilot to produce code that is using the replacement for the deprecation, we can teach it by example. We can take the updated code snippet from the Go documentation (*https://oreil.ly/4vDIl*) and temporarily paste it into the same file in our workspace. (Or we could paste it into a prompt if we're using the chat interface.)

After that, if we repeat our prompt, Copilot will generate updated code that is based on the code snippet we included (Figure 7-16).

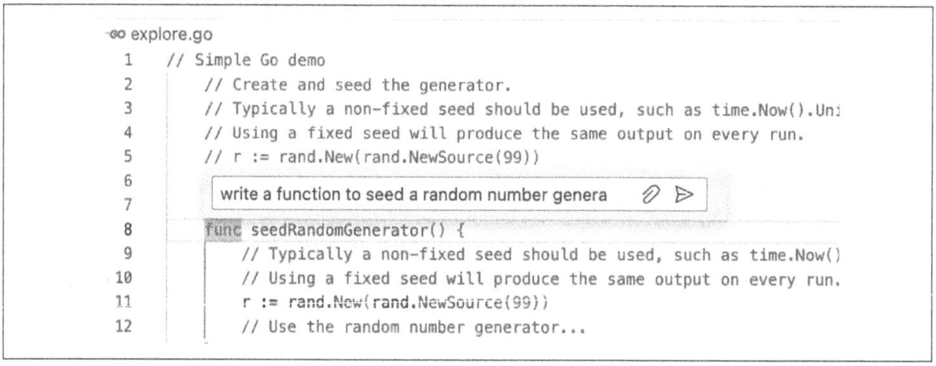

```
-∞ explore.go
1    // Simple Go demo
2        // Create and seed the generator.
3        // Typically a non-fixed seed should be used, such as time.Now().Un:
4        // Using a fixed seed will produce the same output on every run.
5        // r := rand.New(rand.NewSource(99))
6
7        write a function to seed a random number genera
8    func seedRandomGenerator() {
9        // Typically a non-fixed seed should be used, such as time.Now()
10       // Using a fixed seed will produce the same output on every run.
11       r := rand.New(rand.NewSource(99))
12       // Use the random number generator...
```

Figure 7-16. Updated code generated with the code example in place

Obviously, this is a very simple example. In this case, Copilot essentially copied the code verbatim. But, regardless, the end result was still what we needed. After getting the desired result, the example code can then be removed.

Making Updated Code Available

In some cases, for Copilot to draw on separate content, it may be enough to put the content in another file that is opened in your IDE. In other cases, it may be necessary to put the content directly in the file that you're working with. If that is the case, you can add in the content and then remove it when the code generation is correct.

The examples in this section have focused on ways to deal with questions and challenges with content already generated by Copilot. However, you can also employ similar strategies before Copilot generates results to get better results up front. We'll look more at that aspect in the last section of this chapter.

Adding Context to Make Code More Relevant

In addition to compensating for deprecations and missing new features, additional content that you supply to Copilot can help in another way. When you provide more detailed context in terms of definitions or coding examples that are relevant to your project, Copilot can draw on those to generate more thorough, richer, and relevant coding suggestions.

As an example, let's look at creating some SQL content with Copilot. Revisiting a previous example, suppose we are working on implementing a system to manage university courses, students, instructors, registrations, etc. Without any other context, let's ask Copilot to create a general SELECT statement to get students enrolled in a course. We can do this as simply as adding an SQL comment like this in the editor: `-- define a select statement to get all the students enrolled in a course`.

Given this generic directive and no other context, Copilot will produce a reasonable, generalized query like the following:

```
SELECT * FROM students WHERE course_id = 1;
```

There is nothing wrong with this query. It is perfectly valid given the limited context we've provided for Copilot. Assuming that we have the corresponding table and field names in place in our schema, this would work fine.

However, suppose we already have a more extensive set of databases in place for our system (with appropriate tables, data, etc.). We would really like Copilot to generate suggestions that are relevant to those and use the elements that we already have defined. How can we accomplish this?

The mechanism for doing this is similar to what we did for the deprecation example in the last section, adding more context for Copilot to pick up in the workspace. In this case, while we don't have a way for Copilot to dynamically examine our data stores, indices, or stored procedures, we can provide a static representation of them via the schema definitions. We can use either an original SQL definition if we have one or a dump of the schemas from the existing content. A portion of a file that we might use is shown in Figure 7-17.

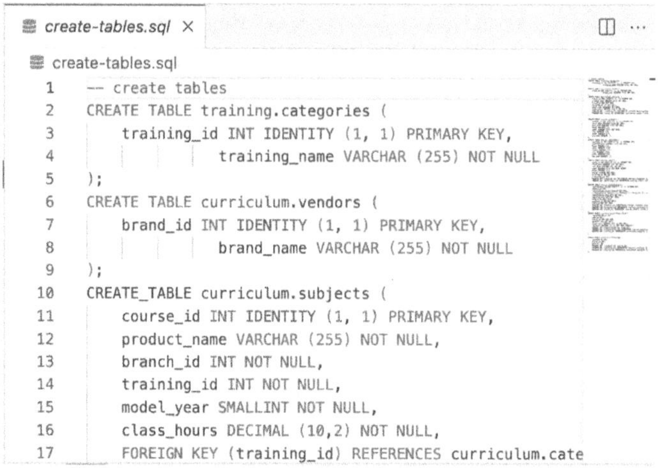

```sql
-- create tables
CREATE TABLE training.categories (
    training_id INT IDENTITY (1, 1) PRIMARY KEY,
    training_name VARCHAR (255) NOT NULL
);
CREATE TABLE curriculum.vendors (
    brand_id INT IDENTITY (1, 1) PRIMARY KEY,
    brand_name VARCHAR (255) NOT NULL
);
CREATE TABLE curriculum.subjects (
    course_id INT IDENTITY (1, 1) PRIMARY KEY,
    product_name VARCHAR (255) NOT NULL,
    branch_id INT NOT NULL,
    training_id INT NOT NULL,
    model_year SMALLINT NOT NULL,
    class_hours DECIMAL (10,2) NOT NULL,
    FOREIGN KEY (training_id) REFERENCES curriculum.cate
```

Figure 7-17. Example extended schema definitions to use for context

This file has specific tables defined for the domains we're working with, along with relevant fields, keys, etc.

Let's add this file to our workspace so that it is part of our project and open it in the editor. Copilot now has this additional context available to draw from. We can go back and provide the same directive in comment form as before: `-- define a select statement to get all the students enrolled in a course`. This time, Copilot produces the following response:

```sql
SELECT students.first_name, students.last_name, students.email,
  students.phone, students.city, students.state, students.zip_code
FROM courses.students
JOIN courses.registrations
ON students.student_id = registrations.student_id
JOIN courses.registration_items
ON registrations.registration_id =
registration_items.registration_id
WHERE registration_items.course_id = 1;
```

Notice that now, with the additional context from the other file available in the workspace, Copilot produced a much richer, more detailed, and more relevant query. It also used specific table and field names provided in the other file.

The key here is that Copilot prioritizes the context you're using in the IDE for deciding how to generate code. Leveraging this kind of approach is a useful and simple strategy to getting much more usable and pertinent coding suggestions and answers from Copilot than would be possible if you simply relied on the model's training data.

Adding the Additional File as Context

In the SQL example shown here, we added the file as an additional one in the workspace and opened it in the IDE. We did not take the contents of the file and paste it into the active file as we did for the deprecation example. While we could have done that, it was not necessary here.

Depending on the use case, you may find that one or the other of these two approaches (inserting content directly into the active file or opening the content as a *peer* file) works better for you. You can always start by opening the content as a peer file and trying that. If you don't get the expected results, then you can add the content directly into the active file.

Another option is to paste relevant examples directly into Copilot Chat for it to work from—if the scope of the example is a good fit for that.

If you are adding content into the IDE either as a new file or an addition to an existing file, be sure to save the changes before querying or prompting Copilot. Copilot relies on persisted (saved) content in the workspace to draw on for context.

The point is that adding richer context up front for Copilot can produce improved results in the form of suggestions or completions. In some cases, it may be more time-consuming to generate files like the schema one we used here, but the trade-off is less time and effort remediating Copilot's suggestions to get to the detail you need.

Miscellaneous Tips for Steering Copilot

Here are a few other tips on ways to help steer Copilot if you encounter content that isn't what you expected and other strategies fail:

- Switching from the inline suggestions to prompting in chat (or vice versa) if you're not getting good results
- If the code that Copilot generates keeps coming up as incorrect, you can try writing part of it (a stub) and then letting Copilot generate a completion to see if you get a better end result
- Adding a more directive comment with clear intent to steer the generation

- Isolating the code temporarily in its own window to remove other context that may be interfering
- Prompting Copilot to explain rather than having it generate
- Changing the filename or even file type to update the context

Conclusion

In this chapter, we've covered the various aspects about how Copilot determines context for its code suggestions and responses, why those may not be up-to-date or accurate, and some ways you can help deal with those situations.

Copilot's core context comes from the training in the underlying models it uses. Since these models are only as current as the point in time when they were last trained, they are missing any updates or changes in the languages and frameworks that were not part of their training. In addition, the content they were trained on will be using older versions of tooling. So, suggestions or responses generated from those can be substantially out of date. This is a key aspect to be aware of and watch out for. One possible quick fix for this is to switch to an updated model if one is available.

Fortunately, Copilot also pulls in context from the available content in the editor and workspace you're using. This context is prioritized over the training data since it reflects what you are doing and using currently. Because of this approach, you can provide Copilot with more up-to-date and more relevant context to draw on. You do this by including your own relevant content in the IDE and workspace. This can be done in most cases by having a file with relevant information open in the IDE. For more explicit direction, the relevant information can be added to the current file for as long as needed for Copilot to draw from.

GitHub Copilot also includes ways to focus the AI on specific content you have. Chat participants can define overall context areas for Copilot to answer questions and respond about. The current set of participants include ones for VS Code, the active terminal, and your workspace.

At a more detailed level, you can steer Copilot's context to particular items within your workspace via chat variables. Examples include the current selection in the editor, the content open in the editor, the last command in the terminal, and more.

In this chapter, you learned how to supply more context for GitHub Copilot when you're working with SQL. This is an example of a nontypical language/framework that you can also use Copilot for. The next chapter explores more examples of how to use Copilot for such nontypical areas.

CHAPTER 8
Other Ways to Leverage Copilot

As we've seen, Copilot provides a lot of value for working with traditional coding flows as well as traditional tasks like testing and documentation. Copilot can also help in many less common use cases encountered by programmers.

We can't cover all those use cases in this chapter or even in this book, but we can cover some representative examples. As a heads-up, the structure of this chapter is different from that of the other chapters. We'll be covering multiple, diverse use cases rather than focusing on one overall feature or functional area. The examples we'll look at are outlined in the next few paragraphs.

You may primarily think of using GitHub Copilot for coding in popular languages like JavaScript and Python. However, Copilot has access to all the languages that the model you're using was trained on. So, you can also use it on ones that we don't think of as traditional programming languages. An example is one we've touched on before—SQL—commonly used to work with relational databases. Copilot can simplify a surprising number of database-related tasks when you're working with queries, schemas, and stored procedures.

Frameworks, such as Kubernetes, also make use of an ordered format (most commonly expressed in YAML). While these frameworks are declarative rather than imperative, their syntax and structure are understood by Copilot. It can provide completion suggestions and answers about how to work with them, just as for any programming language.

Then there are regular expressions—those often complex and cryptic strings of characters. When you need one, they are important to get correct but usually frustrating to try to create. Copilot can make easy work of these.

For testing a regular expression or unit-testing a function, you may also need structured test data. With specific prompting, Copilot can generate nearly any simple data structures needed, although there are a few nuances to be aware of.

Finally, it's worth noting that some Copilot functionality is embedded in the GitHub CLI application. While this is currently limited, it's reasonable to expect more functionality to be added over time.

We'll cover all of these in this chapter, starting with how Copilot can be used when you're working with SQL.

Using Copilot with SQL

While technically a programming language, SQL brings its own unique constructs to data management. These include the standard queries used with the data and schema in the database, indices for efficiencies, and stored procedures for more complex tasks.

In this section, we'll look at three areas where Copilot can help:

- Using Copilot to help with queries
- Working with stored procedures
- Performing optimization

Let's start by looking at the basic ways that Copilot can assist with generating SQL-related queries.

Queries

As you know, Copilot draws from local content to get context. So if you are working in your editor and open a file with an extension of *.sql* or that contains SQL statements, Copilot can pick up on that to know that it needs to generate SQL. You can also use comments to help clue Copilot in further on what you want.

Chapter 7 showed an example of how to add context to make code generation and suggestions more relevant. There we used the technique of opening up an SQL file that had all the database schema definitions for a university student and course registration system to give Copilot more context for generating queries.

You can refer back to "Adding Context to Make Code More Relevant" on page 199 if you need a reminder, but we'll assume the same setup here. Here is a partial schema definition underlying the registration system:

```sql
-- create tables
...

CREATE TABLE courses.students (
    student_id INT IDENTITY (1, 1) PRIMARY KEY,
    first_name VARCHAR (255) NOT NULL,
    last_name VARCHAR (255) NOT NULL,
    phone VARCHAR(25),
    email VARCHAR (255) NOT NULL,
    city VARCHAR (50),
    state VARCHAR (25),
    zip_code VARCHAR (5)
);

...

CREATE TABLE courses.registrations (
    registration_id INT IDENTITY (1, 1) PRIMARY KEY,
    student_id INT,
    registration_status tinyint NOT NULL,
    -- Registration status: 1 = Pending; 2 = Enrolled; 3 = Rejected; 4 = Completed
    registration_date DATE NOT NULL,
    required_date DATE NOT NULL,
    completion_date DATE,
    location_id INT NOT NULL,
    staff_id INT NOT NULL,
    FOREIGN KEY (student_id) REFERENCES courses.students (student_id)
 ON DELETE CASCADE ON UPDATE CASCADE,
    FOREIGN KEY (location_id) REFERENCES courses.locations (location_id) ON DELETE CASCADE ON UPDATE CASCADE,
    FOREIGN KEY (staff_id) REFERENCES courses.staffs (staff_id) ON DELETE NO ACTION ON UPDATE NO ACTION

...

CREATE TABLE courses.registration_items (
    registration_id INT,
    item_id INT,
    course_id INT NOT NULL,
    quantity INT NOT NULL,
    class_hours DECIMAL (10, 2) NOT NULL,
    lab_hours DECIMAL (4, 2) NOT NULL DEFAULT 0,
    PRIMARY KEY (registration_id, item_id),
    FOREIGN KEY (registration_id) REFERENCES courses.registrations (registrations_id) ON DELETE CASCADE ON UPDATE CASCADE,
    FOREIGN KEY (course_id) REFERENCES curriculum.subjects (course_id) ON DELETE CASCADE ON UPDATE CASCADE
);
```

If we open this up in the editor where we are working on our queries and then prompt Copilot via a comment to generate an SQL query to get all students enrolled in a course, we get a detailed result with table names, field names, etc. that match the schema:

```
-- define a select statement to get all students enrolled in a
 course

SELECT students.first_name, students.last_name, students.email,
 students.phone, students.city, students.state, students.zip_code
FROM courses.students
JOIN courses.registrations
ON students.student_id = registrations.student_id
JOIN courses.registration_items
ON registrations.registration_id =
registration_items.registration_id
WHERE registration_items.course_id = 1;
```

By simply having the other file open in the workspace, Copilot was able to draw on that content to create a better query for us.

Save Your Work

Remember to first save any new files as part of the project that you want Copilot to be able to use in context.

As another example, we could ask Copilot to create a table for student attendance to capture attendance by class. Given the same context of the larger schema table, Copilot should respond with a complete table definition:

```
-- define a table for student attendance to capture attendance by
 class
CREATE TABLE courses.attendance (
    attendance_id INT IDENTITY (1, 1) PRIMARY KEY,
    registration_id INT NOT NULL,
    attendance_date DATE NOT NULL,
    attendance_status tinyint NOT NULL,
    -- Attendance status: 1 = Present; 2 = Absent; 3 = Late;
4 = Excused
    FOREIGN KEY (registration_id) REFERENCES courses.registrations
(registration_id) ON DELETE CASCADE ON UPDATE CASCADE
);
```

The format of this table is similar to the format used in the schema file for the *courses.registration* table, as shown next. Notice that both table definitions use status values of 1–4:

```
CREATE TABLE courses.registrations (
    registration_id INT IDENTITY (1, 1) PRIMARY KEY,
```

```
    student_id INT,
    registration_status tinyint NOT NULL,
    -- Registration status: 1 = Pending; 2 = Enrolled; 3 = Rejected;
 4 = Completed
    registration_date DATE NOT NULL,
    required_date DATE NOT NULL,
    completion_date DATE,
    location_id INT NOT NULL,
    staff_id INT NOT NULL,
    FOREIGN KEY (student_id) REFERENCES courses.students
 (student_id) ON DELETE CASCADE ON UPDATE CASCADE,
    FOREIGN KEY (location_id) REFERENCES courses.locations
 (location_id) ON DELETE CASCADE ON UPDATE CASCADE,
    FOREIGN KEY (staff_id) REFERENCES courses.staffs (staff_id)
 ON DELETE NO ACTION ON UPDATE NO ACTION
```

We can also have Copilot generate more complex types of SQL data like stored procedures.

Stored Procedures

A *stored procedure* is prepared SQL code that is saved and can be reused easily. Copilot can help us generate these as well. Continuing with our university registration example, let's ask Copilot to create a new stored procedure for getting a list of enrolled students at a particular location. We can use a simple prompt in chat (similar to the comment form we used earlier) to tell Copilot what we want. The prompt is "define a stored procedure to get course enrollment by location."

With this prompt and the additional context of the schemas, Copilot produces a reasonable result:

```
CREATE PROCEDURE GetCourseEnrollmentByLocation
    @CourseID INT
AS
BEGIN
    SELECT students.city, students.state, COUNT(*) AS
enrollment_count
    FROM courses.students
    JOIN courses.registrations
    ON students.student_id = registrations.student_id
    JOIN courses.registration_items
    ON registrations.registration_id =
registration_items.registration_id
    WHERE registration_items.course_id = @CourseID
    GROUP BY students.city, students.state;
END
```

We can also be more directive. The more prescriptive we are with the prompt, the more likely that Copilot will generate better results. For example, consider the following very specific prompt in the chat interface:

```
define a stored procedure to get instructor details associated with
a location include instructor details, location details, and courses
associated with the instructor use instructor_id as the input
parameter
```

Copilot first explained its thinking in terms of a plan and then generated the detailed code to match the prompt:

Plan
1. Define a new stored procedure named `GetInstructorDetailsByLocation`.
2. Accept `@InstructorID` as an input parameter.
3. Select instructor details, location details, and courses associated with the instructor.
4. Use appropriate joins to fetch data from the `instructors`, `locations`, and [`courses`]
5. Group the results by instructor and location details.

SQL Code
```sql
CREATE PROCEDURE GetInstructorDetailsByLocation
    @InstructorID INT
AS
BEGIN
    SELECT
        instructors.instructor_id,
        instructors.first_name,
        instructors.last_name,
        instructors.email,
        locations.city,
        locations.state,
        courses.course_id,
        courses.course_name
    FROM
        courses.instructors
    JOIN
        courses.locations
    ON
        instructors.location_id = locations.location_id
    JOIN
        courses.course_instructors
    ON
        instructors.instructor_id = course_instructors.instructor_id
    JOIN
        courses.courses
    ON
        course_instructors.course_id = courses.course_id
    WHERE
        instructors.instructor_id = @InstructorID;
END;
```

While it's helpful to have Copilot generating queries and stored procedures for us, that's not its only SQL skill. The AI can also help optimize what we create.

Optimizations

Copilot can make the code we have more efficient and can do so in two main ways. The first is by writing code leveraging built-in constructs that the language or framework provides for optimization. The second is by optimizing existing code.

As an example of the first case, SQL provides indexes to speed up operations. Refer back to the query we worked with earlier in this chapter to get all students enrolled in a course. The complete query is listed here:

```
-- define a select statement to get all students enrolled in a
course

SELECT students.first_name, students.last_name, students.email,
students.phone, students.city, students.state, students.zip_code
FROM courses.students
JOIN courses.registrations
ON students.student_id = registrations.student_id
JOIN courses.registration_items
ON registrations.registration_id =
registration_items.registration_id
WHERE registration_items.course_id = 1;
```

For this query, we can use a separate index to speed up operations. We ask Copilot to create a new index based on this query with the prompt "-- write an index to improve the performance of the query." From this prompt, Copilot might suggest SQL like the following:

```
-- write an index to improve the performance of the query

create index idx_registration_status_date on courses.registrations
(registration_status, registration_date);
```

As with the original query, Copilot was able to draw on the context of available code to create an index that uses the existing field names, table names, etc.

In addition to creating code to help optimize execution, Copilot can optimize static code. This is the second use case mentioned at the start of this section. Suppose we have a query to get all the course registrations for September 2024. It might look like this:

```
select * from courses.registrations where year(registration_date)
= 2024 and month(registration_date) = 9;
```

We can select this query and then prompt Copilot to optimize it via the prompt "optimize this query."

The AI then suggests an optimization that uses direct starting and ending dates instead:

```
SELECT * FROM courses.registrations WHERE registration_date >=
'2023-09-01' AND registration_date < '2023-10-01'
```

In the same output, Copilot also provides additional background on *why* this is an improvement:

```
...using functions or columns in the WHERE clause can prevent the
use of indexes and slow down the query. If registration_date is
indexed, you can optimize the query by avoiding the use of the
YEAR() and MONTH() functions and instead comparing against a range
of dates...
```

Copilot not only suggested an optimization but also told us why and under what conditions this would actually be an optimization. Nice.

Now that you've seen how Copilot works with managing coding for databases, let's look at how it handles a framework by using declarative specifications.

Working with YAML and Kubernetes

YAML is a critical formatting language for many applications today. It can also be painful to work with because of its syntax and strict formatting requirements. But the ability to create specifications and configurations is key for applications like Kubernetes.

Kubernetes itself can also be challenging to work with for multiple reasons. These include learning and remembering how to define objects you want in YAML files. Each native object has a common set of attributes, but then each also has its own specification (spec). The challenges can multiply when trying to scale objects for a service or product. Since any error or incorrect formatting can cause your app not to function, we can leverage AI to good effect here.

Suppose we want to code up a new deployment in Kubernetes. A *deployment* is a type of object in Kubernetes that instantiates and manages multiple instances of a Kubernetes *pod*. The pod, in turn, wraps one or more containers. The containers are based on images and provide a self-contained environment for an app to execute in.

Armed with basic knowledge of the parts, we can prompt Copilot to produce a YAML spec for a deployment via the chat interface:

```
write spec for deployment in Kubernetes with 2 replicas and image
from busybox
add command to run in containers: sleep 3600
add label app: myapp
add label type: front-end
```

After a few moments, Copilot will suggest something like this:

```
apiVersion: apps/v1
kind: Deployment
metadata:
  name: myapp-deployment
  labels:
    app: myapp
    type: front-end
spec:
  replicas: 2
  selector:
    matchLabels:
      app: myapp
  template:
    metadata:
      labels:
        app: myapp
        type: front-end
    spec:
      containers:
      - name: busybox-container
        image: busybox
        command: ["sleep", "3600"]
```

If you don't know Kubernetes, this is valid syntax and mirrors what we would expect to have as a deployment spec. Notice that no personal knowledge of the Kubernetes syntax was needed to generate this other than the type of objects that should be in the spec. We can save this file as *deployment.yaml* and move on.

Now that we have this spec, we will want to execute it at some point. If we're not clear on the process for that, we can ping Copilot about it. We simply go to the chat interface and ask, "How do I execute this?" As shown in Figure 8-1, Copilot references the *deployment.yaml* file we created and then provides instructions to get it into the Kubernetes cluster (a system of machines for running Kubernetes) and verify that the deployment is running. It does this using the Kubernetes CLI called `kubectl`.

Figure 8-1. Copilot explains how to apply the spec to Kubernetes for execution

This is very helpful, but what if at some point we need to move to managing this Kubernetes deployment via the Kubernetes API instead of the CLI? And we'd also like to do it using Python and be able to change (scale) the number of instances of the container it's running.

We can query Copilot about this through another simple natural language prompt in chat:

```
How do I call the K8s API for scaling a deployment to 5 replicas
with Python?
```

Copilot first tells us that we can do this using the Kubernetes Python client library and then dumps out the Python code for the task (Figure 8-2).

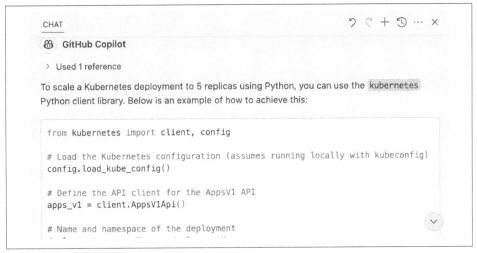

Figure 8-2. Copilot's response to manage Kubernetes in Python

Beyond this, Copilot provides a helpful explanation of the steps needed to run the code (Figure 8-3).

Figure 8-3. Steps for execution

We can then save the suggested code as a new file in the editor and proceed with any edits we want to make, testing the code, etc.

Let's throw one more challenge at Copilot. The more common programming language for Kubernetes is Go. So, if we want to migrate this Python code to Go, can Copilot help? As it turns out, it can! And it's very simple to do. With the Python code selected (and therefore referenced), all we need to do is tell Copilot to "Convert to

Go." Copilot then produces the equivalent pieces for Go code in the chat interface (Figure 8-4).

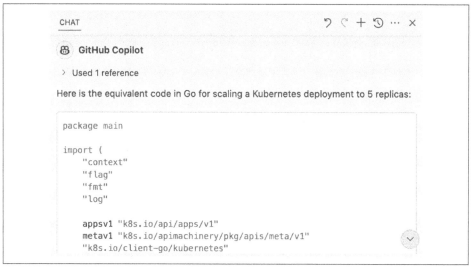

Figure 8-4. Code for Kubernetes deployment in Go

Copilot also provides a corresponding explanation and instructions on execution as it did for the Python version (Figure 8-5).

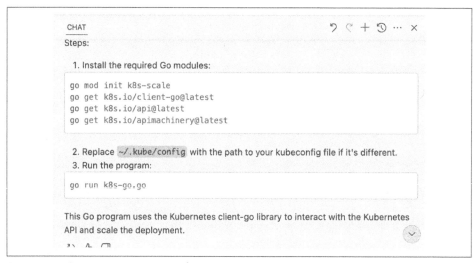

Figure 8-5. Steps to execute Go code

Yet again, we see an example of how Copilot can automate and simplify creating processing for complex tasks.

Another often complex task that Copilot can greatly simplify is creating regular expressions. That's the topic of our next section.

Generating Regular Expressions

Most developers are not a fan of having to come up with the syntax for regular expressions. The process of trying to find a combination of letters, numbers, and symbols to effectively match a set of strings can be time consuming and frustrating. Add to that the need to devise tests that comprehensively test out the expression, and it becomes preferable to try to find something that matches closely from other code or from a resource like Stack Overflow.

However, this is yet another area where Copilot shines. Given a suitable prompt, Copilot can easily create a corresponding regular expression. For example, suppose we tell Copilot to "Create a regular expression to validate a SSN" (where *SSN* stands for a *US Social Security number*). Copilot responds with the following implementation suggestion and explanation:

```
Here is a regular expression to validate a U.S. Social Security
  Number (SSN):

^\d{3}-\d{2}-\d{4}$

Explanation:

  • ^ asserts the start of the string.
  • \d{3} matches exactly 3 digits.
  • - matches a literal hyphen.
  • \d{2} matches exactly 2 digits.
  • - matches another literal hyphen.
  • \d{4} matches exactly 4 digits.
  • $ asserts the end of the string.

Example Usage in Python:

python
import re

def validate_ssn(ssn):
    pattern = r"^\d{3}-\d{2}-\d{4}$"
    return bool(re.match(pattern, ssn))

# Test the function
print(validate_ssn("123-45-6789"))  # True
print(validate_ssn("123-456-789"))  # False

This ensures the SSN is in the format `XXX-XX-XXXX` where `X`
  is a digit.
```

We may also want to generate a function that uses a regular expression for whatever language we're coding in. Assume that we have a JavaScript file (*phone.js*), and we want a function in it to validate any global phone number.

We can prompt Copilot with "create a function to validate any global phone number using a regular expression." Copilot, in turn will produce JavaScript code like this:

```
function validatePhoneNumber(phoneNumber) {
    const phoneRegex = /^\+(?:[0-9] ?){6,14}[0-9]$/;
    return phoneRegex.test(phoneNumber);
}

// Example usage:
console.log(validatePhoneNumber("+1234567890")); // true
console.log(validatePhoneNumber("1234567890")); // false
```

Notice that while the code is short, the regular expression is not simple. And Copilot also provided example calls to use to validate the function. If the use cases in the examples don't match what you were intending, you could reject the suggestion and use a more detailed prompt to get what you need.

After generating a regular expression, you may want some simple data to use for testing it, or you might need some data to do basic testing on some other part of your code. Rather than having to find or create this kind of data yourself, you can create it automatically with Copilot.

Automatic Data Generation

Another area where Copilot can come to the rescue for helping with boilerplate tasks is generating data and data mappings for validating coding approaches and testing after the coding.

The approach here is the same: to use a well-defined prompt to achieve the desired results. Suppose we want some test data to verify a function that looks up area codes for a given state. We can direct Copilot to "Create a mapping of all 50 states to area codes where the key is the state abbreviation and the value is an array of codes with max 10."

Notice that we were specific about what the keys and corresponding values should be for the mapping. Copilot responds with the requested data (Figure 8-6).

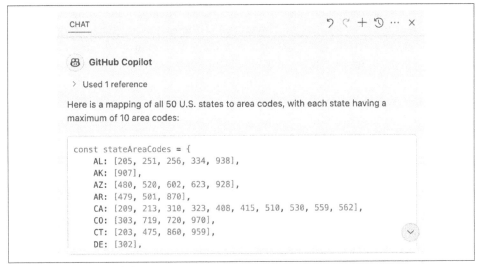

Figure 8-6. Generated data

Sometimes Copilot may include a disclaimer about the accuracy of the generated data. A disclaimer for this data would note that the area codes are placeholders and not guaranteed to be the actual area codes for each state. Repeating a point we made in Chapter 7, Copilot is working only from the data it was trained on. It is not going out and checking to ensure that the data it returns is correct or up-to-date. You must always remember to cross-check results if you need accurate, timely data. You cannot assume that the values provided through Copilot are current and correct.

When you ask Copilot to generate data in this way, you may occasionally encounter two other types of issues.

First, depending on the prompt and amount of data you request, Copilot might return only a portion of the data. This will usually be enough to get you started but not a complete set. For example, if the query left out the *all 50* part and was just "Create a mapping of states to area codes where the key is the state abbreviation and the value is an array of codes with max 10," Copilot might return only a few records:

```
state_area_codes = {
    "CA": [213, 310, 415, 510, 530, 559, 619, 626, 650, 661],
    "NY": [212, 315, 347, 516, 518, 585, 607, 631, 646, 716],
    "TX": [210, 214, 254, 281, 325, 346, 361, 409, 430, 432],
    "FL": [305, 321, 352, 386, 407, 561, 727, 754, 772, 786],
    "IL": [217, 224, 309, 312, 331, 618, 630, 708, 773, 815],
    "PA": [215, 267, 412, 484, 570, 610, 717, 724, 814, 878],
    "OH": [216, 234, 330, 380, 419, 440, 513, 567, 614, 740],
    "GA": [229, 404, 470, 478, 678, 706, 762, 770, 912, 943],
    "NC": [252, 336, 704, 743, 828, 910, 919, 980, 984, 336],
    "MI": [231, 248, 269, 313, 517, 586, 616, 734, 810, 906]
}
```

If you encounter a situation like this, you can prompt Copilot to generate the rest of the data via a prompt like "Create a mapping of the remaining states to area codes where the key is the state abbreviation and the value is an array of area codes with max 10." We added the term *remaining* to tell Copilot to pick up where it left off.

Second, when having Copilot generate data, you may be notified that the generated data matches data in a public repository. If you have the setting enabled to block generated code that matches public code, Copilot's complete response to your prompt will be blocked.

In general, data such as this is less likely to be proprietary. If there is not a concern about license violations, you can usually tweak your prompt to have the AI generate the data with a different dimension. It may be as easy as changing the amount of data requested, as in "create a mapping of the states to area codes where the key is the state abbreviation and the value is an array of area codes with max 5." Note the change in the max value from 10 to 5.

Finally, let's look at one other way you can interact with Copilot. While not as common as the other interfaces we've discussed, the GitHub command line can also leverage Copilot to help you understand and generate answers.

GitHub CLI and Copilot

If you use the GitHub CLI, you can use a couple of subcommands with Copilot. At the time of this writing, there are four.

Before being able to use Copilot with the GitHub CLI, some basic prerequisites have to be met:

- The GitHub CLI has to be installed.
- You must have authenticated to GitHub, such as through the `gh auth` command.
- The Copilot extension must be installed in the GitHub CLI via the `gh extension install github/gh-copilot` command.

After going through the prerequisites, the CLI commands listed in Table 8-1 will be available to you. The table also shows the purpose of each command.

Table 8-1. Copilot commands through the GitHub CLI

Command	Function
alias	Generate shell-specific aliases for convenience
config	Configure options
explain	Explain a command
suggest	Suggest a command

As an example of using the CLI with Copilot, we can ask it to explain a Unix command via a simple invocation of the GitHub CLI like gh `copilot explain "ps -aux"`. The output is shown here:

```
Welcome to GitHub Copilot in the CLI!
version 1.1.0 (2025-02-10)

I'm powered by AI, so surprises and mistakes are possible. Make sure
 to verify any generated code or suggestions, and share feedback so
 that we can learn and improve. For more information, see
 https://gh.io/gh-copilot-transparency

Explanation:

  • ps is used to display information about running processes.
    • -aux is a combination of flags:
      • -a displays information about all processes.
      • -u displays detailed information about the processes.
      • -x includes processes that do not have a controlling terminal.
```

In some cases, you may be asked to select additional options as a follow-up. For example, if you ask Copilot via the CLI to suggest a command to install Python, there can be additional queries from the AI to make sure it provides you with the best response. Here's the output and interactions based on an initial command of gh `copilot suggest "install python"`:

```
Welcome to GitHub Copilot in the CLI!
version 1.1.0 (2025-02-10)

...

? What kind of command can I help you with?  [Use arrows to move,
 type to filter]
> generic shell command
  gh command
  git command

Suggestion:

  sudo apt-get install python3

? Select an option  [Use arrows to move, type to filter]
  Copy command to clipboard
> Explain command
  Execute command
  Revise command
  Rate response
  Exit

Explanation:
```

- sudo is used to run a command with elevated rights, allowing changes to system files.
- apt-get is the package management command for Debian-based systems.
  - install is the sub-command that specifies you want to install a package.
    - python3 is the specific package you want to install, which provides the Python 3 interpreter.

Notice after the original command, there were several follow-up interactions with Copilot. We were given the option to select the context for the command (generic shell, CLI, or Git). Once we selected the shell command, Copilot provided the suggestion. We were then given the option to copy the command, have Copilot explain it, execute it, etc. Selecting the `explain` option provides an explanation like the one in the previous example.

Conclusion

In this chapter, we looked at a set of areas where AI assistance may not be the first option that comes to mind but can prove helpful. Copilot's capabilities can be put to good use in each of these areas.

When you need to interact with databases, Copilot can provide code-completion suggestions and generate full sets of code for SQL just as for more typical programming languages. Copilot can be especially helpful for creating stored procedures and optimizing programming.

Besides generating traditional code that tells the system how to do something, Copilot can also be used to generate declarative specifications that outline the desired end result. A good example of this is using Copilot to help declare Kubernetes specifications. Given a suitable prompt, Copilot can generate the YAML definition for any of the standard Kubernetes objects. In addition, Copilot can tell the user how to use the specification with Kubernetes and even turn it into code with API calls. This kind of help greatly simplifies working with the complexities of different frameworks and their representations in YAML.

Copilot's capabilities can also automate another task that frequently frustrates developers: creating regular expressions. Given a suitable prompt, Copilot will generate the necessary combination of characters for whatever type of matching syntax you need and produce examples of how to validate.

In support of basic testing or demoing, Copilot can create a set of data for the code to operate against. This can be mapped data with keys and values as defined through a prompt or defined from context. The data is not guaranteed to be correct or timely and may be more susceptible to matching public examples, so additional diligence is needed when working with the results.

Finally, in this chapter, we looked at the capabilities that have been added to the GitHub CLI to work with Copilot. Through the CLI application gh, Copilot can help by suggesting commands to do tasks like install applications, as well as by explaining what commands and arguments do. This functionality is limited but will likely expand to other capabilities in the future.

In the next chapter, we'll look further into how Copilot's capabilities are integrated into another core application that users rely on—GitHub itself.

CHAPTER 9
Using Copilot in GitHub

Like many other key software development tools, AI has been integrated into the GitHub ecosystem through Copilot. This means you can chat with Copilot directly in GitHub as well as use the AI capabilities to work directly with key functionality like pull requests and issues.

In this chapter, we'll survey how Copilot has been integrated into GitHub and explain how you can effectively leverage its power when working in GitHub. We'll cover the following:

- Using Copilot Chat with GitHub repositories
- Using Copilot for change workflows
- Copilot and pull requests
- Copilot and GitHub issues

GitHub Interface over Time

As with all information in this book, screenshots and information about what items are present and where they are located is current at the time of writing. Like Copilot integration in the IDEs, integration in GitHub may evolve over time.

To get started, let's explore how Copilot is integrated with your repositories in GitHub.

Using Chat with GitHub Repositories

A chat interface like the ones available in IDEs that integrate with Copilot is also available in GitHub. There is a general one at *https://github.com/copilot*. Also, on the Code page of your repositories, you'll see a Copilot icon in the top row of controls (as shown in Figure 9-1). Clicking the icon will take you to an immersive (full-screen) Copilot chat interface for that project. We'll circle back to that in a moment.

Clicking the drop-down arrow next to the Copilot icon brings up a menu of choices (also shown in Figure 9-1). Of these, the one we're interested in is the Assistive option.

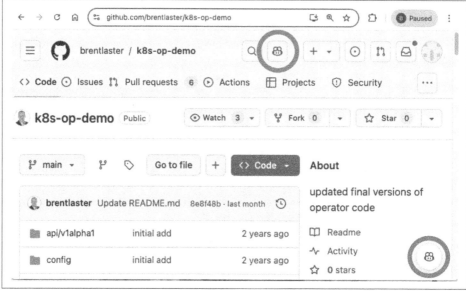

Figure 9-1. Copilot icons in a repository page

Clicking the Assistive menu option brings up a chat interface, pre-populated with suggested questions you can ask about the selected repository, as shown in Figure 9-2.

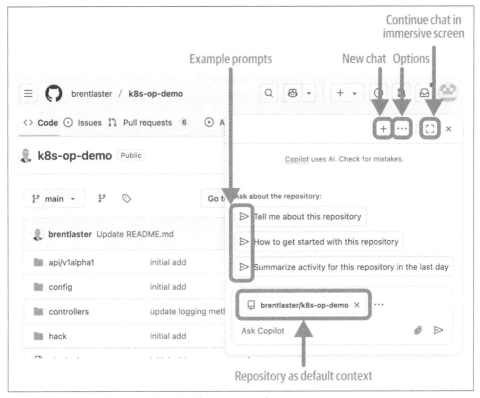

Figure 9-2. Repository questions in the assistive chat

Chat Context in GitHub

New assistive chat instances will be populated with questions relevant to the active GitHub item when the chat is opened. For example, if you are working on a GitHub issue and open a new chat instance, the chat instance will be populated with questions like "Summarize this issue" and "What are the next steps?" Selecting one of these pre-populated questions will fill in a much longer prompt, tailored to specifically get better information.

Choosing the first question, which asks Copilot to tell you about this repository, queries Copilot with a ready-made prompt, as shown here:

```
Please provide answers to the following questions in separate
paragraphs:

 - Provide insights on the purpose of this repository. Please also
provide a summary of its README if it exists.
 - Provide detailed analysis on features and technologies used in
this repository if it contains implementation of software system of
```

Using Chat with GitHub Repositories | 225

```
any kind. Otherwise, provide an analysis on contents of this
repository instead.

Additional guidance:
 - Provide a heading for each paragraph, formatted in bold.
 - Keep your analysis succinct and conversational.
 - Do not repeat or list the context details in your final response.
 - Provide a concise synthesis of the information, avoiding
unnecessary repetition.
```

Copilot's response to the prompt looks like this:

```
Purpose of the Repository

This repository provides a basic example of implementing a
Kubernetes operator. It serves as a training resource for
creating Kubernetes operators using standard toolkits.
The README explains how to set up and run the operator,
including steps for deploying it to a Kubernetes cluster,
testing it, and modifying its API definitions. The project adheres
to Kubernetes' Operator pattern, aiming to synchronize resources
to their desired state.

Features and Technologies Used

The repository is built using Go and utilizes Kubernetes operator
development principles. It leverages Kubebuilder to create
controllers that follow the Kubernetes Operator pattern. The
operator interacts with Kubernetes clusters, managing Custom
Resource Definitions (CRDs) and ensuring the cluster state matches
the desired configuration. Additionally, the repository provides
Makefile targets for tasks such as building, deploying, and
uninstalling the operator.
```

This type of information can be especially useful for someone onboarding or needing to assume responsibility for this codebase.

When interacting, if you prefer an immersive chat experience, you can click the square icon in the upper right to be taken to a full-screen chat session. The immersive option resembles the IDE chat interface, with the repository set as the default context. The immersive option is the same screen you get if you just click the Copilot icon (rather than the arrow next to it) shown in Figure 9-1.

Clicking the icon or going from the Assistive screen to the Immersive one both open *https://github.com/copilot*. The chat interface on that page will have the current repository set as the default context. Figure 9-3 shows the immersive/default screen for Copilot Chat in GitHub.

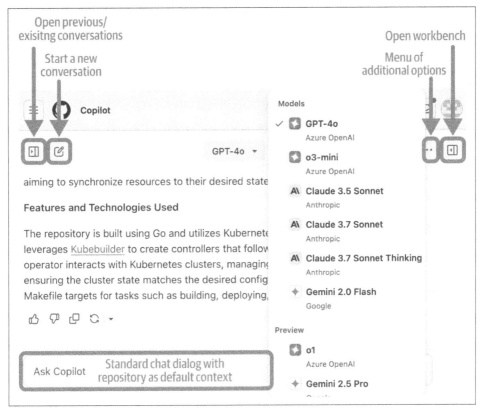

Figure 9-3. Immersive chat

The controls in the main text entry area of the dialog operate nearly the same as the controls in the corresponding area in the IDE chat dialog. One difference is that the Submit arrow button does not have any additional options since we don't have chat participants or other elements to submit the query to.

It's worth spending a few minutes to talk about the other controls and options available in the chat dialog in GitHub. (Some of these may not be visible unless you're in the immersive view.)

The control in the upper left that looks like a square with a strip and right-pointing arrow in it is for opening previous or existing conversations. Clicking this shows a list of all separate conversations you've had in this chat and allows you to select and switch between them.

The next icon to the right that looks like a square with a pencil in it opens up a new conversation.

The control on the far right is identified as *Open Workbench*. At the time of this writing, there doesn't seem to be any real documentation on what this feature is supposed to do.

Another control shows up after you enter your first prompt in a chat conversation: the Share button. This button makes it simple to share a Copilot chat for purposes like peer coding/troubleshooting, adding insights into a pull request, etc.

To share the current conversation and future messages, you click the Share button in the upper right and then click Share again in the dialog that comes up (Figure 9-4).

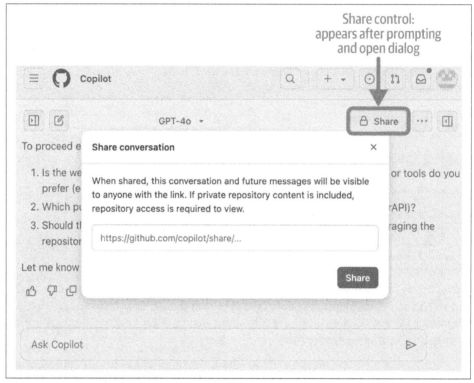

Figure 9-4. A share operation

After this, you can click the drop-down arrow next to the Share button and copy the link for the shared conversation to provide to others (Figure 9-5). You can also unshare if you want.

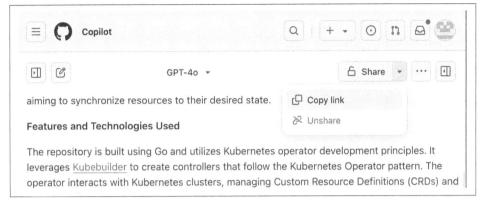

Figure 9-5. Getting the share link

Finally, the Menu control (represented as three dots) to the right of that brings up a menu for accessing advanced functionality, as shown in Figure 9-6.

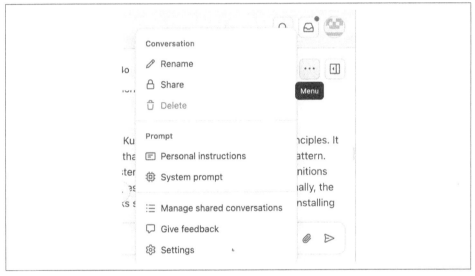

Figure 9-6. Chat menu

The menu items are as follows:

Conversation
  The items in this section are self-explanatory, allowing you to rename, delete, or share the current conversation.

Personal instructions
  These let you customize the way Copilot Chat responds to you on GitHub. Clicking this brings up a dialog where you can specify preferences like language, tone,

or coding style (e.g., "Always answer in Python" or "Be concise"). These instructions override any repository or organization-level settings and apply to all your Copilot Chat sessions on GitHub.

System prompt
This option displays the text of the system prompt that is set for Copilot in GitHub.

Manage shared conversations
This option brings up a list of conversations you've shared and allows you to get a link or unshare each one.

Give feedback
This one is self-explanatory.

Settings
Selecting this option takes you to your personal settings for Copilot.

The chat interface is our gateway for conversing with the AI about the repository, but it is also a trigger for the repository to be indexed. We've discussed how indexes are created and used in the IDE with Copilot. Separate indexes are created for repositories on the GitHub side. The goal, however, is the same: provide Copilot with a much deeper, richer understanding of the repository. The way indexing works for GitHub repositories is described in more detail in the following sidebar.

Indexing in GitHub

When you open GitHub Copilot Chat in a repository on GitHub, the repository is automatically indexed in the background. This process enables Copilot Chat to provide context-aware answers about your codebase, such as explaining code structure or logic, referencing relevant sections of your repository. No manual step is required to trigger this indexing—simply opening Copilot Chat with the repository selected as context will start the process.

Here are some key points about indexing:

Automatically triggered
Indexing starts automatically when you open Copilot Chat with a repository context on GitHub.

Speed
The initial indexing is fast, typically taking only a few seconds to a minute, even for large repositories.

Continuous updates
Once indexed, the repository's index is kept automatically up-to-date, typically within seconds of starting a new conversation.

No indexing limits
> There are no limits to the number of repositories you can index, and this applies to all Copilot subscription levels, including the free tier.

No model training
> The indexed data is not used for model training; it is used only to improve Copilot's ability to answer questions about the code in your repository.

Access control
> Only users with access to the repository can benefit from its indexed context in Copilot Chat.

The chat interface and indexing functionality are useful for understanding and diving deeper into learning about repositories and other objects in GitHub. This can be beneficial for those needing to onboard to a new project or assume responsibility for making changes and fixes.

However, when it comes to working with changes and fixes in GitHub, we can leverage Copilot in other ways to make our coding workflows more efficient and less time-consuming.

Using Copilot for Change Workflows

Copilot provides useful capabilities for code changes—from proposing fixes and helping update issues and pull requests to reviewing code. In this section, we'll take an example of a problem and see all the ways we can put Copilot to use in helping us correct it.

To start, we'll use an example security issue. We have code with a set of database queries that are vulnerable to SQL injections because of the way they are constructed. This sort of issue can be identified easily with GitHub's code scanning done through its CodeQL application (*https://codeql.github.com*).

Code-scanning alerts from a problematic repository are shown in Figure 9-7.

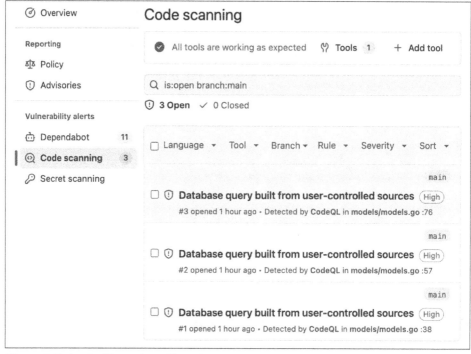

Figure 9-7. A set of issues in coding scans

232 | Chapter 9: Using Copilot in GitHub

Let's pick one of these problems to work with. We'll use the last one. Opening up the
link from the "Code scanning" panel, we see more details about the particular alert
(Figure 9-8).

Figure 9-8. Code-scanning alert

It would be nice if we could have Copilot summarize this alert for us. Unfortunately,
Copilot doesn't have this capability at the time of this writing. However, we do have a
button provided in the same screen to create an issue (as seen in the top right of
Figure 9-8).

Enabling Issues

The Create issue button will be available only if Issues have been
enabled in the repository's Settings.

If we click the Create issue button, we'll get a basic GitHub issue created with a title and a link to the scanning alert, as shown in Figure 9-9. (A warning also results, which is useful, but it's not a concern for what we're doing in this example.)

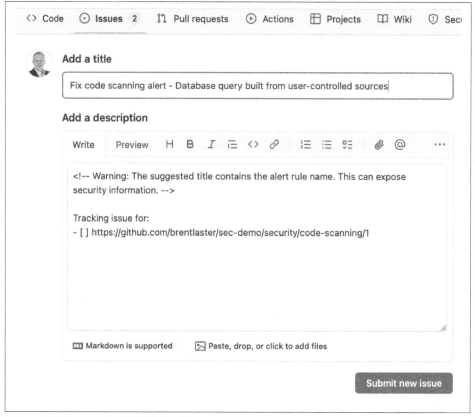

Figure 9-9. A generated draft for the issue

Clicking the Submit new issue button will complete the initial issue creation (Figure 9-10).

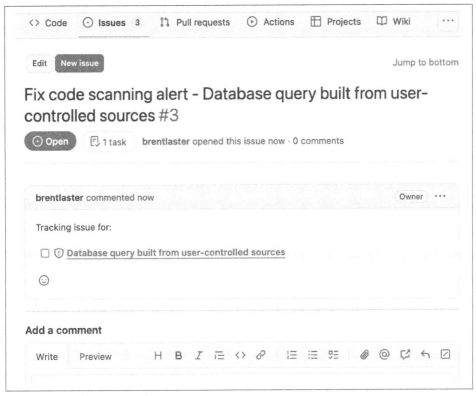

Figure 9-10. The generated issue

After this, if we return to the alert page (Figure 9-11), we can see that it reports that it is "Tracked by #3". The #3 refers to GitHub issue #3 in this repository.

You may have also noticed the banner in the box underneath that mentions "Copilot Autofix for CodeQL" along with a Generate fix button. *Copilot Autofix* is a feature that integrates with GitHub's code-scanning tools (like CodeQL) to analyze your code, identify issues, and create fix suggestions using Copilot.

Figure 9-11. Alert page detail

Clicking the Generate fix button causes Copilot to produce suggested code changes to correct the issues, as shown in Figure 9-12.

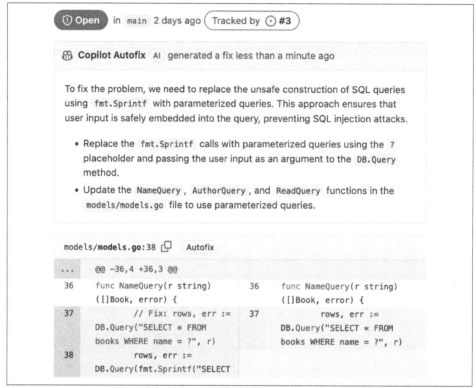

Figure 9-12. A suggested fix from Copilot

At the end of the suggested code changes is a Commit change button. Clicking it sets up a push to a new branch (by default) with autogenerated entries for the branch name and commit message. To ensure this is tied back to the issue we opened for this change, we'll add the extended description `fixes #3`. The commit dialog is shown in Figure 9-13.

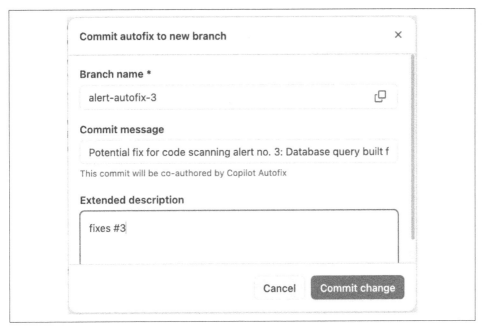

Figure 9-13. Commit setup for autofix

Completing the commit automatically opens a draft pull request that includes running the CodeQL tool again to verify whether the issues are fixed (passing status). In the next section, we'll dive a little deeper into how Copilot can help us with managing pull requests like the one for this change.

Using Copilot with Pull Requests

GitHub pull requests are a tried-and-true method of managing merges in GitHub among multiple repositories or between branches in the same repository. The pull requests offer a means of collaboration to consolidate and vet changes from the source. They also insulate the merge target from bad code by facilitating gates like code reviews and runs of GitHub Actions workflows.

But they're not without their challenges. One of those challenges can be getting and understanding the collection of changes and conversations that are happening in a pull request as it is being worked on. Fortunately, Copilot can provide some help.

Let's pick up with our previous example of security vulnerabilities within our repository that have been addressed in another branch. We now want to merge these fixes back to our production branch (*main* in this case) by using the pull-request process.

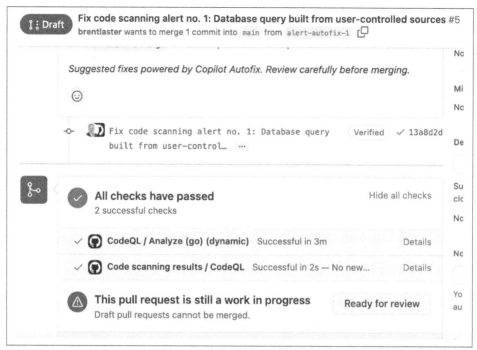

Figure 9-14. Draft pull request from autofix

When we're ready, we can change the draft pull request into one that's ready for review by clicking the "Ready for review" button. After that, we can go through the usual pull-request processes including adding reviewers.

Having Copilot Review Pull Requests

Copilot itself can be added as an automated reviewer to provide feedback on changes. Here's what that looks like. In the Reviewers section of the pull request, you simply click the user area and you'll see Copilot shown as a reviewer option (Figure 9-15).

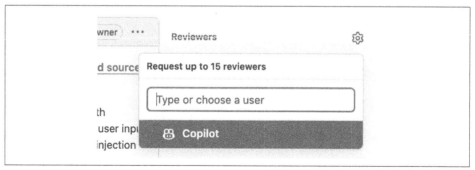

Figure 9-15. Adding Copilot as a reviewer on the pull request

After Copilot has time to review the code, it will post results back to the pull request, as seen in Figure 9-16. In this instance, Copilot had no feedback to offer. This makes sense since Copilot also produced the suggested fix originally.

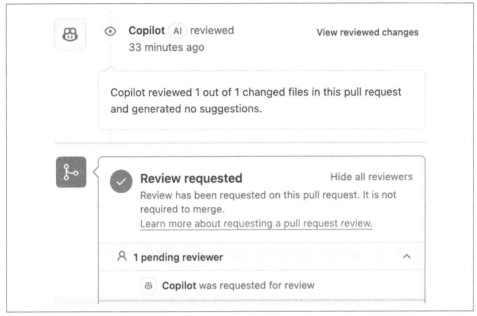

Figure 9-16. Copilot's review

At this point, we're ready to merge the pull request. As a final check, or if we needed to provide an explanation to someone else, we can also ask Copilot to summarize this pull request. We have the buttons to open Copilot chat at the top of the page and also one that is *floating*, usually toward the bottom right (Figure 9-17).

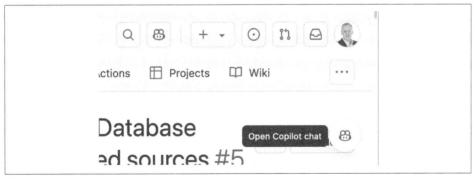

Figure 9-17. Multiple ways to open Copilot chat

You can select one of these to open a chat session. With the session open, we can ask Copilot for tasks related to the pull request, such as "Summarize this pull request" (Figure 9-18).

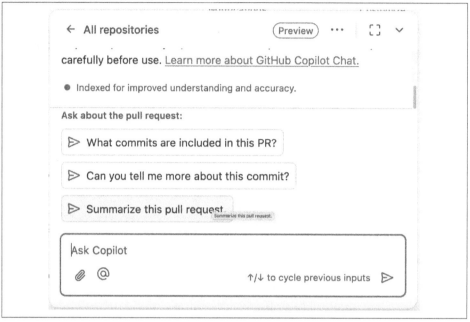

Figure 9-18. Asking Copilot to summarize the pull request

Copilot produces a short summary of the pull-request content that is easily consumable (Figure 9-19).

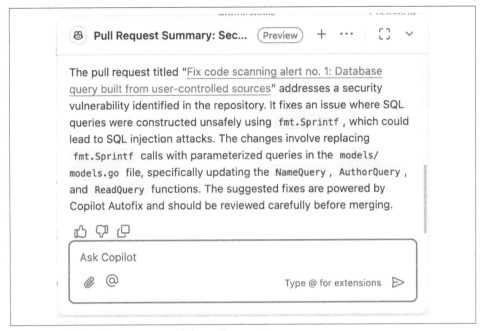

Figure 9-19. Copilot summary of the pull request

Let's look at one more example of how Copilot can help with pull requests: a shortcut method for creating them.

Leveraging Copilot to Simplify Initiating Pull Requests

Assume that in the same repository we've been working in, we create and push fixes for *all three* alerts into a different branch named *dev*. Suppose we want to create a new pull request to merge the *dev* branch into *main*.

We could certainly go through the pull requests menu and follow the steps to create another one. However, with Copilot, we can simplify that process down to a single click. Since most locations and operations in GitHub can be done via visiting a URL, we can ask Copilot to generate a suitable URL for us. To do that, we can open up the Copilot chat interface and use a prompt like the following:

```
Create a link to click on to open a new pull request to merge the
dev branch into main.
```

Afterward, Copilot responds with a link in the chat output, as shown in Figure 9-20. Note that Copilot is only generating a link that you could enter as well.

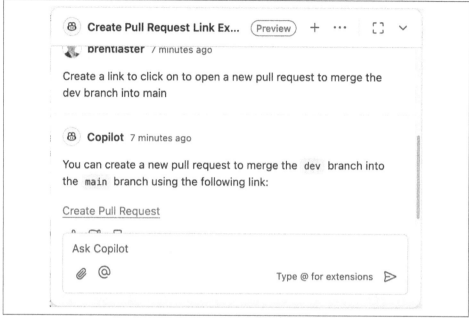

Figure 9-20. A generated link for the pull request

With the link conveniently generated, we can click it to open up the new pull request with the *base* and *compare* components already set up as needed. But beyond just making it easier to create the pull request, we can also have Copilot generate a summary for it based on the changes. Figure 9-21 shows how to do this by clicking the Copilot icon in the description area and then selecting the item to generate a summary. (Note that this is currently only available in paid Copilot plans.)

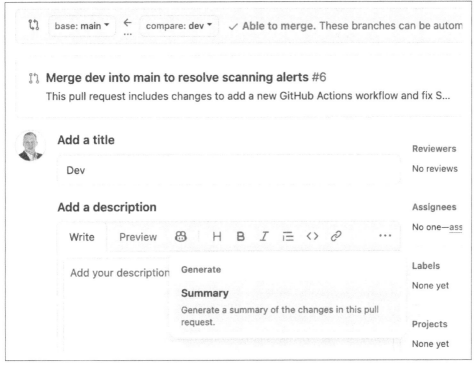

Figure 9-21. A pull request generated through the link

After clicking the control, Copilot will generate a summary of your changes in the description area. The format will be in Markdown and can be edited. Figure 9-22 shows an example of what the summary looks like after the pull request is created. The comments will show up as coming from you even though they were generated by the AI. Details on each change (as well as links to the changed files) are included.

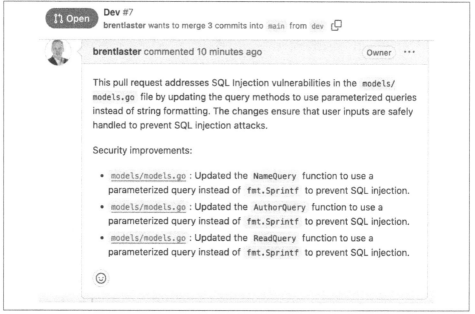

Figure 9-22. Copilot-generated pull-request summary

> **Generating URLs for Other Tasks**
>
> While we had Copilot create a link for a new pull request in this section, you can use that same approach on any action where GitHub provides a corresponding direct URL.

If we need or want to further explore the details of a change, we can also leverage Copilot to help with the exploration.

Exploring Code Changes with Copilot

In the pull request we've been working with, Copilot has supplied links to the changes between the two branches. If we want to further explore a change or set of changes in a file, we can click those links or switch directly to the "Files changed" tab to view the differences (Figure 9-23).

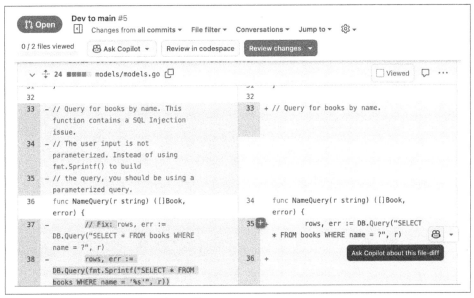

Figure 9-23. Files changed in the pull request

In this tab of the pull request are two links to open Copilot. The one in the lower right is the standard one that opens up a Copilot Chat interface. The one at the top labeled Ask Copilot (next to the "Review changes" button) automatically attaches the current file to the chat context and opens the chat dialog (Figure 9-24).

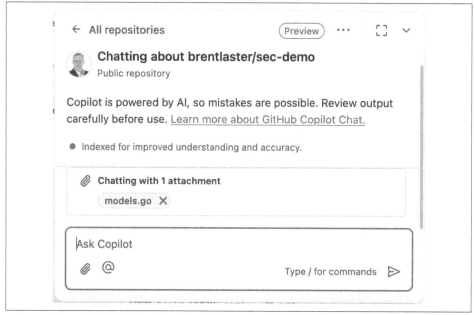

Figure 9-24. Dialog from Ask Copilot

Adding the file as context sets up the context for any subsequent prompts in this dialog to be answered based on the file *models.go*. For example, you can ask Copilot in this dialog to "Summarize the changes in this file," resulting in it giving you info on the file used with the context (Figure 9-25).

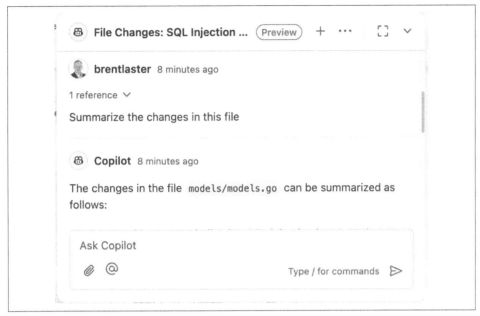

Figure 9-25. File changes from the context of Ask Copilot

There is also a third, sometimes hidden, Copilot access link in a file diff like this. If you scroll up near the start of the selected diff, you will see a small, floating Copilot icon with a drop-down arrow next to it. Clicking this icon gives you two options, Explain and Attach to current thread (Figure 9-26).

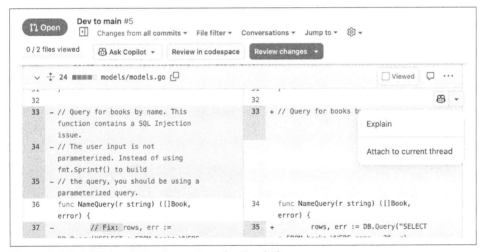

Figure 9-26. Additional Copilot options for the diff

The Explain option is similar to what we've seen before with Copilot's explain functionality. The Attach to current thread option allows us to set this specific diff as the context for Copilot chat. For example, if we select the Attach to current thread option referencing the diff shown in Figure 9-26, then when we next open the chat dialog for Copilot, we can see that it is referencing the single change starting at line 33 as the context rather than the entire file (Figure 9-27).

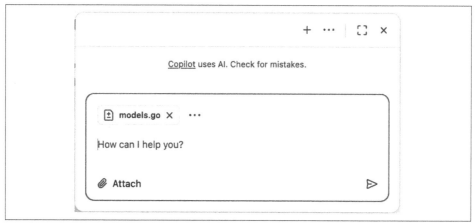

Figure 9-27. Diff-specific context

It's worth noting that we can click Conversation options (displayed as three dots) in the upper right of the diff window to also access some Copilot functionality (Figure 9-28).

Figure 9-28. Accessing Copilot from the Conversation options menu (displayed as three dots)

Both options add the file to the chat context as the Ask Copilot button does.

Lastly in this chapter, let's look at how Copilot can assist with another common GitHub coding aid: GitHub issues.

Using Copilot with GitHub Issues

Copilot has built-in functionality to also summarize GitHub issues. It does this by using tools (like GitHub's own APIs) to parse the issue's content. This includes the issue's body, title, comments, and even linked pull requests (if they exist). The goal is to create a summary overview of the main points you need to be aware of. Depending on the extent of information available in the issue, the summary will typically include the primary problem, the components that are affected, what the functionality should be, and potential fixes.

These summaries provide the following benefits:

Time savings
    Allowing you to quickly understand the core points of an issue without having to spend inordinate amounts of time dealing with long discussions

Better communication
    Providing clear summaries to go along with related tasks or updates at all levels

Efficient triage
    Allowing for better prioritization of GitHub issues based on clarity of severity and impact, and fix complexity surfaced through the summary

Reviewing for Accuracy

As with any output from AI, it is still ultimately up to the user to ensure that the summary information is accurate. Copilot's issue summaries may miss some nuances and/or details that might be important.

Let's work with an issue related to the database query security problem we were using in the preceding section. We can bring up the GitHub Copilot chat screen and provide prompts to get information or help with the issue. Figure 9-29 shows an example of prompting Copilot to Summarize this issue.

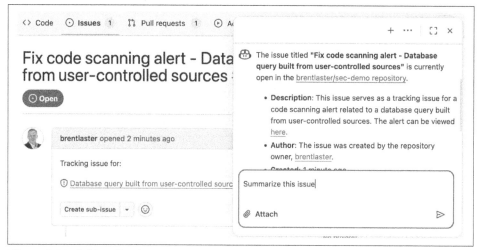

Figure 9-29. Asking Copilot to summarize an issue

We can prompt for more details, ask about the main points, or even get Copilot to suggest next steps. Figure 9-30 shows an example of asking Copilot to "Suggest next steps for this issue."

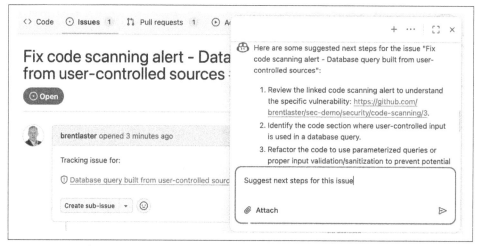

Figure 9-30. Asking Copilot to suggest next steps for the issue

Since generative AI is not deterministic, the quality of the response can vary significantly in terms of detail. You may get more general instructions in some cases and more detailed ones in others.

Conclusion

In this chapter, we've covered the various integration points that Copilot has with the GitHub web interface. By having this direct integration, Copilot's utility is greatly extended and readily available when working with repositories and common GitHub mechanisms such as issues and pull requests.

The integration with GitHub is done mostly through Copilot's chat interface. A GitHub repository has multiple places to invoke the chat dialog and converse with Copilot by using natural language. If you are working on an issue, a pull request, or a fix and start up a new Copilot chat session, Copilot can identify that as the context and offer relevant questions as a starting point.

For more specific responses tailored to one or more files, you can add files as context in a chat. When looking at a change in a pull-request code diff, you can also add individual files or even tell Copilot to reference only part of a file with a particular fix when it generates its responses.

Copilot can also summarize changes made in a pull request as an overall set of comments. Those summary comments will include links to specific changes and allow you to reduce the work of creating a pull request. It can also assist with summarizing and answering questions based on GitHub issues.

Finally, it's worth noting that Copilot can be added and participate as a reviewer on pull requests. Acting as an automated reviewer, Copilot can provide feedback and suggestions in the body of the pull request just as a human reviewer would do.

In the next chapter, we'll look at how to extend the functionality of Copilot and integrate other tools with it through creating Copilot Extensions.

CHAPTER 10
Extending Copilot's Functionality

GitHub Copilot is an amazingly useful tool. It can be made even more useful by extending its capabilities through integration with other tools. This includes ones you can write. The mechanisms for doing this are called *extensions*.

Copilot extensions enhance the functionality of GitHub Copilot by tailoring it to specific use cases or environments. For example, extensions can integrate custom or third-party applications with Copilot through the chat interface. As an example, you can install a Copilot Docker extension (*https://oreil.ly/QS54S*) and then ask questions via chat like "@Docker, how do I containerize this project?"

In this chapter, we'll examine what extensions for GitHub Copilot are and how to find and work with public ones from the marketplace. Then we'll progress to understanding details about the various types, how they work, and their advantages and disadvantages. And we'll cover some details on simple, yet useful, implementation examples. But before we cover those topics, we need to clarify some possibly confusing terminology.

Copilot Extensions Versus VS Code Extensions for Copilot

Extensions for Copilot's functionality can be implemented for one of two different targets. They can be engineered to work on any platform where Copilot Chat is supported (IDEs, GitHub.com, etc.), independent of the platform. Or they can be targeted for VS Code to leverage its underlying functions and only run on that platform (or on another IDE if ported).

Throughout this chapter, we'll use the terms *VS Code extensions for Copilot* or *chat participants* when referring to the ones implemented via VS Code. For the *native* Copilot ones (implemented to be independent of the platform), we'll use the shorter term *Copilot extensions*.

In both cases, the extension's functionality is surfaced through Copilot's chat interface. VS Code extensions for Copilot simply utilize its functionality for both hosting and execution. Copilot extensions require a separately configured and dedicated GitHub App to bridge between the chat interface and the backend code.

We'll be discussing the details of implementation and configuration for both types of extensions later in this chapter. That will include information on what GitHub Apps are and how they are used with Copilot extensions. But, first, let's learn more about what Copilot extensions are in general.

Server-Based and Client-Based Extensions

It may be helpful to think of Copilot extensions as *server-based*, in the sense of needing to communicate back to the app running on the GitHub side to function (although that's not an official description). Likewise, VS Code extensions for Copilot could be thought of as *client-based* since they function utilizing the APIs of the VS Code client where they are installed.

What Are Copilot Extensions?

Copilot has a framework of APIs and lower-level capabilities that underlie its user-facing functionality. That framework can be used by third parties and users to extend Copilot's capabilities. This framework allows other applications to provide their services through Copilot Chat directly to the user. As the user, you get the benefit of being able to invoke and converse with the other tooling, similar to the way you interact with the Copilot AI out of the box.

Extensions have multiple use cases, as noted in Copilot's documentation (*https:// oreil.ly/B7yAU*). They include the following:

Querying documentation
    Allowing Copilot Chat to query a third-party documentation service to find information about a specific topic.

AI-assisted coding
    Using a third-party AI model to provide code suggestions.

Data retrieval
    A Copilot extension can allow Copilot Chat to query a third-party data service to retrieve information about a specific topic.

Action execution
    Allowing Copilot Chat to execute a specific action, such as posting to a message board or updating a tracking item in an external system.

Think of using Copilot extensions as giving Copilot Chat additional knowledge of another application or set of data, and adding specialized skills that you can invoke to help when needed.

Copilot extensions are built to provide cross-platform compatibility, app management, and support. They work anywhere that chat does. They can be private, public and shareable, and listed on GitHub Marketplace, if desired. In fact, the marketplace is a good place to start learning about extensions and the public ones available to use.

Getting Copilot Extensions from the Marketplace

You can write your own extensions (as you'll see later in this chapter), and organizations or companies can create *private* extensions. In addition, *public* extensions from third-party companies and organizations are already available. To see these, go to GitHub Marketplace (*https://github.com/marketplace*) and select Copilot in the left column. Figure 10-1 shows the main screen for Copilot extensions in the marketplace.

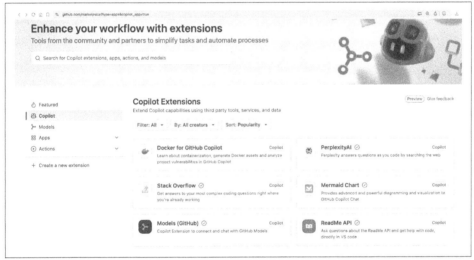

Figure 10-1. Copilot extensions on the marketplace

From here, we'll pick the PerplexityAI extension. This extension allows for gathering responses through real-time web searches. Clicking the link in the marketplace opens up the extension's details page with information about what the extension is and what it can do (Figure 10-2).

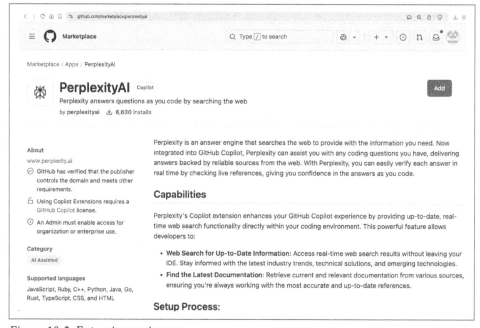

Figure 10-2. Extension main page

Clicking the Add button (in the upper right) or scrolling to the bottom takes you to the section of the page where you can install the extension (Figure 10-3). This one is free.

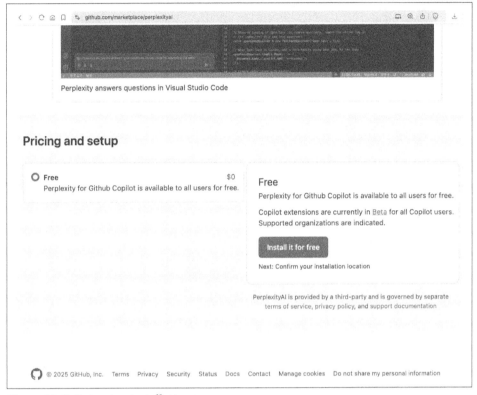

Figure 10-3. Extension installation page

Some extensions may require you to select the user or organization that will be
authorized to use the extension. You can see an example of that if you choose to
install the Docker extension (Figure 10-4). In the case of the PerplexityAI extension,
its functionality is general search, so it is usable for all repos associated with the user
who is installing it.

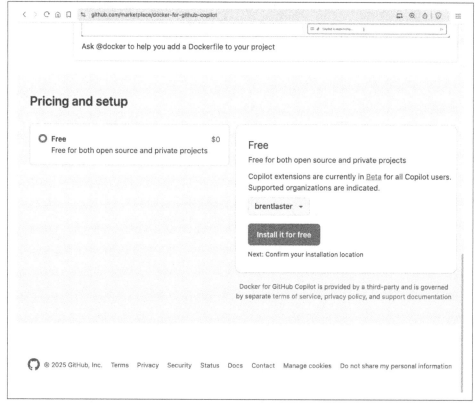

Figure 10-4. Installing the Docker extension with the user or organization selected

Most Copilot extensions get access to repositories and your account through the use
of a *GitHub App*. These are basically backend applications installed and authorized in
your GitHub account to work with your repositories. For Copilot extensions that use
an app, the app serves as the bridge between the chat interface and the code that
implements the extension's functionality. The app provides the access and control
layer between Copilot and the extension's operations.

You can see the app integration once you've done the initial install for the extension. You'll be asked to authorize the associated GitHub App for the account by authenticating to GitHub. After authorizing, you'll be taken to the configuration page for the installed app, as shown in Figure 10-5.

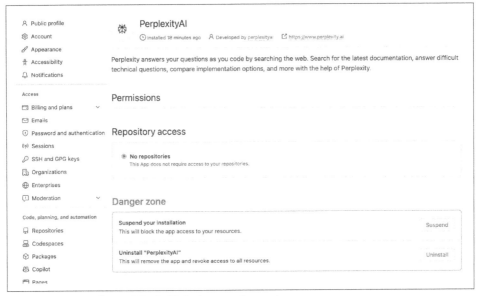

Figure 10-5. PerplexityAI's GitHub App configuration

On this page, you can select specific permissions for the app and/or specific repositories for the app to access. In the case of the app for the PerplexityAI extension, it simply applies to all repositories and does not have any specific permission requirements, so we are good to go. You can also suspend or uninstall the app from this page.

Changing App Configuration

If you later need to change the configuration settings for the app and are logged in, you can go to the applications portion of your settings (*https://oreil.ly/WOBZf*) to modify an installed app's configuration.

Getting Copilot Extensions from the Marketplace | 259

After the install and authorization steps are complete, start or restart any instances of applications where GitHub Copilot is active. Then, type the @ sign and the extension's name in the chat interface to start using the newly installed extension, as shown in Figure 10-6.

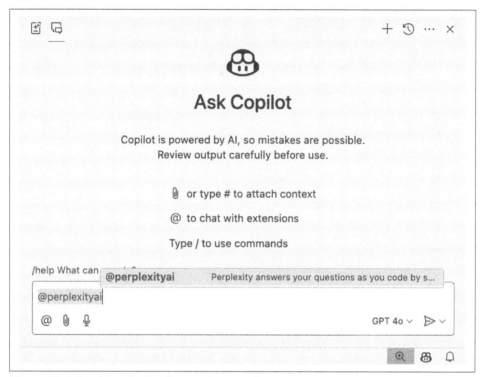

Figure 10-6. Invoking the PerplexityAI app in chat

The first time you attempt to use the new extension via the app after restarting, you may get prompted to authorize it—either for the selected workspace or for all workspaces (Figure 10-7).

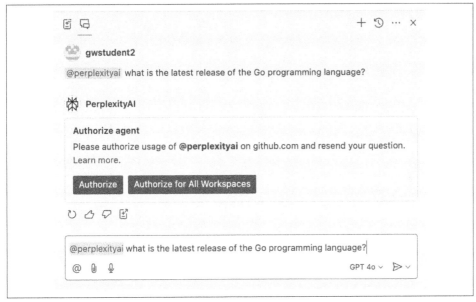

Figure 10-7. Authorization for workspace

This is done in a similar manner to the initial authorization. Once the authorization is completed, you can pose your prompt again, and you should be able to get a response (Figure 10-8).

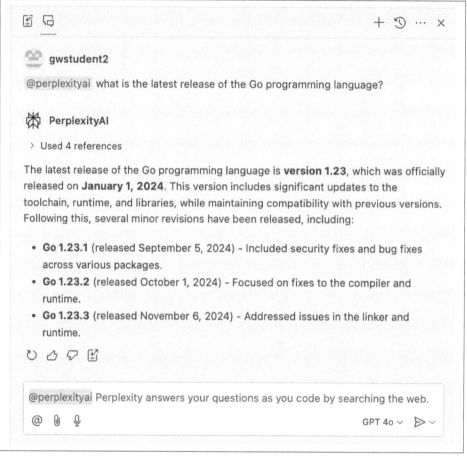

Figure 10-8. PerplexityAI response after authorization

The number of public Copilot extensions is growing regularly. If they fit with an application or purpose you need, they can be a useful option. But if you need functionality that is not already available or need an integration more directly with your data or processes, you may want to consider developing and using your own Copilot extension. To understand more about that option, let's first talk about the two *implementation* types of Copilot extensions that can exist.

Understanding Copilot Extension Implementation Types

Copilot extensions can be implemented as one of two types:

Agent
An extension implemented as an agent serves as a full AI assistant. This means it can handle complex chat conversations, execute custom code, and return very tailored responses.

Skillsets
An extension implemented as a skillset can invoke one or more API endpoints behind the scenes to retrieve specific information or perform basic actions.

You'll see examples of how to build each implementation type later in the chapter. But for now, let's level-set on the general advantages and disadvantages of each.

Agents are the original type of Copilot extension and can provide the most extensive functionality if you need complex or custom processing and integration. They provide full control but also can be complex to implement.

Skillsets make it easy to call other APIs or perform basic operations. They are simpler to implement while being more limited in what they can do and how much control they provide.

Table 10-1 compares the two implementation choices.

Table 10-1. Comparison of Copilot extension types

Attribute	Copilot agents	Copilot skillsets
Complexity	Requires more development effort to manage the entire user interaction flow response and response generation	Designed for easy integration with minimal setup
Control	Provides full control over how requests are processed and responses are generated	Limited control over the user interaction, focus is on data retrieval and basic actions
Use cases	Suitable for complex scenarios where you need to implement custom logic, integrate with other AI models, and manage conversation context	Straightforward tasks like fetching data from an external API or performing simple operations,
Interfaces available	All (GitHub, IDEs)	All (GitHub, IDEs)
Support	GitHub	GitHub

Now that you understand these types, we can look at implementation. The first step in that process is making sure you are clear on some of the building blocks when you are assembling a Copilot extension.

Assembling Building Blocks for Extensions

Building blocks are the components that need to be assembled to allow the extension to be accessed and function. At the core, these are the parts we need when working with a Copilot extension:

- A GitHub App with a specific endpoint that handles interactions between the extension and Copilot Chat.
- A server process capable of hosting the backend and making endpoints available.
- A backend implementation that provides the functionality for the extension. This functionality can involve calls to the LLM along with integration with external tools, services, or APIs.

Figure 10-9 shows an overview of the building blocks we'll be using to construct extensions.

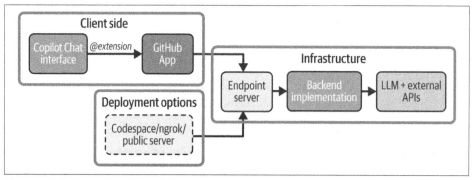

Figure 10-9. Overview of our building blocks

While GitHub apps and endpoint servers are required for agent and skillset extensions, those constructs are not unique to extensions. Next up is some clarification on how these are used for enabling extensions.

GitHub Apps

A *GitHub App* is a tool that integrates with GitHub to extend GitHub's functionality. It can do this in several ways:

- Automating tasks
- Integrating with APIs and webhooks
- Customizing the GitHub workflow

Once created, installed, and registered, a GitHub App can act, independently of the user, as an authorized process to do the type of operations described in the preceding list. The steps involve registering the app (including any manual configuration, if needed), writing any needed code for the functionality, and then setting it up to run via a webhook, callback URL, etc. The App also serves as a gateway for getting authorization to access resources.

Callback URL

In the context of GitHub Copilot extensions, a *callback URL* is a URL that your custom Copilot extension provides to GitHub. The URL serves as the destination where the system will redirect the user after successfully authenticating with your extension. It acts like a *return address* once the authorization is complete.

The app for the PerplexityAI extension discussed previously is a good example. After installing the extension, go to your GitHub profile, and, from the left menu, under Integrations, choose Applications. You'll then see the installed app for that extension (Figure 10-10).

Figure 10-10. PerplexityAI app installed via extension

Link to Install Applications

If you are logged into GitHub, you can also access the list of installed applications via the Installations page (*https://oreil.ly/WOBZf*).

For existing GitHub extensions that are available publicly or in your organization or enterprise, the app is installed and configured automatically as part of the extension's installation and authorization process. For extensions that you implement, you'll need to create and configure a new app as a part of the overall process. We'll cover the creation and configuration steps in more detail later in this chapter.

Next, let's talk about another important piece of how extensions work: the endpoint server.

Endpoint Server

In simplest terms, an agent or skillset Copilot extension can be viewed as an app that connects to an endpoint which handles interactions between the extension and Copilot Chat. The *endpoint* is the API for code that processes a chat input, does some processing, and then streams the output back to the chat. So, having the endpoint available is a key requirement for the flow.

In the case of an extension that you install from the marketplace or an enterprise/organization site, the server will have already been set up and configured. If you are creating your own extension, you need to have it hosted on a publicly accessible server (e.g., via deploying on a cloud service or tunneling). For example, you can use a simple service such as Cloudflare (*https://oreil.ly/m1eVi*) or ngrok (*https://ngrok.com*) to expose a public URL for development and testing.

Both of those services require signing up and then logging in to utilize. Another option, if you are using VS Code or a GitHub Codespace for development and testing, is to expose the port and enable port forwarding (*https://oreil.ly/jgyG3*). This method is free and suitable for use before converting to a formal location when the extension is made public. The key thing to remember if using this method is that the port's visibility must be changed to `public` from the default `private`.

While the app and endpoint provide a way to exchange information with the chat interface, the real work happens with the backend code that implements the endpoint. The rest of this chapter is devoted to looking at and understanding how to do these implementations, starting with creating an extension as an agent.

Implementing an Extension as an Agent

A Copilot Agent is a custom tool embedded in a Copilot extension. Agents augment the capabilities of Copilot by allowing you to build and integrate custom features into the Copilot Chat interface.

Copilot Agent Mode

In Chapter 4, we discussed Copilot's built-in *Agent mode* that allows it to autonomously create code and terminal commands repeatedly to achieve a goal. In this chapter, we're talking about agents again, but as separate functions built for use by extensions.

An agent implementation is appropriate when you need more control over how a request is processed or how a response is generated during a chat interaction. Agents can implement custom logic, integrate with other LLMs and the Copilot API, help with the context for chat conversations, and manage the interaction. But they are also more complex to create and maintain.

Performing a Basic Implementation

In this section, you'll see how to implement a basic but useful agent-based extension named `@meta-files`. Given a programming language in the prompt, our extension will generate example *.gitignore* and *.gitattributes* files. Alternatively, if the user provides an open source license name as part of the prompt, the extension will generate an example of the open source license. If the license has a placeholder for the user's name and the current year, the extension will attempt to fill those in. Finally, the extension will also provide some guidance on when that type of license is useful.

Examples of using the extension are shown in Figures 10-11 and 10-12. The prompts used to invoke the extension are shown in the upper right: `@meta-files Python` for Figure 10-11 and `@meta-files MIT` for Figure 10-12. The code is based on examples in the Copilot extensions (*https://oreil.ly/pWQcX*) and can be found in the book's GitHub repository (*https://oreil.ly/93ZY_*).

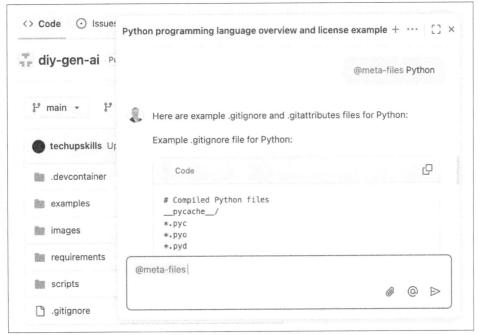

Figure 10-11. Extension generating meta files for Python

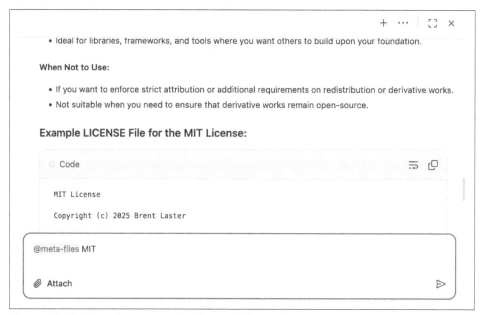

Figure 10-12. Extension generating license information

Figure 10-13 shows at a high level how an agent extension works. I'll have more to say about the individual pieces in the following sections.

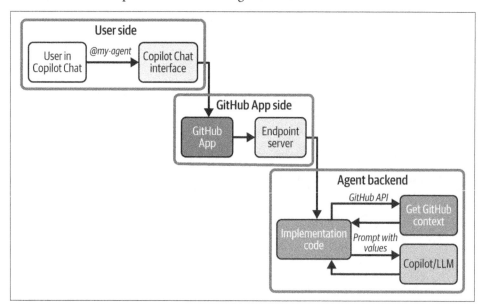

Figure 10-13. Agent extension overview

For the sake of brevity, we won't dive into all the code here. We'll just hit some key points. This example is written in JavaScript, but your extension can be written in nearly any modern language.

This simple example focuses on only two standard JavaScript files: *package.json* (*https://oreil.ly/vowZU*) and *index.js* (*https://oreil.ly/k16Kn*). Let's take a look at the *package.json* contents first. The contents are shown here:

```
{
  "name": "metafiles-extension",
  "private": "true",
  "description": "Generate metafiles for a GitHub repository",
  "scripts": {
    "start": "node index.js",
    "dev": "node --watch index.js"
  },
  "type": "module",
  "dependencies": {
    "@octokit/core": "^6.1.2",
    "express": "^4.19.2"
  }
}
```

The structure of this is standard boilerplate for this type of file. We could have multiple other fields, but we're keeping the example simple. The only pieces that warrant additional explanation are the dependencies.

Express (*https://expressjs.com*) is a simple, backend web application framework. It's designed to make it easy to build web apps and APIs with Node.js. When we create our agent extension, we are essentially creating a web app with an endpoint that is surfaced via the GitHub App.

The other dependency we're using, Octokit (*https://github.com/octokit*), is a set of libraries provided by GitHub to let code interact with its REST and GraphQL APIs. It facilitates programmatically automating tasks and managing repositories and allows you to manipulate GitHub resources like pull requests and issues in code. We use it here to help get and work with a token for the user's information.

The file with our main logic is *index.js*. You can look at the file in GitHub (*https://oreil.ly/GJW8z*) if you want to see the entire code. The logic at the top of the file does the necessary imports, starts an Express app, posts a welcome message, and then goes into the main processing.

The main processing uses Octokit to get a token, then moves into a standard cycle:

- Getting the payload coming to us from the chat interface (via the GitHub App)
- Augmenting the prompt to tell the AI what we're looking for

- Sending the prompt off to the underlying LLM to get a response from the AI
- Passing the response to the chat interface

The mechanics are fairly straightforward. The real magic happens where we augment the prompt to tell the AI what we're looking for. Here's the code for that part:

```
// Define the LLM's role and what it should look for and do

const messages = payload.messages;

messages.unshift({
  role: "system",
  content: "Search for a programming language name in the message
 from the user. If you find one, generate example .gitignore and
.gitattributes files for that programming language",
 });

messages.unshift({
  role: "system",
  content: "Search for an open source software license name, type,
 or abbreviation in the message from the user. If you find one,
 do the following: Provide a few key bullet points about the
 license and when it should/should not be used. Then generate an
 example LICENSE file for that license. If the example file contains
  the text [NAME] or [YOUR NAME], replace that text with " +
 user.data.name + ". If the LICENSE file contains the text [YEAR],
 replace [YEAR] with the current year.",
  })
```

We are adding content to the prompt we received from the chat to tell the LLM what we want it to look for and how to respond. This is the key to making an agent extension work—providing a detailed prompt to the LLM to tell it what we want it to pay attention to and the kind of output we require. Think of it as similar to interacting directly with a model like ChatGPT. The more details we can provide in our prompt conversation, the better response we can expect from the AI. The logic we use in our agent code to get the desired outcome really comes down to crafting a good prompt.

Crafting a Good Prompt

Any number of resources are available with guidance on crafting a good prompt. Ultimately, the best prompt is the one that works as you intend in terms of parsing out the right information and returning a meaningful response.

One simple approach to this is trying out and then refining your prompt through the Copilot Chat interface (or an AI model) directly first. Once you have found a prompt that works, you can add it into your extension's code.

With this basic setup, we have the core code we need for our extension. The necessary code for running this extension was created in a *nonproduction* environment. Taking this to production would require more implementation.

To help simplify the larger implementation for production, GitHub has made an SDK available that implements some of the core functionality needed for production extensions. At the time of this writing, the SDK is only an alpha release and only suitable for extensions implemented as agents. You can learn more about it in the sidebar.

> ### GitHub Copilot Extensions SDK
>
> To simplify some common tasks when building an extension as an agent, GitHub has provided an SDK. The *GitHub Copilot extensions SDK*, also known as the *Preview SDK*, is a tool designed to simplify and speed up implementation of GitHub Copilot extensions written as agents. The SDK can be used to automate common tasks such as the following:
>
> *Request payload verification*
> : Ensures that incoming requests are valid and secure
>
> *Payload parsing*
> : Simplifies the extraction of relevant data from requests
>
> *Response building*
> : Formats responses in a way compatible with Copilot Chat
>
> *Streamline API interactions*
> : Provides utilities to integrate external tools, APIs, or data sources directly into Copilot Chat without needing to write repetitive integration code
>
> By handling these kinds of boilerplate tasks, use of the SDK lets developers focus on the extension's core functionality. The code for the SDK is located in GitHub's Copilot extensions area (*https://oreil.ly/Dgdr4*). For the sake of brevity and because it is still early in the SDK's development, we won't go into how to use the SDK's functionality, but you can find basic examples of common tasks in the project's *README.md file* (*https://oreil.ly/G_IfL*). An examples folder (*https://oreil.ly/PjTdz*) also includes a couple of basic examples of how to use the SDK.

We need a server and an app to complete the implementation. Let's look at how those can be set up.

Configuring a GitHub App for a Copilot Agent Extension

In this example, we're leveraging a GitHub Codespace to provide the runtime environment and server for the endpoint. Using a codespace is not something you would do in production use, but it simplifies the process quite a bit for our basic demo and testing scenarios. You could also use a service like ngrok if you preferred.

The steps for creating a codespace from a GitHub repository are outlined in the documentation (*https://oreil.ly/DCh4K*). Once the codespace is started, you just need two commands to get the server going:

```
npm install
npm start
```

> **Node App and npm**
>
> The code here is a node app (*https://nodejs.org/en/about*), and npm (*https://npmjs.com*) is a node tool used to run it.

At this point, you'll have a server running from the codespace on port 3000. You need to take two steps prior to configuring a GitHub App for the extension. First, you need to make the port serving the endpoint *public* instead of *private*. To do that, switch to the Ports tab in the codespace, right-click the port in the list, and change its Port Visibility setting to Public, as shown in Figure 10-14.

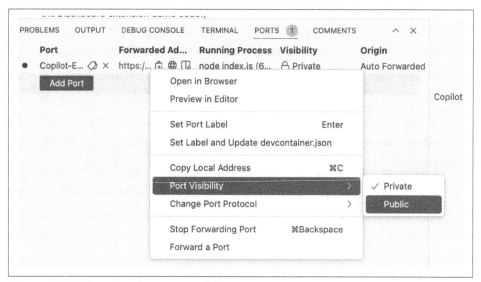

Figure 10-14. Changing the port to public

Then copy the server address from the same location (Figure 10-15).

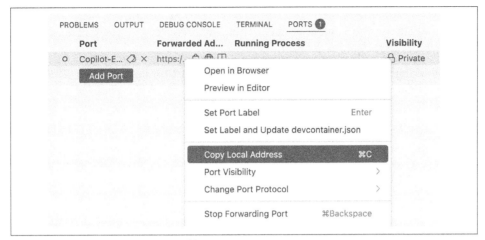

Figure 10-15. Copying the port address

Behind the Scenes

If you want to understand more about how the codespace is configured and how the server is started, the port selected, etc., take a look at the files *.devcontainer/devcontainer.json* (*https://oreil.ly/E9daL*) and *.vscode/launch.json* (*https://oreil.ly/HTlM8*) in the GitHub repository.

With the code implemented for the extension agent and the server running, we're now ready to complete the implementation of the extension itself by creating and configuring a corresponding GitHub App.

For Development and Test Purposes Only

In our examples in this chapter, we are creating code, setting up simple servers, and implementing user-specific agents for demo purposes. To convert these examples to production-ready instances, you would need to add functionality for security, hosting, and more.

To set up the app, log into GitHub with the same ID as the the one used to run the codespace. Then go to your developer settings and create a new app. The shortcut link for this is *https://github.com/settings/apps/new*.

Next, fill in the required fields. The App Name should be a unique name. This is the name that you will use in the Copilot Chat interface to invoke your extension. For example, if you choose *my-app* for the name, you would use `@my-app` in the chat interface to invoke your extension.

For the Homepage URL field, you can provide a URL that goes to a web page about your app/extension if you have a page. If not, you can just put in the link to the GitHub repository for your extension or even just *https://github.com*.

The Callback URL field is where you place the public URL address from the port you set as public in the codespace. This must be in place in order for your extension to send and receive responses for its code. You should also add `/callback` at the end of the URL.

For the examples we're using here, we can disable any other selected options on this page, such as *Webhooks*. Next is the app's visibility setting. You can make it accessible only to you for development and testing purposes. Later, you can enable public access when you're ready to share. Figure 10-16 shows an example page with completed fields.

When you have completed this screen, you can click Create GitHub App to complete the registration.

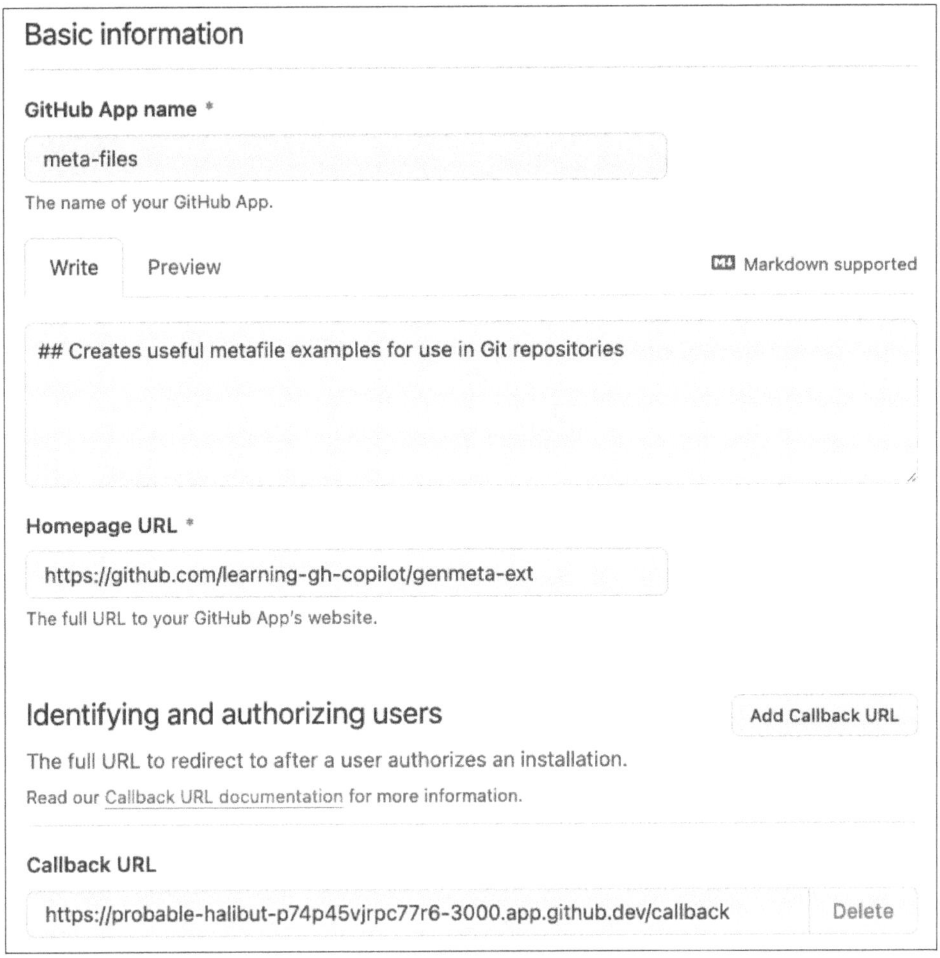

Figure 10-16. Initial agent extension configuration

At this point, you'll need to generate a private key in order to install your app and sign access tokens. GitHub will provide you with a link to generate and download the key (Figure 10-17). The key will then be automatically added to your app's configuration.

Figure 10-17. Generating a private key to install the app

Once you've created the app on the General page, you need to do a bit more configuration by using the selections on the left. On the Permissions & Events page, the only option you must set for dev/test purposes is in the Account Permissions section. Give Copilot Chat read-only permissions (Figure 10-18). Then save those changes.

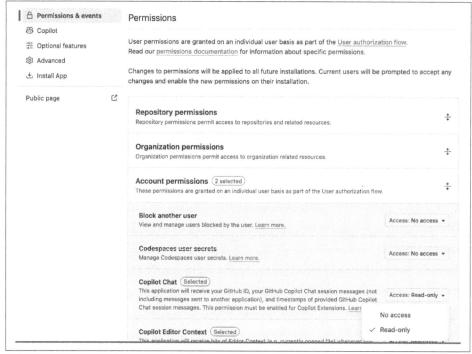

Figure 10-18. Adding permissions for Copilot Chat

On the Copilot-specific settings page, change the app type from Disabled to Agent (since we're implementing our extension as an agent). Then, in the URL section, paste the public URL from your codespace.

Lastly on this page, add content in the "Inference description" field. This information is used to provide a brief description of your agent to help users understand the purpose of the extension. The contents are displayed to users when they hover over the extension's slug in the chat area. After completing this, you can save your changes. Figure 10-19 shows the completed page.

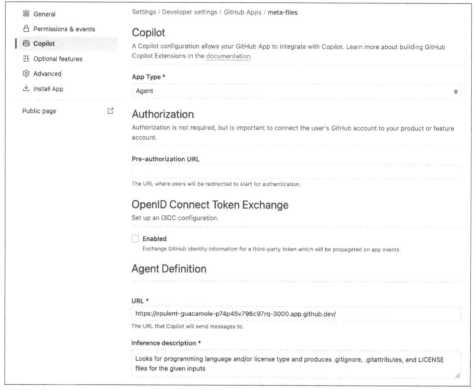

Figure 10-19. Copilot settings for the app

These are all the required fields you need to set up for the app to work with your agent. An Optional Features page only allows you to opt out of token expiration, and an Advanced page handles Danger Zone types of options for transferring ownership of the app, deleting the app, or making it public.

After completing the preceding steps, you can install the app in your personal or organizational account for testing. To do this, click the Install App page and follow the instructions.

The first time you attempt to use the extension, you'll need to authorize access for it to continue (Figure 10-20).

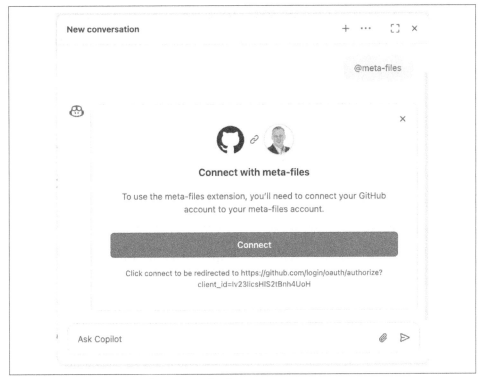

Figure 10-20. Connecting the app on the first use

After clicking the Connect button, you'll need to authorize the app to access the relevant resources (Figure 10-21).

Implementing an Extension as an Agent | 279

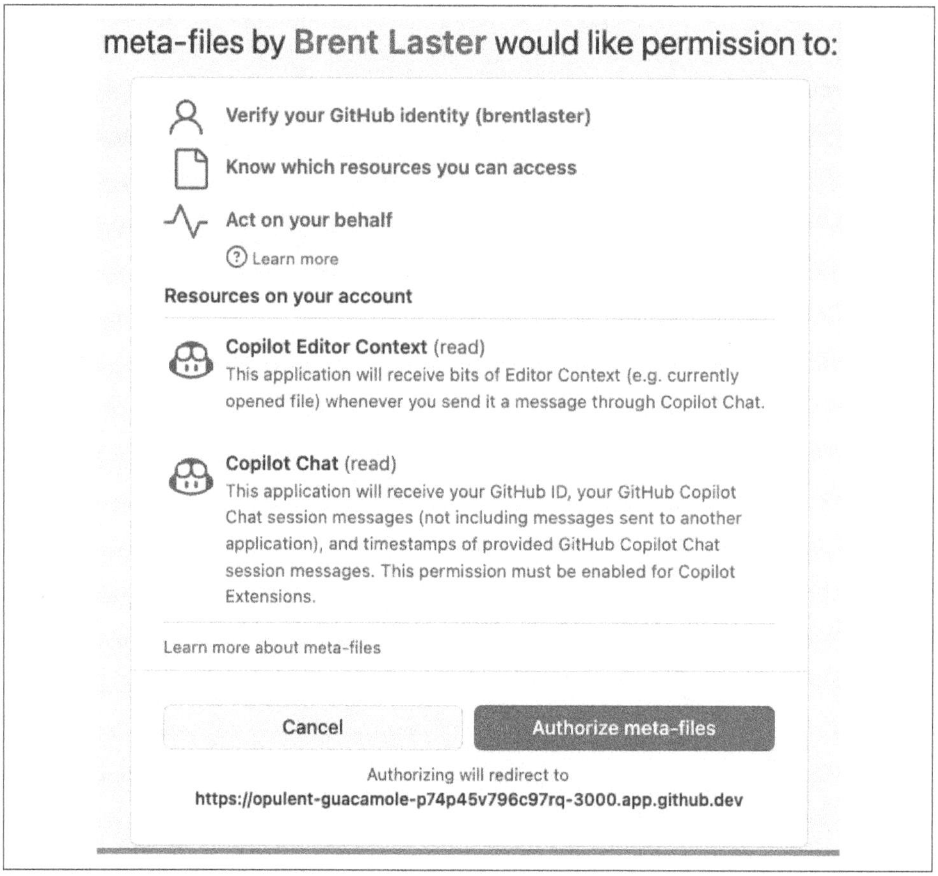

> **meta-files by Brent Laster** would like permission to:
>
> - Verify your GitHub identity (brentlaster)
> - Know which resources you can access
> - Act on your behalf
>   - ⓘ Learn more
>
> **Resources on your account**
>
> **Copilot Editor Context** (read)
> This application will receive bits of Editor Context (e.g. currently opened file) whenever you send it a message through Copilot Chat.
>
> **Copilot Chat** (read)
> This application will receive your GitHub ID, your GitHub Copilot Chat session messages (not including messages sent to another application), and timestamps of provided GitHub Copilot Chat session messages. This permission must be enabled for Copilot Extensions.
>
> Learn more about meta-files
>
> [Cancel]   [**Authorize meta-files**]
>
> Authorizing will redirect to
> https://opulent-guacamole-p74p45v796c97rq-3000.app.github.dev

Figure 10-21. Authorizing the app

Once the app is authorized, you're ready to use the extension as shown earlier.

Another way to create an extension is to utilize the *skillsets* pattern. This implementation choice works well for allowing Copilot to get real-time targeted information or do simple API processing easily. But while it can be a simpler coding implementation, it does require a more complex app configuration. We'll explore extensions implemented via skillsets in the next section.

Implementing an Extension via Skillsets

While agents provide a powerful and flexible architecture for implementing Copilot extensions, they can be overkill. If all you need to do in response to a chat prompt is invoke a specific tool or call an API, you can implement your extension by using skillsets instead.

A single *skill* in Copilot is a tool that the model calls to do a specific task in response to a prompt—for example, calling an external API. A collection of up to five skills is called a *skillset*. These skillsets allow for integration of external services or custom API endpoints into the Copilot workflow, without the complexity of agents.

Skillsets are more lightweight and simpler than agents. They are a better architecture choice when you need to do simple, specific tasks without a lot of setup. They can automatically handle tasks like routing, prompt crafting, function evaluation, and response generation.

Figure 10-22 shows at a high level how a skillset extension works. I'll have more to say about the individual pieces in the following sections.

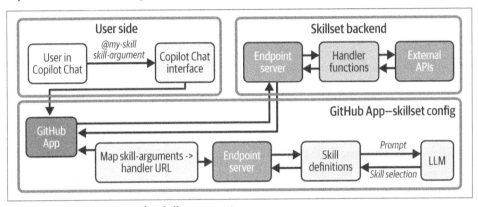

Figure 10-22. Overview of a skillset extension

Performing a Basic Implementation

As an example for the book, I've created a simple Copilot extension, implemented with skillsets, that allows you to do three basic operations for Go releases:

- Find out the latest release of Go
- Find out the currently supported releases of Go
- Determine whether a given release of Go is supported or when it reached its end of life (EOL)

The code for this example lives in book's GitHub repository (*https://oreil.ly/n13JY*). To show an example of implementing an extension in a different language, the code for the `gover-ext` extension is written in Go. It is modeled after the Copilot skillset extension example (*https://oreil.ly/WWZxW*).

A *main.go file (https://oreil.ly/8dk9j)registers* handler functions for specific URL patterns related to each of the capabilities of the extension. The core logic is shown here:

```go
func main() {
    if err := run(); err != nil {
        fmt.Println(err)
        os.Exit(1)
    }
}

func run() error {
    http.HandleFunc("/latest-version-go", handlers.LatestVersionGo)
    http.HandleFunc("/supported-versions-go",
handlers.SupportedVersionsGo)
    http.HandleFunc("/is-supported-or-eol",
handlers.IsSupportedOrEOL)
    http.HandleFunc("/_ping", func(w http.ResponseWriter,
r *http.Request) {
        w.Write([]byte("OK"))
    })

    http.ListenAndServe(":8080", nil)
    return nil
}
```

For each of the handlers, we implement a separate function that invokes an API, checks for errors, and returns the desired results. For example, in the handler for getting the latest version—LatestVersionGo (*https://oreil.ly/TxXMz*)—the key parts of the code are implemented as follows.

First, we implement a structure to hold the version and make a call to the Go site's API to get the latest version:

```go
type GoVersion struct {
    Version string `json:"version"`
}

func LatestVersionGo(w http.ResponseWriter, r *http.Request) {
    fmt.Println("Latest Go Version Called")
    req, err := http.NewRequestWithContext(r.Context(),
http.MethodGet, "https://go.dev/dl/?mode=json", nil)
    if err != nil {
        http.Error(w, "Failed to create request",
http.StatusInternalServerError)
        return
    }
```

After doing some error checking to make sure the call was successful, we buffer the response and then parse it to get the latest version and write that back to the stream:

```go
// Buffer the response body for decoding
    var bodyBuffer bytes.Buffer
    tee := io.TeeReader(resp.Body, &bodyBuffer)

    // Drain the tee to ensure we can parse the body later
    if _, err := io.Copy(io.Discard, tee); err != nil {
```

```go
        http.Error(w, "Failed to process response body",
http.StatusInternalServerError)
        return
    }

    // Parse the JSON response
    var versions []GoVersion
    if err := json.NewDecoder(&bodyBuffer).Decode(&versions);
err != nil {
        http.Error(w, "Failed to parse JSON response",
http.StatusInternalServerError)
        fmt.Printf("Failed to decode JSON: %v\n", err)
        return
    }

    // The latest version is the first item in the array
    if len(versions) > 0 {
        trimmedVersion := strings.TrimPrefix(versions[0].Version,
"go")
        fmt.Fprintf(w, "%s", trimmedVersion) // Write the version
to the HTTP response
        return
    }
```

The handler for the supported versions query uses a similar approach. There's a structure to hold the data and a call to a different API to get the raw information:

```go
type VersionInfo struct {
    Cycle       string      `json:"cycle"`
    ReleaseDate string      `json:"releaseDate"`
    EOL         interface{} `json:"eol"`
}

func SupportedVersionsGo(w http.ResponseWriter, r *http.Request) {
    fmt.Println("Supported Go Versions Called")
    req, err := http.NewRequestWithContext(r.Context(),
http.MethodGet, "https://endoflife.date/api/go.json", nil)
    if err != nil {
        http.Error(w, "Failed to create request",
http.StatusInternalServerError)
        return
    }
```

Then after some error checking to make sure the call was successful, and buffering the response, the results are parsed and converted into a single string that is written back to the stream:

```go
    // Parse the JSON into a slice of VersionInfo
    var versions []VersionInfo
    if err := json.NewDecoder(&bodyBuffer).Decode(&versions);
err != nil {
        http.Error(w, "Failed to parse JSON response",
http.StatusInternalServerError)
```

```go
        fmt.Printf("Failed to decode JSON: %v\n", err)
        return
    }

    // Filter versions with eol == false and collect the results
    result := make([]struct {
        Cycle       string `json:"cycle"`
        ReleaseDate string `json:"releaseDate"`
    }, 0)

    for _, v := range versions {
        // Check if EOL is a boolean and is false
        if eolBool, ok := v.EOL.(bool); ok && !eolBool {
            result = append(result, struct {
                Cycle       string `json:"cycle"`
                ReleaseDate string `json:"releaseDate"`
            }{
                Cycle:       v.Cycle,
                ReleaseDate: v.ReleaseDate,
            })
        }
    }

    // Convert the result to a single string
    var builder strings.Builder
    for _, r := range result {
        builder.WriteString(fmt.Sprintf("Version: %s, Release Date: %s\n", r.Cycle, r.ReleaseDate))
    }

    // The versions are all in one string now
    if len(builder.String()) > 0 {
        fmt.Fprintf(w, "%s", builder.String()) // Write the list of supported versions to the HTTP response
        return
    }
```

The flow for the other function to determine whether a version is supported or has reached EOL is similar.

Since the coding is pretty basic and makes no mention of the AI or inferences, you may be wondering how the prompts in Copilot Chat ultimately end up invoking the respective handlers. The secret is in the GitHub App configuration when you are creating an extension that uses skillsets.

Configuring a GitHub App for a Copilot Extension Using Skillsets

Like extensions that are implemented as agents, extensions implemented as skillsets need a GitHub App to act as a bridge between Copilot's chat interface and the underlying extension implementation. Much of the setup is similar to that done for agents, but we'll cover some significant differences here. (For any other details on app setup and configuration, you can refer back to "Configuring a GitHub App for a Copilot Agent Extension" on page 272.)

The first difference is that, on the General page, you do not have to put in an extension-specific Callback URL. You will need a callback URL for authentication, but it can be a simple URL like *https://github.com*.

The other changes for configuring the app, and the most significant ones, are done on the Copilot page. On this page, you need to set the App Type field to Skillset. Doing this will then bring up a section called Skill definitions (Figure 10-23).

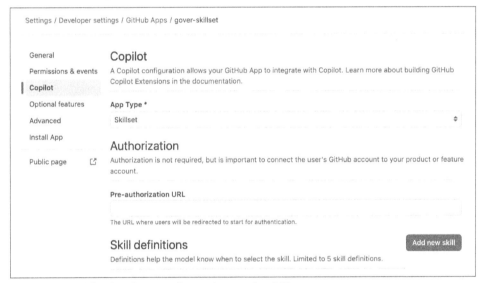

Figure 10-23. The Copilot page for setting up the skillset app

The "Skill definitions" section is where the mapping happens from the prompt in chat to the handlers in the code. For each skill that we are handling in our code, we need to go through the process of adding a new skill. We'll look at one as an example. The others follow the same pattern.

When you click the "Add new skill" button, you get a dialog with various fields to fill in, including Name, Inference description, URL, and Parameters (Figure 10-24).

Figure 10-24. New skill definition screen for the app

In the Name field, we put the name of the skill to be used by the model, and that is shown to the user when it is invoked.

In the "Inference description" field, we are explaining to the model *what/when/how* this skill should be invoked. This description should be meaningful enough that the model can understand what is intended.

Think of this as the direct prompt that you might supply to the model if you wanted it to execute this skill. While we are using a simple prompt here, depending on what your skill does and how complex it is, you may want to define additional details. Examples could include expected inputs and outputs, especially if other skillsets are very similar. Figure 10-25 shows an example definition including the inference description matching one of the skills we are using.

Figure 10-25. Skill definition in the app

Based on the prompt in the chat and how well the model can match it up with the Inference description, the process will invoke the endpoint specified in the URL field. This field is where you put the endpoint server address with the path specified in the extension code. In this case, since our extension code is looking for `latest-version-go` to know to invoke the handler for getting the latest Go version, we can put the API endpoint in this field with `latest-version-go` at the end.

Implementing an Extension via Skillsets | 287

In production, we would have a designated public URL that this would be directed to. But if we're using ngrok, a codespace, or something similar to serve this, we would put the public URL being served from those applications with *latest-version-go* appended. For an ngrok (*https://ngrok.com*) instance, the entire URL would look something like this:

```
https://8fa7-2605-a601-a6ca-f00-1466-39cc-11f7-7f71.ngrok-free.app/
latest-version-go
```

Localhost URL and ngrok

ngrok lets you create secure tunnels from a public internet endpoint to a locally running service on your machine. This cross-platform tool lets you easily expose local web servers to the internet for testing and sharing without having to set up complex networking configurations.

While you would typically start ngrok serving on localhost:8080, you cannot use localhost in the skill configuration because it is not publicly reachable. Instead, you'll need to grab the actual public URL that ngrok is forwarding to localhost:8080.

If we were using a codespace, the URL might look like this:

```
https://turbo-dollop-p74p45vgx739pqj-8080.app.github.dev/latest-
version-go
```

The Parameters section is for defining the parameters of the skill in JSON. Since each of our skillsets keys off the prompt string, we can simply use the following in this field:

```
{ "type": "object" }
```

Once we have the implementation completed and the app set up and configured, we can run the app in the same way as we did for the agent one. Figure 10-26 shows an example of trying out the various skills from the extension. Notice the specific prompts that are being used: "@go-versions supported versions" and "@go-versions 1.21" (as shown on the right).

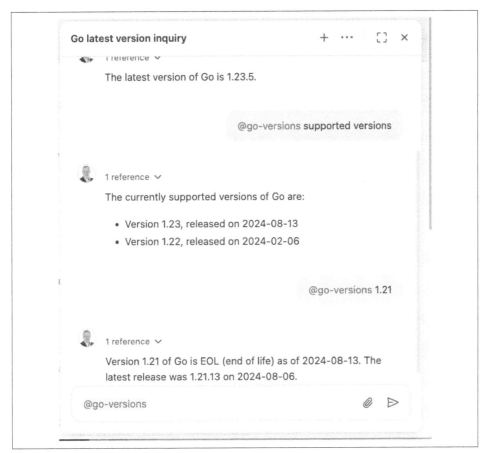

Figure 10-26. Running the `go-versions` extension

Extensions implemented as agents and skillsets provide maximum flexibility with their ability to be run in any of the integrated chat interfaces (GitHub, IDEs). Now that we've covered those, it's time to look at the other alternative for adding capabilities into the IDE mentioned at the start of the chapter—VS Code extensions for Copilot.

Creating VS Code Extensions for Copilot

Like Copilot extensions, VS Code extensions for Copilot provide additional capabilities for the user through Copilot Chat. Unlike Copilot extensions, VS Code extensions are implemented using the VS Code platform and APIs. Because of that implementation approach, the VS Code extensions have access to broad and deep VS Code functionality and can have tight integration. And they don't require a separate GitHub App to use. The disadvantage is that you can't use them in other non-IDE clients (like a chat interface in GitHub). Table 10-2 shows an updated version of our earlier comparison table with an added column for VS Code extensions for Copilot.

Table 10-2. Comparison of Copilot extension types

Attribute	Copilot agents	Copilot skillsets	VS Code extensions for Copilot
Complexity	Requires more development effort to manage the entire user interaction flow response and response generation	Designed for easy integration with minimal setup	Can be complex or simple, depending on VS Code APIs used
Control	Provides full control over how requests are processed and how responses are generated	Limited control over the user interaction, focus is on data retrieval and basic actions	Most control as written for VS Code only
Use cases	Suitable for complex scenarios where you need to implement custom logic, integrate with other AI models, and manage conversation context	Straightforward tasks like fetching data from an external API or performing simple operations	Tasks for working with code in the IDE and, optionally, providing additional commands for the participant
Interfaces available	All (GitHub, IDEs)	All (GitHub, IDEs)	Limited to VS Code to get full advantage of all VS Code APIs
Support	GitHub	GitHub	VS Code Team

Ultimately, what the user sees when we add a VS Code extension for Copilot is a new chat participant.

A *chat participant* is a domain expert that can answer questions about a specific topic, or perform specific tasks, when you are working with Copilot Chat in an IDE. We've discussed these before in the context of participants that come built-in with Copilot (see Chapter 3). For example, the built-in `@workspace` participant can respond relative to your entire VS Code workspace. To do this, it uses integrated tools such as semantic search and code indexes. Other examples we've discussed include `@terminal` and `@vscode`.

Chat participants are invoked using the same `@identifier` syntax as for other extensions. Once a participant is invoked and passed a prompt, the code for the participant can use one of several approaches to handle the prompt. These include the following:

- Calling an AI model to interpret and respond
- Forwarding the request to a backend service
- Using built-in logic and/or APIs to do the processing

Because of the underlying tight integration with VS Code, chat participants can return responses that include interactive elements like buttons, file trees, or progress updates. The chat participants can also provide follow-up suggestions and their own slash commands (as in previous examples, such as /explain and /fix) that are related to the participant's domain.

In short, VS Code extensions for Copilot can provide rich *client-side* experiences. These extensions have access to the VS Code client context and interfaces on the frontend, while utilizing the power of Copilot on the backend.

Chat Participants in Other IDEs

While we are focusing on VS Code in this chapter, chat participants are available in other IDEs as well. Likewise, depending on the capabilities of the underlying IDE platform, VS Code extensions for Copilot could be ported to other IDEs where Copilot also runs.

The implementation example we'll use for this extension is an *API finder*. This extension, when installed in VS Code, allows the user to search for APIs that perform a certain function and stream back information in the chat interface on the APIs and how to use them.

Figure 10-27 shows at a high level how a VS Code extension for Copilot works. I'll have more to say about the individual pieces in the following sections.

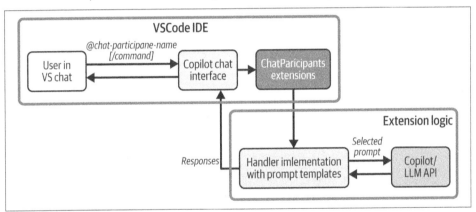

Figure 10-27. Overview of a VS Code extension

Figure 10-28 shows an example of using the extension's user-facing functionality to find suitable APIs.

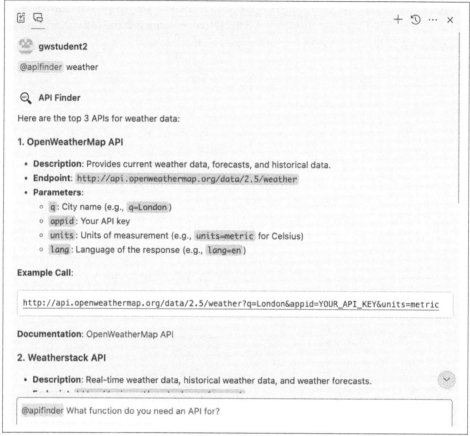

Figure 10-28. Using the API Finder chat participant to find weather APIs

This extension also has an additional command built-in that can be invoked as /examples. Figure 10-29 shows an example usage of the command.

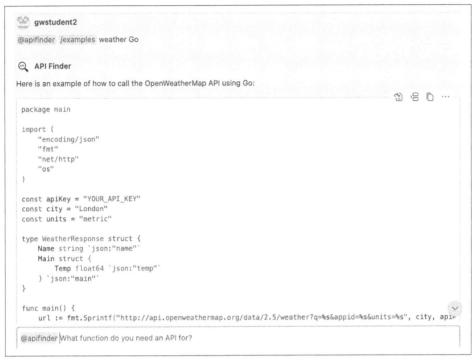

Figure 10-29. Using the command from our chat participant

The code for the extension is located in the book's GitHub repository (*https://oreil.ly/ RUAtr*). This one is implemented in TypeScript, with the main logic in the file *src/ extension.ts* (*https://oreil.ly/VSPMM*). This is based on the example (*https://oreil.ly/ uRBxt*) in the VS Code extension examples in GitHub.

The code starts off by importing dependencies from VS Code's libraries. Then it defines the prompt to send to the model for the base functionality and the one to send for the code font command:

```
import * as vscode from 'vscode';

const BASE_PROMPT = 'You are a helpful API finder. Your job is to
  locate and provide documentation on the top 3 APIs that match the
  prompt. Respond with basic documentation about the API, how to call
  it, and its parameters. Cite your sources and provide links to more
  information where appropriate.  Use bullet points in explanations
  wherever possible. If the user asks a question that is not relevant
  to APIs, politely decline to respond.';

const SAMPLE_CODE_PROMPT = 'You are a helpful source of API examples.
```

```
Your job is to locate the top 3 APIs that match the prompt and
provide simple example code for how to call them. Keep the code as
short as possible to still provide a usable, relevant example.
If the user asks a question that is not relevant to APIs, politely
decline to respond.';
```

Notice that we are being explicit about how we want the LLM to process our query by supplying detailed prompts to use.

Specifying the Language for /examples

In the previous example shown in Figure 10-29, we specified the language Go as a second argument on the prompt to @api finder /examples. However, our prompt does not explicitly reference the programming language. This is a benefit of using the AI to handle the request. It infers additional context and meaning that we don't have to explicitly call out.

Code at the bottom of the file instantiates the chat handler and adds an icon to it for use in chat:

```
// create participant
const apifinder = vscode.chat.createChatParticipant("chat-tutorial.
api-finder", handler);

// add icon to participant
apifinder.iconPath = vscode.Uri.joinPath(context.extensionUri,
'apifinder.jpeg');
```

The main processing function selects the prompt (based on whether we want the core functionality or are using the `examples` command). It then combines the prompt and any previous messages, sends that to the model, and streams the response:

```
export function activate(context: vscode.ExtensionContext) {

    // define a chat handler
    const handler: vscode.ChatRequestHandler = async (request:
vscode.ChatRequest, context: vscode.ChatContext,
stream: vscode.ChatResponseStream, token: vscode.CancellationToken)
    => {
        // initialize the prompt
        let prompt = BASE_PROMPT;
        if (request.command === 'examples') {
            prompt = SAMPLE_CODE_PROMPT;
        }
        // initialize the messages array with the prompt
        const messages = [
            vscode.LanguageModelChatMessage.User(prompt),
        ];
        // get all the previous participant messages
```

```
        const previousMessages = context.history.filter(
            (h) => h instanceof vscode.ChatResponseTurn
        );
        // add the previous messages to the messages array
        previousMessages.forEach((m) => {
            let fullMessage = '';
            m.response.forEach((r) => {
                const mdPart = r as vscode.ChatResponseMarkdownPart;
                fullMessage += mdPart.value.value;
            });
            messages.push(vscode.LanguageModelChatMessage.Assistant
(fullMessage));
        });
        // add in the user's message
        messages.push(vscode.LanguageModelChatMessage.User
(request.prompt));
        // send the request
        const chatResponse = await request.model.sendRequest
(messages, {}, token);
        // stream the response
        for await (const fragment of chatResponse.text) {
            stream.markdown(fragment);
        }
        return;
    };
```

Testing this extension is as simple as opening the folder in VS Code, installing the dependencies with `npm install`, compiling the code via `npm run compile`, and then running the extension in a new VS Code instance.

Running a Participant with the Debugger

Probably the simplest way to test your participant code is to load it into a VS Code instance, run the `npm` commands, and then use the Start Debugging option from the Run menu to spin up a new instance of VS Code. The new debug instance will have the participant installed and active, so you can use it in that instance's chat interface. Instructions can be found in the repository's README file (*https://oreil.ly/QXsC_*).

As with the other types of extensions, you would want to make additional changes before rolling this out to production, such as ensuring that authentication works as needed. The VS Code documentation (*https://oreil.ly/UH18y*) describes implementation in much more detail. You can also find information on publishing your finished extension to the VS Code Marketplace (*https://oreil.ly/HGZkA*).

Conclusion

GitHub Copilot extensions and VS Code extensions for Copilot provide a way to augment the built-in capabilities of GitHub Copilot. These extensions are accessed via the Copilot Chat interface and the @ prefix.

The backend code for Copilot extensions can be architected in one of two ways. Agents are the most flexible option but also the most complex in general to implement. Extensions that use the skillsets architecture call one or more skills on the backend to get additional information. A skill can be as simple as an API call.

VS Code extensions for Copilot are architected on top of VS Code's platform. They have full access to the underlying VS Code APIs and rely on VS Code to function. From a user-facing perspective, they provide VS Code chat participants, similar to the built-in ones like @workspace and @terminal.

The backend code for extensions can be implemented in several languages, including JavaScript, TypeScript, and Go. For extensions using the agent approach and JavaScript, GitHub has provided an early version of an SDK that can be used to simplify coding and help fill in production needs like authentication.

Copilot extensions (implemented as either agents or skillsets) require a GitHub App to bridge the connection between the Copilot chat interface and the backend code. While both use GitHub Apps, the configuration for each is different. Agents rely on a single callback URL defined in the app. Apps for skillsets require additional inference details in their configuration so that the AI can map the prompt to the correct skill API endpoint.

Since Copilot extensions utilize a GitHub App, they can run in any Copilot chat interface, including in an IDE or on GitHub. In contrast, since VS Code extensions for Copilot rely on VS Code APIs and functions, they can only be used in that environment.

Index

Symbols
symbol, 83
#file variable, 173
#selection variable, 173
#terminalLastCommand keyword, 174
+ symbol, in Copilot Chat, 59
/ (slash character), 74
/doc command, 157, 158
/explain command, 119
/fix command, 119
/setupTests, 129, 192
/startDebugging command, 120, 122
/tests command, 67, 133-136
@ symbol, 66, 76, 77, 260
@apifinder /examples, 294
@github, 77
@project, 77
@terminal chat participant, 77, 81-83
@vision, 77
@vscode chat participant, 77, 80-81
@workspace chat participant, 77, 78-80, 129, 147, 167, 173, 192, 290
"rerun without" link option, 67

A
accuracy, 14, 249
actions, Copilot extensions for executing, 254
advanced editing mode, 24
Agent mode, 18, 24, 104-110, 266
    requests, 18
    using for testing workflows, 151-153
agents, 263, 266-280
AI (artificial intelligence), 2-3
    Copilot Chat and, 54
    Copilot extensions for AI-assisted coding, 254
    generative, 126
    pair programmer, 17
alternative suggestions, 28-30
Anthropic's Claude, 5
API finder, 291
APIs, generating documentation for, 164-165
applications
    CodeQL, 231, 235
    configuring, 259
    links for installing, 265
Apply Changes button, 128
arguments, specifying, 193
Ask Copilot button, 249
Ask mode, 52-53
Attach to current thread option, 247
automatic data generation, 216-218
autonomous workflows
    Agent mode, 104-110
    Copilot Vision, 111-119
    debugging, 119-123
    in IDE, 93-124
Azure Data Studio, 22

B
bad answers, in Copilot Chat, 90-91
batch editing, 45
    functionality of, 97
building blocks, assembling for Copilot extensions, 264-266
Business plan, 18, 19

C

C#, 162
callback URL, 265
Change Completions Model, 46
change workflows, using Copilot for, 231-237
Chat (Copilot) (see Copilot Chat)
chat models, 5
chat participants
    adding using prompt dialog, 66-66
    Copilot Chat, 77-83, 127, 130-131, 290
chat request, 18
chat sessions, managing in Copilot Chat, 59-62
chat variables, 68
ChatGPT, 5, 6, 17-18, 51
circular arrow, 71
Claude (Anthropic), 5
CLI (command-line interface), 218-220
client-based extensions, 254
cloud-based, 2
Cloudflare, 266
code
    changes with Copilot, 245-249
    completions, 18, 45
    documenting, 155-179
    explaining logic used in, 172-173
    explaining what may go wrong, 173
    generated, 170-171
    generative AI and, 5-6
    Go, 169-170
    reviewing with GitHub Copilot, 39-44
codebase, 13
CodeQL application, 231, 235
Codespaces (see GitHub Codespaces)
command line, 177
Command Palette, accessing through GitHub Copilot, 38
comments, 7
    creating unit tests using, 137-139
    directive, 31-34
    documentation from, 158
    documentation versus, 161
    leveraging, 30-35
    questions via, 34-35
Commit change button, 236
commit messages, generating automatically using GitHub Copilot, 44
completeness, 13
contents
    deprecated, 186
    documenting, 156-168
    explaining, 169
context
    adding additional files as, 201
    adding elements using prompt dialog, 64-66
    adding to make code relevant, 199-201
    misplaced, 188-189
    missing, 189-190
    origins of, 182-183
    telling Copilot what to use for, 191-193
context menus, 35-39
controls, changing, 135
Conversation option, 229
Copilot (see GitHub Copilot)
Copilot Autofix, 235
Copilot Chat, 6, 35, 51
    accessing main interface, 52-55
    bad answers, 90-91
    bypassing default participants, 130-131
    copying conversations, 168
    creating custom code-generation instructions, 87-90
    exporting conversations, 168
    generating documentation through, 159-161
    hallucinations, 90-91
    in the terminal, 86-87
    inline Chat interface, 69-73
    managing chat sessions, 59-62
    output, 55-59
    participants, 77-83, 127, 290
    prompt dialog, 63-69
    prompt engineering for, 62-63
    Quick Chat interface, 73-74
    running participants with debugger, 295
    shortcuts, 74-76
    specifying variables for, 193
    using with GitHub repositories, 224-231
    variables, 83-86
Copilot Docker extension, 253
Copilot Edits, 97-103, 110
Copilot Free, using Agent mode with, 110
Copilot Language Server SDK, 7, 22
Copilot Vision, 111-119
copilot-debug command, 122
coping strategies, user-based, 191-199
copying chat conversations, 168
cost, 20
Create issue button, 233
current file, 7

current version, 12
custom code-generation instructions, creating, 87-90
custom reviews, creating instructions for, 42-44

D

data generation, automatic, 216-218
data retrieval, Copilot extensions for, 254
debugging, 119-123, 295
deleting chats, 61
deployment, 210
deprecated contents, 186
directive comments, 31-34
Disable Completions option, 47
Docker extension, 258
documentation
    comment versus, 161
    content, 156-168
    creating functional, 165-167
    extracting summary, 167-168
    for code, 155-179
    from comments, 158
    generating for APIs, 164-165
    generating framework-compatible, 162-164
    generating inline, 156-159
    generating through chat, 159-161
    querying, 254
Done button, 101, 109
dot inside a square symbol, 101

E

Eclipse, 22
Edit Settings option, 47
editing
    advanced editing mode, 24
    Copilot Edits, 97-103
    files via settings, 48
    in IDE, 93-124
    predictive edits with Next Edit Suggestions (NES), 93-97
endpoint server, 266
Enterprise plan, 18, 19
examples command, 294
exception helper, 121
experimental features, 47, 145
explaining content, 169
explanation use cases, 55
explicit prompts, creating unit tests using, 136-137

explicit references, 147
exporting chat conversations, 168
Express, 269
Extensions (GitHub Copilot), 66, 188
    implementing as agents, 266-280
    installing, 77
extensions (GitHub Copilot), 254-255
    assembling building blocks for, 264-266
    configuring GitHub Apps for using, 272-280
    configuring GitHub Apps for using skillsets, 285-289
    creating with VS code, 289-295
    getting from the GitHub Marketplace, 256-262
    implementation types, 263-263
    implementing via skillsets, 280-289
    VS code extensions for Copilot versus, 253-254
external dependencies, 141

F

files
    editing via settings, 48
Files changed tab, 245
Fix functionality, 186
Fix using Copilot option, 36
four-point star symbols, 35
framework-compatible documentation, generating, 162-164
frameworks, leveraging, 145-153
framing questions, 196
Free plan, 18, 19
frequency, of training, 184
functional documentation, creating, 165-167

G

Gemini 2.5 Pro, 195
Generate fix button, 235
generated code, 170-171
generative, 2
generative AI
    code and, 5-6
    testing and, 126
gh auth command, 218
git status command, 175
GitHub App, 258, 264-266
    configuring for Copilot Agent extensions, 272-280

configuring for Copilot extensions using skillsets, 285-289
GitHub Codespaces, 7, 16-17
GitHub Copilot
    accessing through Command Palette, 38
    as a teacher, 170
    capabilities, 1
    ChatGPT versus, 17-18
    code changes with, 245-249
    command-line interface (CLI), 218-220
    configuring in IDE, 44-49
    context menus, 35-39
    debugging with, 119-123
    default review options, 39-41
    documentation, 21
    generating automatic commit messages, 44
    guiding by example, 198-199
    how it works, 3-11
    indexing in, 230
    plans, 18-22
    relevance of, 181-202
    reviewing code using, 39-44
    telling it what to use for context, 191-193
    testing with, 125-154
    timeliness of, 181-202
    usage considerations, 11-15
    using for change workflows, 231-237
    using with GitHub issues, 249-250
    using with pull requests, 237-244
    using with SQL, 204-210
    what it is, 2-3
GitHub Copilot extensions SDK, 271-271
GitHub Marketplace, getting Copilot extensions from, 255-262
GitHub repository, 160, 165, 166, 173, 224-231, 267, 281, 293
GitHub Trust Center, 15
GitHub, using Copilot in, 223-251
Give Feedback option, 230
Go code, 169-170, 185, 213
Google Gemini, 5
gutter, 94

H

hallucinations, 90-91, 186-187
high-level flow, 7-11
hover menu, 58
Hugging Face Spaces, 195

I

icons, changing, 135
IDEs, 3, 23, 25
    advanced editing in, 93-124
    autonomous workflows in, 93-124
    chat participants in other, 291
    configuring Copilot in, 46-49
    specific features of, 121
implementation types, for Copilot extensions, 263-263
indexing, 8, 230
initiating pull requests, 241-244
inline Chat interface, 54, 69-73
inline documentation, 156-159
inline mode, 23, 182
inline suggestions, 24-28
inputs, validating during testing, 139-141
Insert at Cursor option, in Copilot Chat, 59
installing
    Copilot Extensions, 77
    Maven, 151
integration tests, creating, 141-144
interfaces
    accessing for Copilot Chat, 52-55
    Editor Inline Chat, 54, 69-73
    Quick Chat, 54, 73-74

J

Javadoc, 163
JavaScript, 162
JetBrains, 7, 22
JSDoc, 162

K

key combinations, 24
Kubernetes, 203
    operators, 170
    pods, 210
    working with, 210-215

L

language, specifying, 294
LatestVersionGo, 282, 288
left arrow, in Copilot Chat, 59
links, for installing applications, 265
LLMs (large language models), 4-5, 68
local index, 8
localhost URL, 288

logic, explaining logic used in code, 172-173
LSP (Language Server Protocol), 22

M

Manage Models link, 69
Manage Shared Conversations option, 230
Markdown format, 168
Marketplace, getting Copilot extensions from, 255-262
matching content, 16
Maven, 151
MCP (Model Context Protocol) standard, 106
Meta notation, 24, 157
Microsoft 365 Copilot, 2
misplaced context, 188-189
missing context, 189-190
Mockito, 145
mocks, 141
models
    accessing, 18
    changing, 194-195
    multipliers, 19
    querying, 195-197

N

Neovim, 7
NES (Next Edit Suggestions), 110
    activating, 94
    predictive edits using, 93-97
ngrok, 266, 288, 288
node app, 272
nonproduction environment, 271
npm, 272

O

Octokit, 269
Office 365 Copilot, 2
Open Completions Panel, 46
Open Workbench, 228
OpenAI, 5
Operator SDK, 170
optimizations, SQL, 209-210
output, for Copilot Chat, 55-59

P

participants (chat)
    adding using prompt dialog, 66-66
    Copilot Chat, 77-83, 127, 130-131, 290

peer file, 201
PerplexityAI, 256, 258, 259, 265
Personal Instructions option, 229
pod, Kubernetes, 210
port forwarding, 266
predictive edits, with Next Edit Suggestions (NES), 93-97
premium requests, 18, 19, 197
preview features, 47
Preview SDK, 271-271
print-ready, 164
privacy, 14-15
private extensions, 255
Pro plan, 18, 19
Pro+ plan, 18, 19
prompt dialog, 63-69
    adding context elements, 64-66
    adding participants, 66-66
    options for submitting prompts, 67-69
prompt engineering, for Copilot Chat, 62-63
prompts, 5, 15
    accuracy and, 14
    creating, 270
    creating unit tests using explicit, 136-137
    specificity of, 141
ps command, 174
public extensions, 255
publish-ready, 164
publishable, 164
pull requests, using Copilot with, 238-244
pydoc, 162
Python, 162

Q

queries and querying
    documentation, 254
    models, 195-197
    specificity of, 127
    SQL, 204-207
questions
    framing, 196
    via comments, 34-35
Quick Chat, 54, 73-74
quick validation, 183

R

rand.NewSource function, 195
rand.Seed function, 195
Ready for review button, 238

reference, 55
Regenerate option, 71
regular expressions, generating, 215-216
relevance, 13, 181-202
remote index, 8
renaming suggestions, 96
repositories
    GitHub, 16-17, 160, 165, 166, 173, 224-231, 267, 281, 293
repository indexes, 66
return address, 265
review feedback dialog, 41
reviewing
    for accuracy, 249
    pull requests, 238-241
right arrow, in Copilot Chat, 59

S

security, 16-17
Seed function, 185
SELECT statement, 199
Send button, 67
Send to New Chat option, 68
Send with #codebase option, 68
server-based extensions, 254
Settings option, 230
settings, editing files via, 48
shortcuts, Copilot Chat, 74-76
Show Chats icon (Copilot Chat), 61
skill, 281
skillsets, 263
    configuring GitHub Apps for Copilot extensions using, 285-289
    implementing Code extensions via, 280-289
slash commands, 74, 81, 127, 130-131
sparkle icon, 35
SQL (Structured Query Language), 203
    optimizations, 209-210
    queries, 204-207
    stored procedures, 207-208
    testing SQL code, 131
    using Copilot with, 204-210
Stack Overflow, 127
stored procedures, SQL, 207-208
Submit new issue button, 234
suggestions, 15
    accepting, 26
    alternative, 28-30
    completeness of, 27
    fit of, 27
    pausing for, 27
summary documentation, extracting from code, 167-168
Swagger, 164, 165
System Prompt option, 230

T

TDD (test-driven development), 145-153
terminal
    Copilot Chat in, 86-87
    explaining how to do something in, 177
    explaining items from, 174-176
Test Explorer, in Visual Studio 2022, 121
TestDrivenio, 145
testing, 125-154
    creating integration tests, 141-144
    creating unit tests, 132-141
    defining custom instructions, 144-145
    generative AI and, 126
    process of, 126-132
    SQL code, 131
    test-driven development (TDD), 145-153
time, for Agent mode, 108
timeliness, 12-12, 181-202
traditional LLMs, 4
training cutoffs, 183-186
training frequency, 184
Trust Center (GitHub), 15
trust, for generated tests, 132
TypeScript, 293

U

Undo option, 101, 109
unit tests, creating, 132-141
URLs, generating, 244
user engagement, 15
user-based coping strategies, 191-199

V

validation
    lack of real-time, 187-188
    of inputs during testing, 139-141
variables
    Copilot Chat, 83-86
    specifying for chat, 193
Views and More Actions control (Copilot Chat), 61

Vim/Neovim, 22
Visual Studio, 7, 22, 121
VS Code (Visual Studio Code), 7, 22, 23
    creating Copilot extensions, 289-295
    documentation, 295
    extensions for Copilot versus Copilot extensions, 253-254
VS Code Marketplace, 295

W

workflows
    autonomous, 93-124
    testing using Agent mode, 151-153
workspace environment, 47
workspace index, 66

X

X, in Copilot Chat, 61
Xcode, 22
XMLDoc, 162

Y

YAML, working with, 210-215

About the Author

Brent Laster is an experienced industry technologist and leader. He's a global trainer, author, and the founder of Tech Skills Transformations, a company dedicated to helping people take their technical skills to new levels. Brent creates and conducts training courses on GitHub Copilot as well as helping organizations with adoption.

Colophon

The animals on the cover of *Learning GitHub Copilot* are Ecuadorian hillstars (*Oreotrochilus chimborazo*). This species of hummingbird is found almost exclusively in the Ecuadorian Andes, though its range extends into part of Colombia. Its primary habitat is mountain grasslands, ranging from about 11,500 feet to 17,000 feet in elevation.

The Ecuadorian hillstar reaches about 12 centimeters long, with a long, curved beak. Males and females have strikingly different appearances; males have a vibrant purple hood, a bright white chest with a black stripe down the middle, and iridescent green patches on the wings and body. One subspecies also has a turquoise patch on the throat. Females and immature males are much more drab in appearance, with greenish-brown plumage and a lighter-colored speckled belly. They are often found near chuquiraga bushes, whose orange flowers are one of the Ecuadorian hillstar's main sources of nectar.

The Ecuadorian hillstar is considered a species of least concern, since its population is stable. Many of the animals on O'Reilly covers are endangered; all of them are important to the world.

The cover illustration is by Monica Kamsvaag, based on an antique line engraving from Lydekker's *Royal Natural History*. The cover fonts are Gilroy Semibold and Guardian Sans. The text font is Adobe Minion Pro; the heading font is Adobe Myriad Condensed; and the code font is Dalton Maag's Ubuntu Mono.

O'REILLY®

Learn from experts. Become one yourself.

60,000+ titles | Live events with experts | Role-based courses
Interactive learning | Certification preparation

Try the O'Reilly learning platform free for 10 days.

www.ingramcontent.com/pod-product-compliance
Lightning Source LLC
LaVergne TN
LVHW080407120725
815951LV00002B/2